DATE DUE			

FOUNDATIONS
OF
WEAVING

FOUNDATIONS OF WEAVING

Mike Halsey and Lore Youngmark

Photographs by Edwina Ferguson   Drawings by Mike Halsey

Watson-Guptill Publications

New York

'The greatest freedom comes from the greatest strictness'
Paul Valéry

To Raie Barnett

First published in the United States 1975 by Watson-Guptill Publications,
a division of Billboard Publications, Inc.,
One Astor Plaza, New York, New York 10036

Copyright © 1975 by Mike Halsey and Lore Youngmark

First published 1975 in Great Britain by David and Charles Limited,
South Devon House, Newton Abbot, Devon, England

Printed in Great Britain by Biddles Limited Guildford Surrey

Library of Congress Cataloging in Publication Data

Halsey, Mike.
    Foundations of weaving.

    Bibliography: p.
    1. Hand weaving. I. Youngmark, Lore, joint
author. II. Title.
TT848.H28 1975   746.1'4   73-14777
ISBN 0-8230-1916-0

CONTENTS

INTRODUCTION

The aim of this book is to encourage exploration and experiment, leading to the production of exciting, imaginative and original fabrics. The only specific instructions given are for methods and samplers. If these are followed, they will help the weaver to design and make items such as dress and upholstery lengths, and rugs or wall hangings to his own specifications. Suggestions for these and many ideas for samplers and exercises are given.

The weaving processes and techniques described are those that can be done on simple and four-shaft looms. We do not include equipment so bulky or expensive that it would normally be used only by handweavers who make their living by this craft. These exclusions in no way limit the understanding and exploration of weaving.

The first easy steps using household items for looms, exercises on simple and table looms, floor looms, drafting, and the construction of more complicated weaves are all included. These are explained in a sequence that leads easily from one technique to the next.

We have both taught for a number of years and it is this experience that has been our guide in preparing this book. We have tried to answer the questions that beginners usually ask and also to deal with the theoretical and practical problems of more experienced weavers.

The methods described in the following pages are those we have found most suited to our way of working and those we have found easiest to explain to our students. Alternative techniques, descriptions and explanations can confuse, and where there are different methods, we describe the simplest and most direct in the main text. Some alternative methods of historical or specialised interest are given in the appendices.

There are probably as many variations as there are weavers and it is likely that no two weavers in the world use exactly the same methods. This highlights the marvellous freedom which the individual has. No matter what your experience of weaving, we recommend that you read this work from the beginning. You will see how we relate the various aspects of weaving and this may encourage you to experiment with methods you had previously not known or not tried.

With the constant development and improvement of industrial weaving machinery, there are very few hand-weaving techniques that cannot be reproduced on power looms. The manufacturer cannot profitably weave small quantities, or start new colours, textures or techniques, that are not included in the original design and costing. The handweaver can do these things, without considering yardage, production costs and the 're-tooling' of the loom.

Unless you are working on a commission, you do not have to think about pleasing others. You are probably weaving to please yourself and to satisfy some indefinable instinct to create. It may then come as a pleasant surprise that others so admire your work that they are willing to buy it.

M.H. and L.Y.

ACKNOWLEDGEMENTS

Our grateful thanks to: Hilary Haywood who made the initial introductions; Muriel Nicholas who did so much of the typing; Roy Evans for proof-reading; Jack Youngmark for proof-reading and many helpful suggestions; Nancy Lee Child for her comments and criticism; and to Edwina Ferguson for all the black and white photographs.

1

BASIC STRUCTURE

EARLY WEAVING

Weaving is certainly one of the oldest surviving crafts in the world, although its exact origins are obscure. We can only guess at the steps that led man to the discovery of this craft. It is likely that he started by interlacing branches and twigs to make protective fences and shelters. As soon as the practicability of interlacing flexible branches and twigs at right angles to each other was understood, other natural and accessible materials could be experimented with. Rushes, reeds, canes and certain types of bark and leaves were all suitable materials for primitive weaving. At this stage a loom was not required. The resilient but flexible nature of the raw materials and their naturally limited length, made them easy to manipulate.

Two-element structure

Those early experiments were the beginnings of the *two-element structure* of weaving. The two elements were worked at right angles to each other, being interlaced to form firm but pliable fabrics. This pliability could be employed to make useful objects such as bowls and baskets, as well as flat pieces for mats and protective coverings. Some early pottery bowls were moulded on pre-formed woven shapes. All these materials are still being used today to make similar articles.

PAPER WEAVING

Warp and weft

Experimental weaving with paper or thin card is a useful exercise that will help to clarify the relationship and interaction of the two elements. If two colours of paper are used, one for each element, this will make the relationship more obvious. A few identical strips of paper are cut and laid parallel to each other. These are then secured at one end to a board or stiff card with pins, glue or self-adhesive tape (Fig 1a). The strips should have small spaces of about 1mm between them and should lie parallel. The spaces will have to be slightly wider if you are using thin card instead of paper for the strips. These are called the *warp* and it is the warp that runs along the length of the fabric. The second element, the *weft*, runs across the warp and is interlaced with it. The weft strips should be the same dimensions as the warp strips.

Weaving

To commence weaving, lift the odd numbered warp strips 1, 3, 5 etc and insert the first weft under these. Place the first weft so that it lies adjacent to the closed end of the warp and at right angles to it (Fig 1b). The second weft strip is inserted by lifting the even numbered warp strips 2, 4, 6 etc and is pushed against the first (Fig 1c). Continue these two steps, lifting the odd and even warp strips alternately, until the warp is filled (Fig 1d). This simple exercise can be used in a number of ways. Experiments can be tried with different colours and in varied widths of paper, or with strips of any natural or man-made materials.

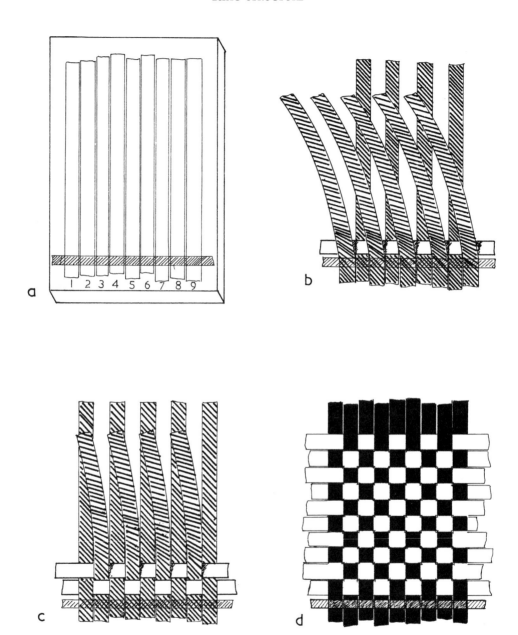

Fig 1   Paper weaving

Plain weave

The name of the weave structure which this exercise produces is *plain weave*. It is the simplest and the firmest of weave structures and is used when strength and stability are required in a cloth.

All the threads interlace alternately and so each thread supports and binds those that surround it.

PROPERTIES OF THREADS

Before you start weaving with threads, you will need to know something about them. We will first describe the basic types and their properties. This, together with the information given later, should help you to choose your initial stock of yarn.

Selecting yarns from the huge variety available is entirely personal and is not easy, especially if your budget is limited. We suggest that you choose a strong cotton or wool yarn of medium thickness and in a few colours for these early samples. Black and white, or a light and dark colour, will make the construction of these easier to see. Ordinary knitting yarns like 3ply, 4ply, quick-knit etc, are best avoided (but can be used until you can buy weaving yarns). They are spun specifically for *single element structures* such as knitting and crochet, and usually give very unsatisfactory results if used for weaving. Some of the novelty knitting yarns can be used for special effects as these are very often spun in a similar way to novelty weaving yarns.

Natural fibres

The natural fibres divide into three basic groups, animal, vegetable and silk. Silk is in a class of its own, both in its quality and in the way it is produced, and is often called the queen of fibres because of its beautiful appearance and texture. The beginner is advised to wait until he is more experienced before using silk in a warp. It is not particularly easy to use and is expensive to buy.

Of the vegetable fibres, the one most used by the handweaver is cotton. It is a very practical yarn, being strong, smooth and easy to handle. Cotton yarns can be bought in a wide range of colours and thicknesses. The natural colour is creamy white (App 1.1).

Animal fibres subdivide into two basic groups: wool and hair. Some animals grow a coat of each, a top coat of hair for protection and an under coat of wool for insulation. They can be obtained in a fairly limited range of beautiful natural colours, from very dark brown (or black) to pale cream (or white). Very few animals produce a pure black or white coat that is suitable for spinning. Hair is difficult to dye but wool can be dyed easily and can be bought in a wide range of colours, qualities and sizes (App 1.2). As we have said, several animal species produce a coat of wool, but when we refer to wool, we shall mean the wool from sheep.

Man-made fibres

Because of the very complex variety of man-made fibres and yarns, we advise you to refer to specialised books on this subject. It will suffice to say that the majority have similar properties and characteristics to one or more of the natural fibres. In very general terms, the following are the most common man-made fibres and their nearest natural fibre equivalents. Polyamide (nylon), polyester (terylene) and acrylic (acrilan) fibres have some of the properties of wool. Viscose rayon has similarities to cotton, as acetate rayon has to silk. It must be stressed that these are generalisations. Each fibre group can be treated with a variety of processes that alter its basic characteristics, and the above are only a few of the many types of man-made fibres.

YARN PACKAGING

Skeins

There are a confusing number of names for yarn packages (see Glossary). Most kinds of yarns are available in skeins. These are tied in two or more places in a figure-of-eight to prevent the skeins from tangling (Fig 2a). One of these ties holds the

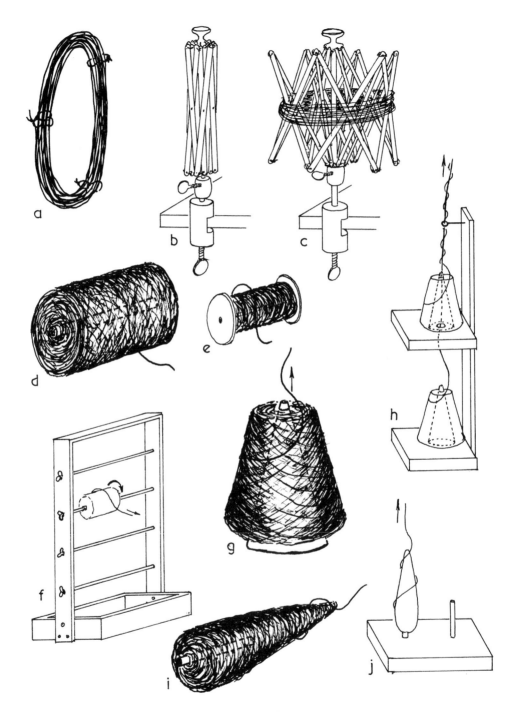

Fig 2   Yarn packaging

two ends of the skein. The skein must be handled with care and the ties should never be undone unless the skein is held open securely. They can be easily muddled and can become unusable if these precautions are not followed. A *skein holder* is recommended to make unwinding easier (Fig 2b) (these are sometimes called *skein winders* as they can be used for making skeins), but a chair back can be used in place of one of these. Before unwinding, tidy the skein by holding it on your outstretched hands; make sure you have opened the complete skein correctly and jerk your hands away from each other a few times. Being careful to keep the skein tidy, place it on the holder, which is opened until it supports the skein (Fig 2c). Select one of the ends from the tie and if it unwinds from the inside, tuck it back into the skein and use the other end, as the skein should be unwound from the outside. Make sure it is only one skein you are trying to unwind as they are sometimes tied together to form *hanks*.

There is a ball winding machine for use with home knitting machines, that can be bought for unwinding skeins and rewinding yarns into balls, otherwise they should be wound by hand.

Spools

If the yarn is not packaged in skein form it will be wound onto one of the several types of commercial holders or bases. The most common of these is the tube of card or plastic. The yarn is wound round the tube in a to-and-fro movement that builds up a firmly packed cylinder (Fig 2d). This type of package is known by several names but we will use the most common one, *spool*. Slippery or very fine yarns are often wound on flanged spools (Fig 2e).

A spool requires a *spool rack* or some means of supporting the tube so that the spool can revolve for unwinding (Fig 2f). This can be improvised with lengths of thin dowelling or metal rods or

strong knitting needles held horizontally and firmly enough to support the spool.

Cones, doubling and pirns

A third method of packaging yarn is similar to the previous one, but a cone shaped holder is used instead of a tube as a base. The package is called a *cone* and is unwound by placing it on the floor or stand and taking the yarn vertically from above (Fig 2g). Yarns on cones can be easily *doubled* (loosely twisted together) by supporting one cone above the other and threading the bottom yarn through the centre of the top cone and unwinding the two yarns together. This makes the top yarn twist around the bottom one (Fig 2h). This method of doubling can be used in several ways to mix a limited range of colours on cones and create a wider variation of colourways. Try doubling two contrasting colours or two shades of the same colour, and then reverse the positions to get the opposite colour twisting around the central one. These will all produce slightly different colour textures when used as wefts (App 1.3).

Another method of packaging yarns is the *pirn*. This is similar to the cone in that it is wound to a tapering point, but it is wound on a tube base (Fig 2i). There is a danger of the pirn collapsing unless it is handled with care and it should never be bent or pulled. It is unwound by supporting the tube on a short vertical rod (not longer than 10cm or 4in) and unwinding vertically (Fig 2j).

CARD LOOM WEAVING

Having explored the relationship of warp and weft in paper, we can start experimenting with threads. It is fairly obvious that it would not be practicable to attempt to weave with soft pliable threads in the same way as we described for paper. This is where a loom becomes essential for weaving.

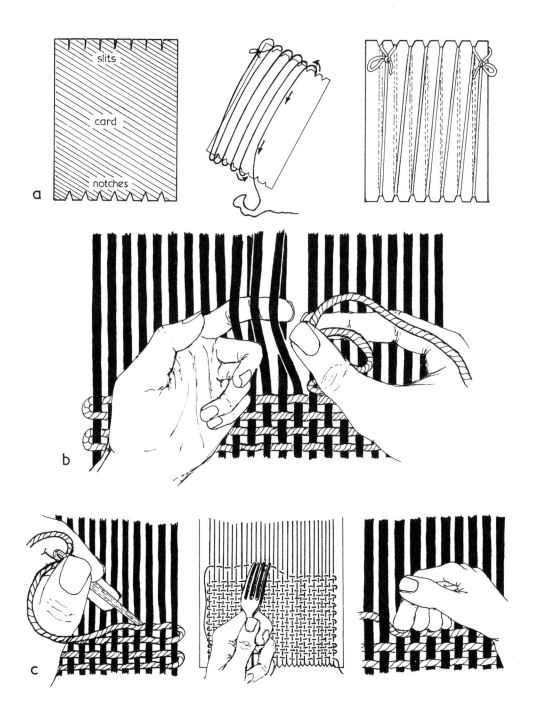

Fig 3   Card-loom weaving

The definition of a loom is a device which will hold the warp under tension (App 1.4). The tension of a warp must be tight enough to hold the threads in place but not so tight that it puts too great a strain either on the warp or on the loom. It is important that the warp is evenly tensioned with no warp threads tighter or slacker than the rest.

One of the simplest ways of making a loom is to wind the warp around a piece of stiff card. To prevent the warp threads from slipping, the card can have notches or slits cut at opposite ends with the thread passing through these (Fig 3a).

If the card loom is small it will be easier to darn the weft in with a blunt needle or bodkin. With a larger card loom the warp can be picked up with the fingers of one hand and the weft inserted with the other (Fig 3b).

To avoid getting the weft tangled, use fairly short lengths at this stage. The weft is pushed or *beaten* into place with a bodkin, a fork, or the tips of your fingers, and is beaten towards you (Fig 3c).

Card looms can be used the other way round but this would mean weaving 'upside down' in relation to most other types of loom.

For your first sampler follow the directions given for paper weaving to produce a plain weave in two colours.

Warp, weft, shed and fell
When we wish to describe a single warp thread we refer to it as an *end*. This is easy to remember if you think of it as having two 'ends' to its length and that the fabric when woven and taken from the loom has cut ends. When referring to the number of ends in a centimetre (inch) in notation, we use shorthand. Ends per centimetre (ends per inch) is written *e/cm* (*epi*). The equivalent name for an individual weft thread is *pick*. The warp ends are 'picked up' to insert the weft, hence the term weft pick, and picks per centimetre (picks per inch), written *p/cm* (*ppi*). When the warp ends are picked up or opened they form the *shed*, which is the name for the space between the two layers of warp into which the weft picks are put (Fig 4). The last working pick is called the *fell* of the cloth.

Sett
The *sett* of the cloth refers to the relationship of the number of ends to picks in a square area of

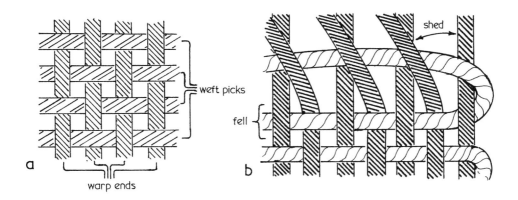

Fig 4   Warp and Weft

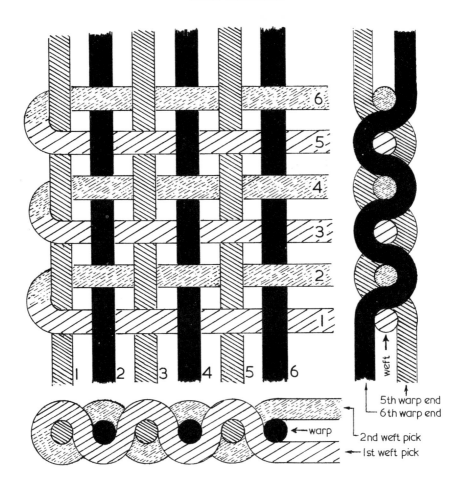

Fig 5   Balanced plain weave

cloth (including the spaces between the threads), e/cm (epi) to p/cm (ppi). The sett has a direct bearing on the type and quality of the cloth. In the first piece of paper weaving, where the warp and the weft are of equal width and equally spaced, a *balanced* plain weave sample is produced. Plain weave can be unbalanced by having more weft picks than warp ends, or vice versa, in an area of cloth. This is explained in more detail in later chapters.

In the paper weave sample, because of the flat ribbon nature of the paper, there were very small spaces between the strips. As soon as three-dimensional materials such as threads are used, their diameter has to be considered. It is because the threads have a diameter that they have to be given enough room between them to bend over and under each other (Fig 5).

Balanced plain weave sett
The relationship (sett) of e/cm to p/cm (epi to ppi) must be 'calculated' in order to produce a

balanced plain weave with any given thread. It is the diameter of the thread that determines the sett. The sett for balanced plain weave is found by wrapping the thread that you are going to use for the warp round a ruler or stick. We will describe how to find the sett for other weaves later. The threads should just touch without being crammed together. Wind them in this way for 1cm (1in) and count the number of threads within this distance. The number is *halved* to give the e/cm (epi) for a balanced plain weave. For greater accuracy when using very thick threads for warp, wind a wider unit than 1cm and calculate the sett from this. The reason for halving the total number is to give the threads a space, equal to their own diameter, between them so that they have room to bend round each other (Fig 5). If the same or similar thread is used for the weft and beaten to give the *same* p/cm (ppi), a perfectly balanced plain weave will result (Plate 1a).

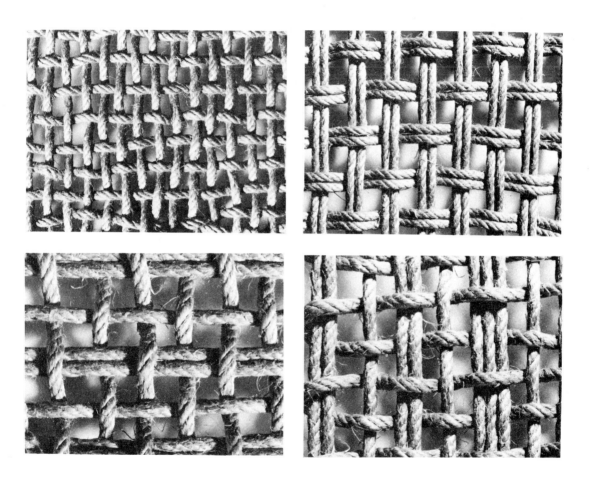

Plate 1   Card loom weaving
a (above left) Balanced plain weave. b (above right) Hopsack. c (below left) Weft rib.
d (below right) Warp rib.

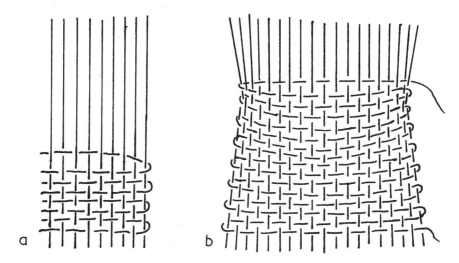

Fig 6 Selvages and waisting

Once you have mastered calculating and weaving balanced plain weave samples, you can experiment on your card loom with different threads and setts. This will give you practice and experience in prejudging the kind of cloth a particular sett or type of thread will produce. It will be obvious without experiment that a thick soft string would not be set to the same e/cm (epi) for balanced plain weave as an embroidery cotton. What will not be so obvious is the result that will be produced in weaving.

Selvages and waisting
The *selvage* (self-edge) is the firm finished edge on each side of the cloth, running parallel to the warp and preventing the edges unravelling. It is formed by one weft turning at the end of a pick and returning into the next shed to form the next pick (Fig 6a). It is created quite naturally as soon as a continuous weft is used. Paper weaving

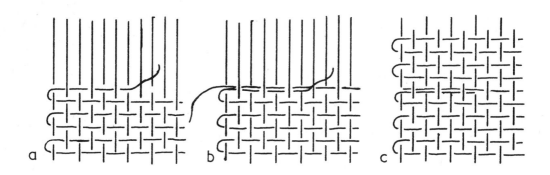

Fig 7 Weft joins

with individual wefts for each pick leaves raw edges (no selvage) to all sides of the fabric.

When turning the weft at the selvage, care must be taken to avoid pulling the weft too tight to the edge, or the fabric will begin to *waist* (Fig 6b), and unless compensated for this will become progressively worse. It is better in the early samples to be slightly over generous with the weft to avoid waisting. Loops may form at the selvage, but this can be corrected in later weaving when you have gained more confidence and skill.

Weft joins

It is impracticable (usually impossible) to weave a length of cloth with one continuous weft thread, so new lengths of weft will have to be joined in as weaving progresses. The new weft should be overlapped with the end of the old one for at least four raised ends. With a closely set warp this overlap may be shorter, and for widely set warps it may have to be increased. On a small sampler the join is best made at the selvage. If the last bit of weft will not complete a pick, take it into the

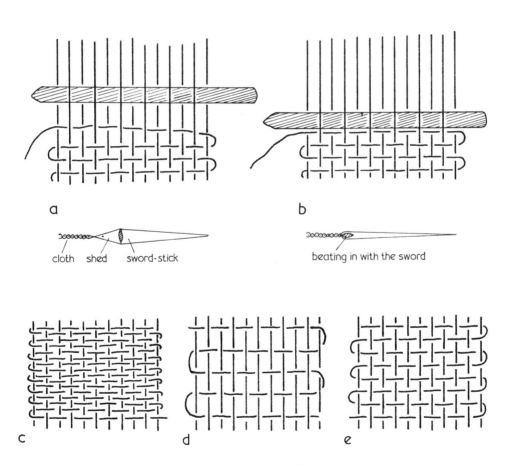

cloth   shed   sword-stick

beating in with the sword

Fig 8   Sword-stick and beat

next shed for the first 2cm (¾in), bring it out between two warp ends and leave it lying on the surface of the cloth (Fig 7a). Take the new weft and pass it through the same shed leaving a couple of centimetres hanging out of the selvage at the join (Fig 7b). Continue weaving, and when you have completed the next few picks, the two trailing ends of the join can be trimmed flush to the cloth face (Fig 7c).

On a larger piece of weaving, longer lengths of weft are used and the joins are spaced well apart. It usually does not matter where a join is made, it can be at the selvage or in the width, but if it is at all obvious it should be made at the selvage.

Sword-stick

We suggest that you use fairly thick yarns for the early card loom samples as they are easy to handle and push into place. As soon as you start using less bulky yarns a new method will be necessary to keep the weft even and horizontal—therefore the use of a *sword-stick* is recommended. This, as its name implies, it a flat stick with a fine smooth edge and pointed at one or both ends. It is put into the shed to beat the weft into place. Care must be taken to keep the sword at right angles to the warp or the weft will begin to slope and distort the weave. (This slope can be used to great effect as a design element if done consciously and systematically.) The shed is picked up by passing the sword over and under alternate warp ends (Fig 8a). To open the shed turn it on edge, insert the weft and turn it flat again. The weft is beaten into place by pulling the sword towards you, holding it at both ends (Fig 8b). The sword-stick is then removed and the next shed is picked up with it. Before inserting the next weft, the previous one can be beaten again to make sure it is lying straight. Remember that if you are trying to produce a balanced plain weave you must not beat the weft too hard or it will pack down too tightly and show more than the

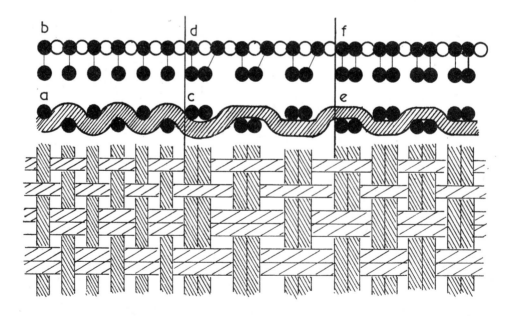

Fig 9   Variations of plain weave—sett

warp. Figure 8c–e shows the weft beaten (c) too hard, (d) too soft and (e) correctly to produce a balanced cloth.

Variations of plain weave

Hopsack is the name of a plain weave structure that has two ends up, two ends down in alternate sequence, with *two* threads in one weft pick (Plate 1b). This weave can be extended by using a sequence of ends: 3 up, 3 down alternately, with a triple thread weft; 4 up, 4 down with a quadruple weft, etc. The more this is extended the less stable the cloth becomes, even though it is still theoretically a balanced weave. The loss of stability is caused by the threads bunching together and thus upsetting the relationship of *thread* to *space* in the sett, as is illustrated in Fig 9a–f below.

Fig 9a shows the normal relationship of warp to weft in the plain weave and again illustrates the reason why half the number of ends are used as will lie side by side and just touching on a stick (Fig 9b). Fig 9c shows the relationship of warp to weft when the hopsack is *unbalanced* (Fig 10a). It can be seen that if the number of ends used remains constant, but the weft intersections are fewer, the width of the intersections will be greater than the thickness of the weft. This can be counteracted by using a thicker weft, or by using more strands twisted together. The bunching of the threads is shown in Fig 9d. Fig 9e shows the relationship of warp to weft in a balanced hopsack weave (Fig 10b). The sett of the warp has been altered and in this case there are more warp ends and fewer intersections. This works out at *two-thirds* of the total number of threads per centimetre (inch) as will lie side by side and touching on a stick (Fig 9f).

Cording

Another variation of plain weave, which makes use of the unbalanced sett as shown in Fig 9c, is a *weft cord*. The extra room between the threads of the warp is used to pack varying numbers of weft threads into successive picks. This produces cords of different thicknesses and can be done on any *even* grouping of warp ends, eg 2 up, 2 down; 3 up, 3 down; etc (Fig 9c, 10c and Plate 1c).

The above grouping can be turned through 90° so that it becomes a *warp cord* (Fig 10d and Plate 1d). This is done by lifting varied groupings of ends, eg 3 up, 3 down, 2 up, 1 down, 3 up, 3 down etc. As plain weave has only two sheds the other shed will be the reverse. The weft can be either single, double, treble or more (depending on the thickness of the weft thread used) woven throughout.

Warp cord and weft cord can be combined to make a corded check cloth. The same sequence of grouping the warp ends is used for grouping the weft picks. If the above sequence for warp cord were used, it would need four picks of weft to complete the pattern. The first pick would have three threads, the second would have three, the third would have two, and the fourth would have one. The fifth pick would be the same as the first, the sixth the same as the second, etc (Fig 10e). The resulting fabric is an even check of warp cords and weft cords.

Uneven checks and random textures can also be woven in this way, by varying the grouping sequences of the warp and weft (Fig 10f).

Tubular cloth

Both sides of the card loom can be woven on to make two or more samples using the same warp and different wefts or weaves. If the selvage threads are near to the edges of the card, both sides can be woven alternately with the same weft to produce either a *tubular* or a *double-width* cloth. A tubular cloth is produced by weaving from right to left (or vice versa), continuously.

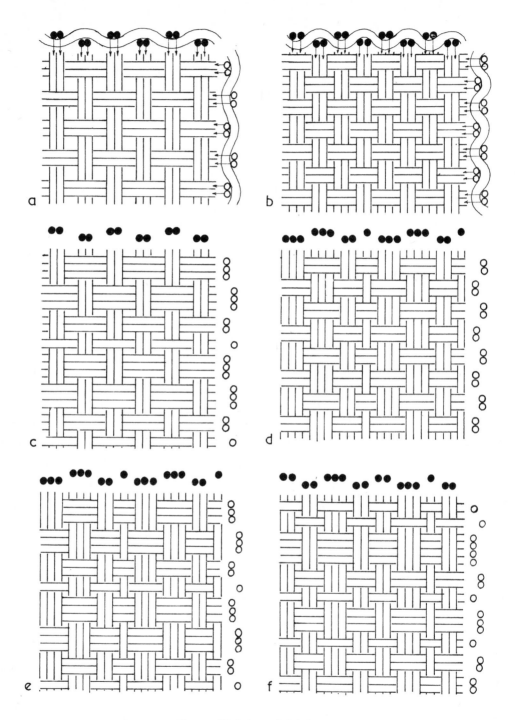

Fig 10   Variations of plain weave

Weave first on one side of the card and then on the other and then back to the first again. This will make the weft pass in a circular course from the front to the back of the card and a tubular cloth with no selvages will result. In order to keep the alternate sequence of the warp ends correct, one side of the card should have an even number of warp ends and the other an odd number. When the weft passes *under* the last warp end on one side of the card it must pass *over* the first warp end on the other, and vice versa.

Double width cloth

A *double width* cloth is woven in a similar way to the above, but the weft does not travel in a circular motion but in a to-and-fro direction. The first pick is woven on side *a*, the card is turned over for the first pick on side *b*, the second weft is woven on side *b* before turning the card over and weaving the second pick on side *a*. This sequence continues: third pick *a*, third pick *b*, fourth pick *b*, fourth pick *a*, etc. If you weave from left to right for the first pick, the open edge will be on the left hand on side *a*, and on the right hand on side *b*. It will not make any difference to the weaving if you have odd or even numbers of warp ends in this case. However, you must remember to pass the weft under the first thread of side *b* if it went over the last warp thread on side *a*, and vice versa, or the cloth will have a double warp end running through the centre of the cloth (App 1.5).

Card looms are very useful for sampling and for learning about weave-structures. Even when you have progressed to the more sophisticated looms do not forget that card looms can be used to test the qualities of yarns, colours or textures quickly. Keep all your samples, preferably in a notebook, together with details of the yarns used. These will prove invaluable as your knowledge of weaving increases, and new ideas can very often be developed from old samples.

2
FRAME LOOMS

The card looms described in the last chapter can be used as experimental and sample looms, and also for weaving small articles. Square or strips of cloth can be sewn together to make larger items, but the looms described in this chapter are also very inexpensive and easy to make, and are just as easy to use. They are sturdier and more practical for weaving larger pieces of cloth.

FRAME LOOMS

The frame loom is one of the easiest to make or buy because of its simple construction, and for the same reason it is one of the simplest to use. Any rectangular frame that is strong enough to support the warp, and of a convenient size, can be used as a loom. Plain picture frames make good sample looms. They can be made stronger with braces across the corners. (The finished fabric can be left on the picture frame, if it is to be hung on a wall and the warp needs to be kept under tension.)

Rugs or tapestries require the use of a strong, rigid frame because the warp must be held at a high tension during weaving. Painters' canvas stretchers are very suitable, being strong, rigid and easily assembled. The sides are interchangeable and are usually sold in pairs. By combining pairs of different lengths, a variety of frame proportions and sizes can be made.

The frame will need to be slightly larger than the intended fabric. As the first 5–10cm (2–4in) of the warp are not woven, and the last 15–25cm (6—10in) become increasingly difficult to weave,

the inside length of the frame should be about 30cm (12in) longer than the length you wish to weave. The inside width of the frame should be about 20cm (8in) wider than the warp to give a clearance on either side.

DIRECT WARPING
Figure-of-eight
One way of making a warp on a frame is to wind it in a continuous figure-of-eight (Fig 11a). This makes the warp threads cross past each other *alternately* at the centre of the frame (Fig 11b and c). The *cross* has the primary function of keeping the threads in the correct sequence before weaving commences. As the warp threads cross past each other in the same way as they do between two picks of a plain weave (Fig 11d), they are held in position in the same way and cannot become muddled or twisted.

Winding the warp
When the purpose of the cloth, the yarns to be used and the sett of the warp have been decided (drawing on the experience of the experiments in Chapter 1 on card looms), the warp can be wound on the frame (Fig 12a). It is important when making the warp to keep the threads at an *even* tension. As long as it is even, the tension of the entire warp can be increased after it has been wound.

When the warp has been made it is spread to the weaving width. Insert a smooth, strong, flat stick

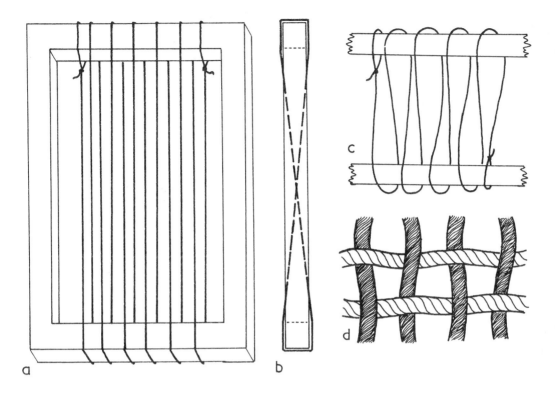

Fig 11 Direct warping—figure-of-eight

into the bottom half of the cross and push this *heading-stick* to the top of the frame (Fig 12b). The warp is spread to give the correct e/cm (epi) by counting and spacing the threads evenly from the heading-stick (Fig 12c). Remember that each warp loop passing over the top of the frame is *two* warp ends. When the warp has been spread at the top of the frame the heading-stick is removed and replaced in the top half of the cross and pushed to the base of the loom. The warp is spread (Fig 12d), and the heading-stick is secured to the base of the frame with string ties (Fig 12e). The stick pushes the cross down and brings the two layers of warp together (Fig 12f), which is its main purpose. It can also be used to increase the tension. The closer

it is pulled to the base of the frame the more it will increase the tension of the warp (Fig 12g). Make all the ties of equal length or the heading-stick will bow and the tension of the warp will be uneven. If the warp is wider than about 30cm (12in), more ties will be needed between the centre and outside ties.

The top half of the cross will now open from the heading-stick, forming a shed that is as deep as the thickness of the frame (Fig 13a). If the shed is not deep enough for the weft to pass through easily, it can be made deeper by inserting a thick rod or shed-stick (Fig 13b). The shed-stick is tied to the top of the frame to prevent it slipping. The *counter-shed* or second shed is picked up with the fingers as described in Chapter 1, Fig 3b.

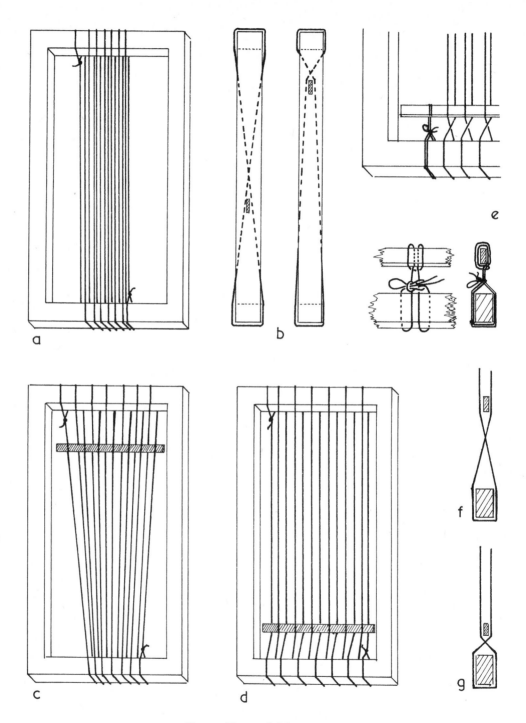

Fig 12   Figure-of-eight warping

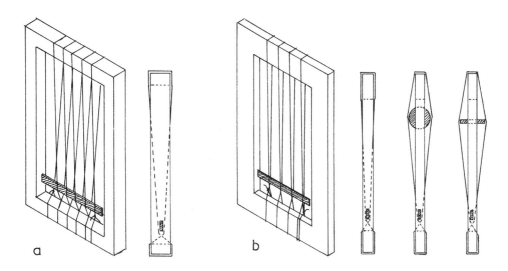

Fig 13   Heading-stick and shed-stick

The loom is now prepared for weaving. Even though all plain weave structures are possible on this loom, it is most suitable for weft-faced fabrics or finger manipulated fabrics (see Chapter 5, *Finger Manipulated Weaves*).

Circular warping

Although circular warping is not as direct as the figure-of-eight method, it has several advantages. It creates *two* layers of warp, making it possible to weave double cloths (see Chapter 1 and App 2.1), without having to turn the frame over; individual pieces can be woven separately, one on each side of the frame but using the same length of warp; or one continuous piece can be woven if the warp is pulled around the frame as the weaving progresses. The latter is the main advantage because a length of cloth, almost twice the length of the frame, can be woven on a circular warp.

The warp has to be tied to a stick so that it can be pulled around the frame. The *tie-stick* is lashed to the sides of the frame while the warp is being made (Fig 14a). The first warp thread is tied to the stick and passed around the frame until it returns to the tie-stick. It is wrapped around the tie-stick for a few turns and then passed around the frame again (Fig 14b). The warp is spread on the tie-stick according to the number of turns, to give the correct sett. Remember that although the warp threads form two layers, one on each side of the frame, both layers are part of the same continuous warp. (In some of the illustrations, the lower layer of warp is not shown, to avoid confusion.) Figure 14c shows a closely set and a widely set warp. Wrapping the warp around the tie-stick also helps to hold the tension while the warp is being made. The thread should be made into a *finger skein* to make the winding of the warp easier.

Finger skeins

A length of yarn can be wound into a firm and compact bundle that will unwind easily as it is

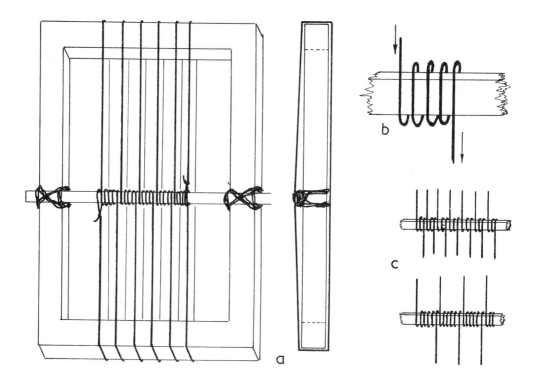

Fig 14   Direct warping—circular

needed. The yarn is wound into a figure-of-eight around the thumb and little finger of one hand. The first end is left hanging between the thumb and first finger and when the skein has been wound the last end is wrapped tightly around the middle of the bundle for half a dozen turns and fastened with a couple of half hitches (Plate 2). About 9m (10yd) can be wound in this way, although the actual length will depend on the thickness of the yarn and the span of your hand. Do not make the finger skein too bulky or it will become tangled. Thick yarns will require the full span of the hand, but finer yarns should be made into smaller skeins by holding the finger and thumb closer together. Do not try winding very fine or slippery yarns into finger skeins. The skein is used by pulling

on the free end, which releases the yarn from the inside of the skein.

Picking up the cross

Circular warping does not produce a *cross* and, as the cross is essential for accuracy in finding the shed and counter-shed, it will have to be made. Two smooth sticks which have holes through the rounded or pointed ends are needed and are called *cross-sticks*. They should be the same width as, or slightly wider than, the width of the frame. The tie-stick is unlashed from the frame and positioned near the bottom edge. The cross-sticks are inserted one at a time, about 20cm (8in) above the tie-stick. One cross-stick is passed over and under alternate warp ends and the other is passed over and under

Plate 2 Finger skeins
a (left) Winding the finger skein. b (right) The completed skein.

the *opposite* ends (plain weave sequence), following the thread order on the tie-stick (Fig 15a). Make sure you pick the cross up in the correct sequence. The cross-sticks are kept in place by tying a piece of string from the hole in one end of each stick, across the warp to the hole in the other end (Fig 15b).

Leashes

Having tied the cross-sticks in place, *leashes* are tied around the warp ends that pass over the lower stick. The upper cross-stick is pushed to the top of the frame while the leashes are tied. Leashes are loops of strong thread, used to raise alternate warp ends to create one of the sheds for weaving.

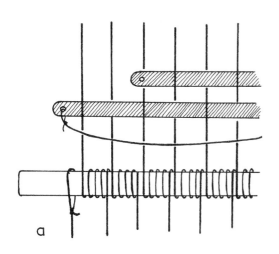
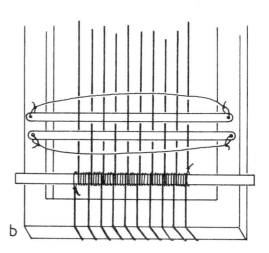

Fig 15 Picking up the cross—cross-sticks

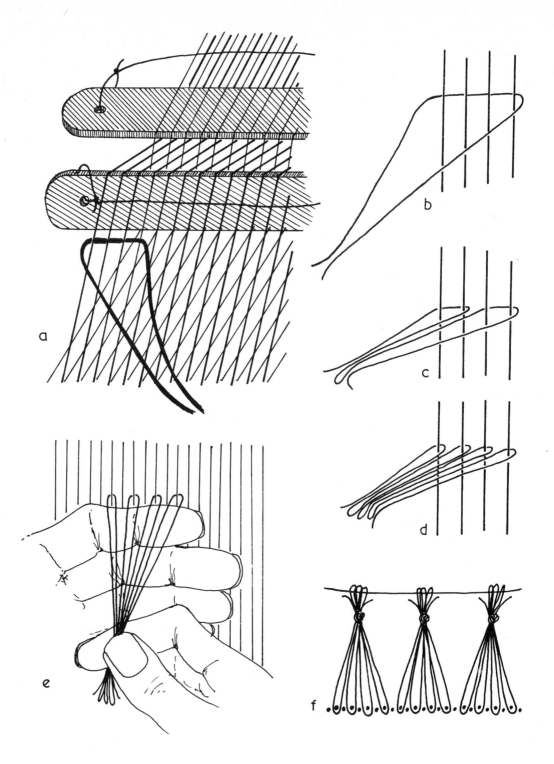

Fig 16   Leashes

The thread should be strong and smooth to withstand the friction caused in using the leashes.

Cut a number of leash threads about 90cm (36in) long. Each of these will make four leash loops. Turn the lower cross-stick on edge to form a shed and pass a leash thread under four warp threads (Fig 16a). Bring the two ends of the leash thread together (Fig 16b) and hold them in one hand. Pick up a loop with a finger of the other hand, between the first two and last two warp threads, pull it level with the two ends (Fig 16c), and transfer it to the other hand. With a finger for each, pick up two more loops: one between the first and second warp threads, and the other between the third and fourth (Fig 16d). Pull them level and transfer them to the other hand. This will produce four loops around four warp threads. Make sure the loops are all the *same* length or the shed will be uneven. To equalise the length of the leashes before they are tied off, hold the group fairly close to the warp and place the fingers of one hand across the warp ends under the leashes (Fig 16e), and pull gently on the group with the other. Allow them to slide between the fingers but do not let them go. Tie the ends of the loops in a thumb knot (overhand knot) (see Fig 23). Tie groups of leashes on all the threads passing over the lower cross-stick. If there is an odd number of warp threads, the last group can be tied with individual leashes which are then knotted together.

The completed leashes should be approximately 8cm (3in) long from the thumb knot (overhand knot) to the warp. To keep the leashes tidy and to prevent them falling to the back of the warp, a string is passed through the small loops at the

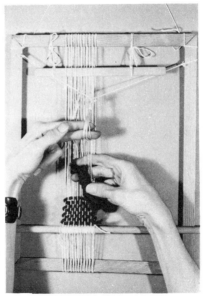

Plate 3 Frame loom and leashes
a (left) Direct circular warp with plain weave and finger skein inserted in the shed.
b (right) Inserting the finger skein into the counter-shed, using the leashes.

knotted end of the leashes (Fig 16f). The string is tied to the sides of the frame to support the leashes about 30cm (12in) above the tie-stick. The lower cross-stick is removed from the warp, but the upper stick is left in. If it is broad enough to give a deep shed it can be used as a *shed-stick*. If it is not suitable, turn it on edge and insert a broader stick into the open shed. The cross-stick is then removed from the warp. The shed-stick is tied with lengths of string to the top of the frame. These ties prevent the stick slipping and support it just above the leashes (App 2.2).

Weaving on the frame

The loom is now prepared for weaving. One shed is opened by turning the shed-stick on edge, and the other is opened in sections, by pulling each of the leash groups in turn (Plate 3). The weft can be inserted with the fingers, using short lengths. Longer pieces of weft can be used by winding them into finger skeins. The weft can be 'beaten' with a fork or the fingers as described in Chapter 1.

Rugs or tapestries need to be beaten very firmly and you will need a *rug beater*. This is a weighted multi-pronged fork and is made either of metal, usually brass (Fig 17a), or a hard wood that is weighted with lead (Fig 17b). A wooden beater is less tiring to use than a metal one because the weighting is balanced. Beat with a flexing movement of the wrist, not the whole arm, to prevent muscle fatigue. The beater should not be dropped or the prongs will be bent or split and will damage the warp. Light fabric structures require the use of a sword-stick for beating if the weft is to be kept horizontal and straight and does not need to be beaten hard (see Chapter 1).

The working height of the weaving can be adjusted to keep the fell of the cloth at a convenient height. Pull the tie-stick further around the frame after weaving about 10–20cm (4–8in). If the tension of the warp needs to be increased after it has been made, a stout stick or *tensioning bar* is passed under the entire warp with its ends resting on the sides of the frame (Fig 18a). A second tensioning bar can be inserted on the

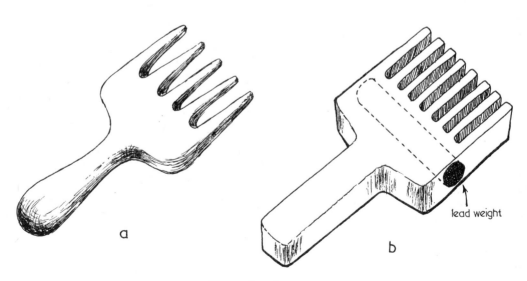

lead weight

Fig 17   Rug-beaters

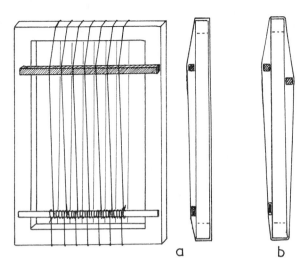
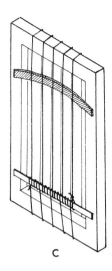

N B Shed-stick and leashes not shown in above figure

Fig 18 Tensioning bars

other side of the frame to increase the warp tension even more (Fig 18b). One or both bars may have to be removed when the warp needs to be moved around the frame. The tensioning bars should be very rigid or they will bow in the centre (Fig 18c). The bars will also help to separate the layers of warp if the frame is not very thick.

Chapters 4 and 5 give ideas and examples of weaves that can be done on the frame loom. It is most suitable for rugs and tapestry weave, but many other fabric structures can be made on it (App 2.3).

3

SIMPLE LOOMS

BOX LOOMS

The method described for circular warping can be used on a *box loom*. The sheds can be made in exactly the same way as on a frame loom, using a shed-stick and leashes. The loom is easy to make, or can be improvised by using a drawer, salvaged from an old piece of furniture. It should be sanded smooth on all edges so that it will not snag the warp or weft threads. If the drawer has to be replaced after use, make the warp around the sides of it so that only these edges need to be sanded smooth. Any box, provided that it is strong and smooth, can be used as a loom. Because of the depth of the box loom and the separation of the two layers of warp, it can also be used with a *rigid heddle*.

RIGID HEDDLES

The rigid heddle is a simplification of the heddle, and a heddle is a development of the leash. Like the leash, the heddle is used to open a shed. It is a length of string or wire, knotted or twisted to form a loop at the centre (Fig 19a). A warp thread that passes through the loop can be raised or lowered by pulling the heddle up or down (Fig 19b). The rigid heddle is a number of stiff heddles made of wood or metal joined at the top and bottom with cross pieces. Small slits are left between the strips (Fig 19c).

Warp ends are threaded through the holes and slits (Fig 19d). When the warp is tensioned the rigid heddle can be raised, lifting all the threads in the holes, or lowered, pushing the *same* threads down. The warp threads in the slits remain stationary and horizontal throughout weaving (Fig 19e). The rigid heddle is also used to position the weft by pulling it forward to the fell of the cloth.

Because the heddle strips are joined, the number of holes and slits per centimetre (inch) remains constant. Metal rigid heddles usually have larger holes and slits than the wooden type. The sett of the rigid heddle will determine the sett of the warp, and the thread used will have to be suitable to the sett and not vice versa as is usual. The size of the holes and slits will also determine the maximum thickness of the warp thread (App 3.1).

SIMPLE WARPING

As the rigid heddle has to be threaded, a continuous warp made on the loom would be impractical. The warp is made on a *warping frame* or *warping board* and then transferred to the loom. Warping boards can be improvised, but you will need a well constructed board for longer warps and we suggest that you buy or make one.

Warping Board

The warping board is used to make the required number of warp threads of the same length and tension, and to keep the threads in the correct sequence.

The board has a series of holes drilled into it (Fig 20a). Posts or pegs of dowelling are fitted

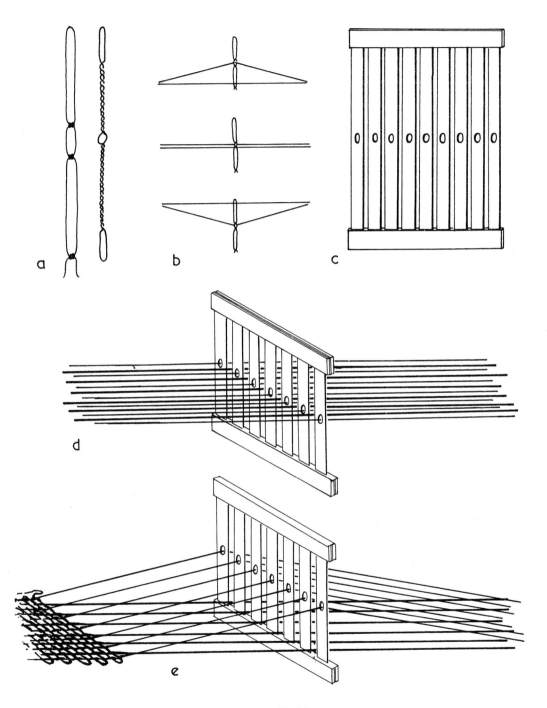

a   b   c

d

e

Fig 19   Rigid heddles

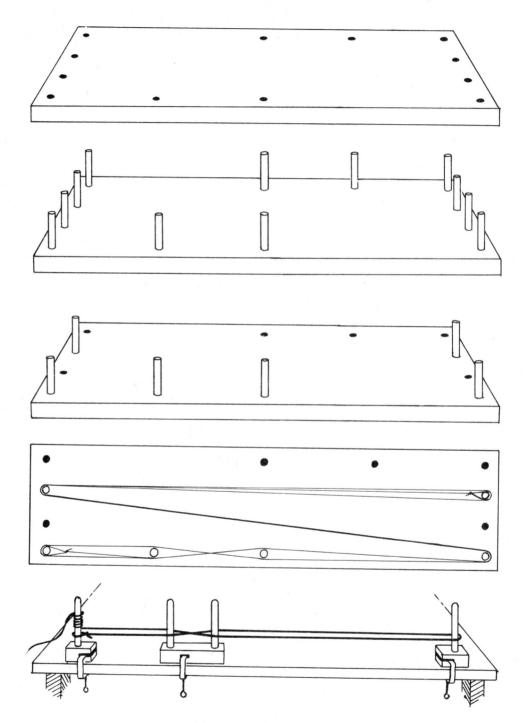

Fig 20   Warping board

into the holes (Fig 20b). The pegs must fit tightly, to prevent them working loose while the warp is being wound, but not so tightly that they cannot be removed from the holes. Fig 20c shows the standard layout of pegs and Fig 20d the path of the threads for a short warp. In place of the frame or board, a set of warping posts can be used. These are independent posts or pairs of posts, fixed into blocks, which are clamped to a table top (Fig 20e).

Warp planning and recording

We strongly recommend that you keep a record, together with a sample of the cloth, for each piece of work. Before you make a warp you will need to know the length, width and e/cm (epi). These should be recorded together with the type of yarn used, the purpose of the cloth and any other details, such as stripe or threading sequence.

To calculate the length of warp for a box loom, measure the distance around the loom and add at least 20cm (8in) to this. The extra length is required for tying the warp on the loom.

Making the warp

The warp is made with a *singles-cross* at one end and a *counting tie* at the other. The singles-cross is most important when making a warp off the loom. Without it the threads would be muddled, tangled and in no order for threading. The singles-cross is made by crossing the warp threads alternately between two pegs (Fig 21a).

The counting tie is made at the other end of the warp and is used to group the threads into convenient units for counting. The units can be used to mark a stripe repeat or to group the threads to equal the e/cm (epi). A length of contrasting thread is crossed between the units to form a figure-of-eight chain (Fig 21b).

It is not necessary to know the *total* number of threads in the warp. It is much easier to remember

the e/cm (epi) of the warp and to count these units and the number of units (centimetres or inches) in the width of the warp. Thus if the warp has 5 e/cm and is 40cm wide (or if working in half inch units, 10 epi and 20in wide, as a convenient example) the counting tie will cross around each group of five threads and there will be forty groups. This is much easier to count than 200 threads.

When using two or more colours to make a stripe, join the yarns with knots at one of the end pegs. Keep all knots as close to an end peg as possible (Fig 21c).

There are two important points to remember when making a warp: to make the cross correctly, and to keep the tension even. It does not matter if the tension is high or low, but it must be even throughout the warp. Loose or tight threads will create difficulties in weaving. The tension should be high enough to prevent the threads drooping between the pegs, but not too high or the pegs will bend. This may happen if the pegs are not firmly bedded into the board and they will begin to slope inwards with the pressure of the warp (Fig 22a). If a warp is made on sloping pegs (and provided that the pegs do not pull out of the holes), the threads at the top of the pegs will be slightly shorter than those at the base (Fig 22b). If this happens while the warp is being wound and it is impossible to push the pegs securely back into their holes, it is better to unwind the warp and begin again.

Having made a note of the length, width and e/cm (epi) of the warp, make a loop at the end of the warp yarn by turning the yarn back on itself and tying a thumb knot (overhand knot) (Fig 23).

The loop should be about 8cm (3in) long and is placed over peg *a*. The thread is taken behind peg *b* and in front of peg *c*. It then passes around pegs *d* and *e* and is turned back around peg *f* to begin the *second* warp thread. This follows the

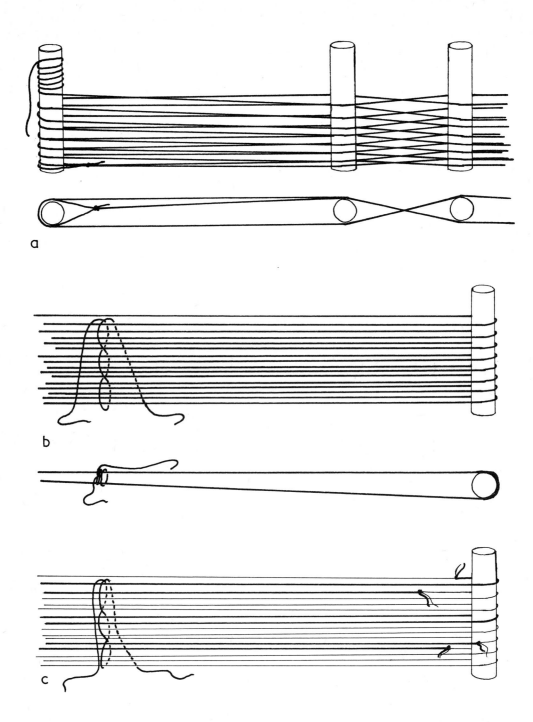

Fig 21   Simple warping—making the warp

same course as the first thread as far as peg *d*. It is taken behind peg *c* and in front of peg *b*. The first warp thread is shown by a solid line and the second by a dotted line in Fig 24a. All threads travelling from peg *a* to peg *f* follow the course of the first thread, and all threads returning from peg *f* to peg *a* follow the course of the second. Do not create a second cross between pegs *a* and *b* as this would make threading difficult. Keep the threads away from the top of the pegs by pushing them down after each group has been counted and the counting tie thread has been crossed (Fig 24b). If you have to let go of the thread during warping, it should be wound around a peg at least half a

dozen times to hold the tension (Fig 21a). Do not forget to unwind it before continuing with the warp.

A longer warp can be made by using more pegs after peg *f* (Fig 24c), or a shorter warp by turning the warp around peg *d* or peg *e* (Fig 24d). If you make your own warping board, it will be practical to make the distance between the sides (pegs *a*, *e*, *g* etc, and pegs *d*, *f*, *h* etc) one metre (or yard) (App 3.2). You are more likely to calculate your warps to the nearest metre (or yard), and sub-divisions can be made by using two pegs on one side of the warping board as shown in Fig 24e and f.

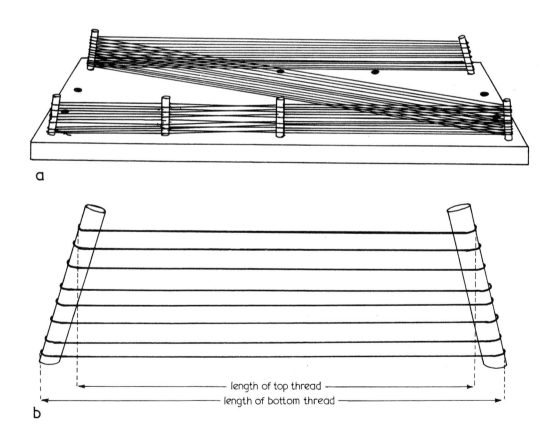

Fig 22 Loose warping pegs

Fig 23   Thumb knot and loop

Tying up the warp

Before the warp can be removed from the board it must be securely tied in the following places. The thread used must be strong and smooth and should be a contrasting colour to the warp. Check and double check the ties before you remove the warp.

A long tie string is passed down through the triangular space between peg *b* and the cross, under the cross and back up through the other triangular space by peg *c*. The two ends are knotted firmly with a thumb knot to form a loop enclosing the cross (Fig 25a). A firm tie is made through the loop at peg *a* to hold this end of the warp tidy. The warp must also be tied to hold the loop around peg *f*, and a tie is made on each side of the loop (Fig 25b). A third tie is made around the whole warp about 20cm (8in) away from peg *f*. Further ties are made around the whole warp at approximately one metre (yard) intervals to keep the warp tidy. These should be made quite tight (Fig 25c).

Having tied the warp and having *checked* that no ties have been forgotten, (check with Fig 25c)

the warp can be taken off the board. Peg *f* may have to be removed to release the warp tension. If the warp is longer than a couple of metres (yards) it will be easier to handle (and to store if necessary) if it is *chained*. The end of the warp is held in one hand and the warp is made into a loop (Fig 26a). The warp is pulled through the loop (Fig 26b) to form a second loop (Fig 26c). The warp is pulled through the second loop to form a third, etc (Fig 26d). Chain the warp from the counting tie end so that the cross is at the open end of the chain ready for threading (Fig 26e). The singles-cross must *not* be pulled through the last loop. The chain will undo easily when pulled from the open end.

Threading the rigid heddle

The rigid heddle should be secured to a table surface so that the holes overhang the edge of the table by approximately one centimetre (half an inch) (Fig 27). It can be taped (Fig 27a) or clamped (Fig 27b) in place. The warp is laid on the table with the cross about 15cm (6in) away from the holes of the rigid heddle, leaving about 20cm

(8in) of the end loop hanging over the front edge (Fig 27c). The warp is held in place either by placing a heavy weight on it about 40cm (16in) behind the cross or, if the warp is long enough, by tying it to the leg of the table.

The warp threads have to be entered through

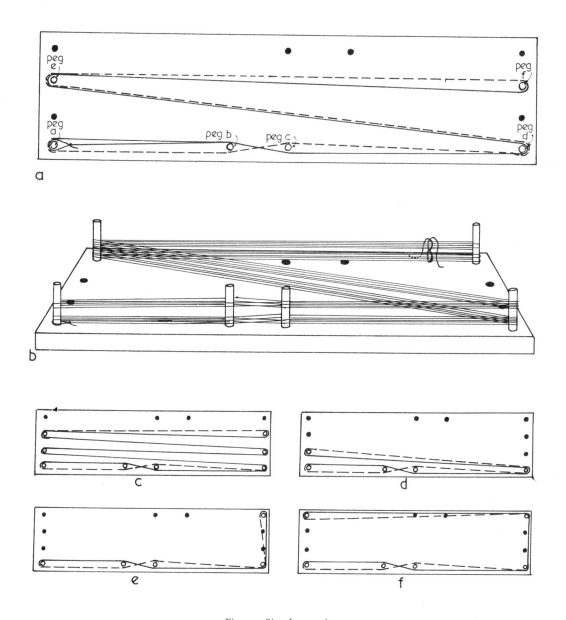

Fig 24   Simple warping

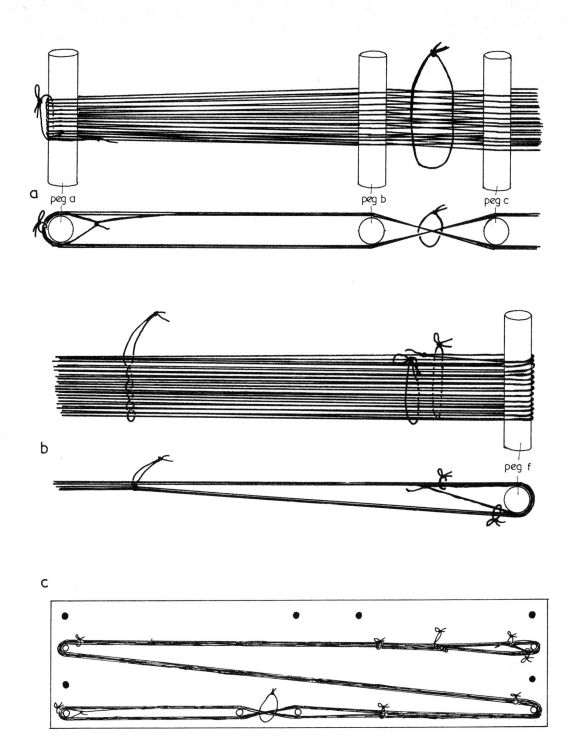

peg a   peg b   peg c

a

b

peg f

c

Fig 25   Tying up the warp

the rigid heddle in the *same* sequence in which they were laid on the board. The cross-tie holds this sequence but prevents the warp being spread to the full width of the rigid heddle. Insert a cross-stick into each side of the cross, and make sure that it has been picked up correctly. Tie the sticks together securely, leaving about 1cm (½in) gap between them (Fig 27d), and remove the cross tie.

Cut through the loop that was formed round peg *a* to release the warp ends for entering. The rigid heddle is entered by threading one warp end in each slit and one in each hole alternately, taking the threads in the order held between the cross-sticks (Fig 27e). Check that none of the slits or holes are left unthreaded or are threaded twice and tie each centimetre (half-inch) group with a *slip-thumb knot* (overhand slip knot) (Fig 28a) or a *half-knot* (Fig 28b) as it is entered. This prevents the threads being pulled out of the rigid heddle accidentally (Fig 27f).

If the full width of the rigid heddle is not being used, the warp must be centred in it or the rigid heddle will dip on the empty side and will make weaving very difficult.

When the whole warp has been entered and tied off in slip-thumb knots, the rigid heddle is released from the table top and pushed along the warp to the cross-sticks. Make a final check that the threads are entered in the correct sequence. All the thumb knots (overhand knots) are gathered into a bundle and tied together with a piece of string. Pull gently on each group to straighten and tension the threads and tie the group firmly. Undo the cross-sticks and remove them. They are *only used for threading* and must *not* be pushed along the warp. We stress this because some people think that the cross-sticks must be kept in the warp under all circumstances. This is not true and gives rise to the idea that the cross must be corrected on the cross-sticks if a mistake is found during entering. This is not true either, and if attempted a lot of time can be wasted, the order of the threads may become more muddled in the process and the mistake may simply be shifted across the warp.

A common mistake in early warps is that of two or more threads crossing over one stick and under the other together. This mistake is caused

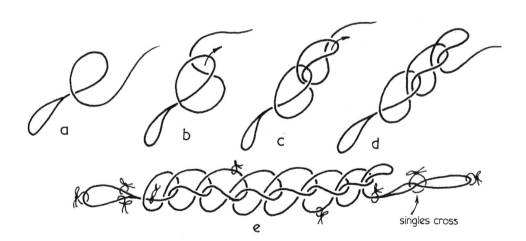

Fig 26 Chaining the warp

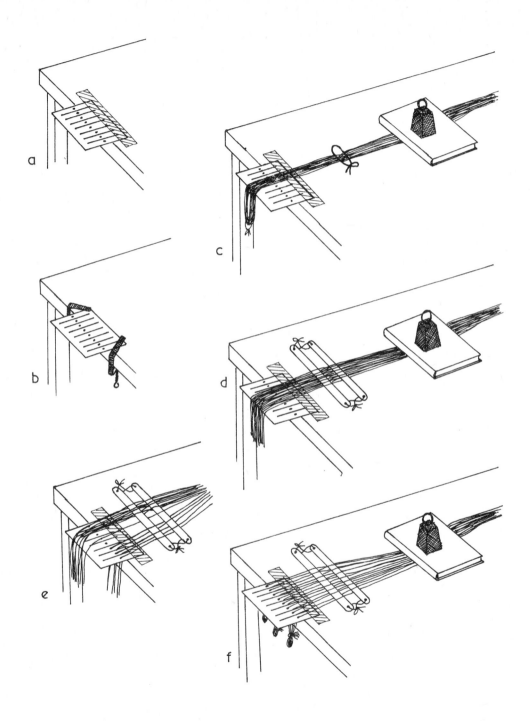

Fig 27 Threading the rigid heddle

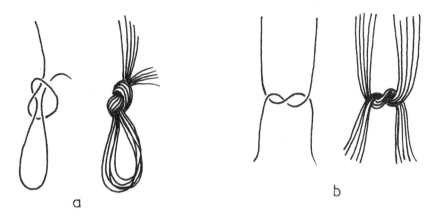

Fig 28   Slip thumb-knot—half knot

by careless warping as the threads were not laid in the correct position on the warping board. It is *too late* to correct this, and it is impossible (except by tracing the threads to the other end of the warp) to tell which thread should be in what order. Enter the threads through the rigid heddle and by chance you may get them in the correct sequence. It will not be too serious if you have not, as the threads will either cross once (if the mistake is a pair), or twice (if it is a group of three), and this should not cause too much trouble during weaving. Another common mistake is a warp end that has been left out of the cross altogether. If this is the only mistake in the warp it will mean that there are two threads passing together between the cross-sticks. The thread that is out of the cross should pass between these, though again you will not be able to tell which is the *first* of the two ends. If there are other mistakes and you are not sure of the position of the thread, it should be left out altogether. It will have to be tied off in an end loop at the other end of the warp to secure its counterpart in the warp. This is done at a later stage in preparing the loom.

Dressing the loom

After removing the cross-sticks undo the ties holding the warp, with the exception of the tie in front of the rigid heddle and the last three holding the end loop (Fig 29a). Push the rigid heddle along the warp, holding the warp under slight tension, to the first of the three remaining ties. Lay the warp on the table with the end loop towards you, and keep it in place by putting a heavy weight on it on the other side of the rigid heddle.

Place a smooth *end-stick* through the end loop. The end-stick should be a few centimetres (approx two inches) longer than the width of the warp and have a hole through each end. Tie the stick with a piece of string from hole to hole so that it cannot fall out of the loop (Fig 29b). Undo the remaining ties and spread the loop across the end-stick so that the threads lie parallel between the rigid heddle and the end-stick (Fig 29c).

If any thread is not entered in the rigid heddle, but is part of a counter-thread that is entered, it must be tied to the end-stick to secure the counter-thread.

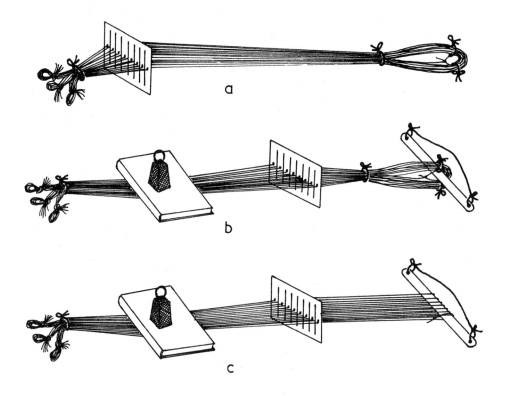

Fig 29   Spreading the warp on the end-stick

The end loop can be kept in order by placing a strip of self-adhesive tape across the end-stick. Fix the rigid heddle to the back of the loom, on the inside, with the holes level with the top edge of the loom and the end-stick hanging over the back (Fig 30a). Use strips of tape or clamps to fix the rigid heddle.

Temporary end-stick strings are attached across the top of the loom (Fig 30b) to hold the end-stick steady when the warp is being tied on. These strings are two double lengths, tied with a loop at their centres just large enough to grip the end-stick. These loops must be tied accurately so that the stick is held parallel to the front of the loom. The strings are fixed to the top of the loom with drawing pins (thumb tacks), small nails or hooks.

They are tied off under tension with a bow knot so that they can be removed easily after the warp has been tied to the end-stick.

The warp is pulled around the loom with the end-stick passing under the base, up the front and over (Fig 30c). As the warp is pulled around the loom the rigid heddle will spread it. Place the ends of the end-stick into the loops of the temporary strings and release the warp. Be careful not to disturb its position on the loom. Temporary strips of self-adhesive tape can be used to keep the warp in place (Fig 30d).

Remove the tie holding the thumb knots (overhand knots) and undo the centre group. Pull it gently through the first finger and thumb of one hand and take hold of the tensioned group with

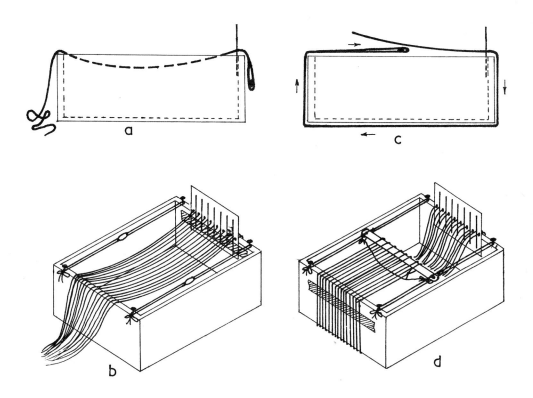

Fig 30   Dressing the box loom

the other. Pass the group over and back under the end-stick, divide it into two halves and bring these up on either side (Fig 31a) and tie into a half knot (Fig 31b).

Tie the warp groups alternately from left to right working to the outside edges. The groups are then tensioned equally working from the centre. Hold the split groups in each hand and pull firmly at an angle of 45° away from the end-stick (Fig 31c). When the right tension has been reached pull at right angles to the warp to close the half knot (Fig 31d). To check that all the groups are at an equal tension, run the back of the fingers across the warp. All the threads should feel the same. If any are too tight or too loose they should be re-tensioned. When all the

groups have been pulled to the same tension they are tied off with bows (Fig 31e–f).

The loom is now dressed and the rigid heddle can be released from the back of the loom. The tension of the warp should be high enough to support the rigid heddle and to keep the threads in the holes level with the threads in the slits. If the rigid heddle drops more than $\frac{1}{2}$cm ($\frac{1}{4}$in) fix it to the back of the loom again and re-tension the warp to a higher tension.

Remove the temporary strips of tape and the end-stick strings. The loom is now prepared for weaving.

Weaving with a rigid heddle
Plain weave is produced by lifting the rigid heddle

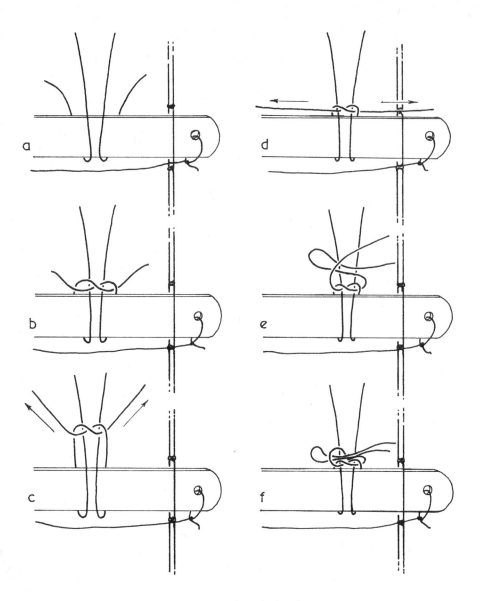

Fig 31   Tying on and tensioning the warp

to insert one weft pick (Fig 32a) and pushing it down for the other (Fig 32b). The weft is beaten into place with the rigid heddle by pulling it forward (Fig 32c).

If your grip is not very strong and you have any difficulty in holding the rigid heddle up or down while inserting the weft, the shed can be held open by using a shed-stick. This is turned on edge to hold the shed open while the weft is inserted (Fig 32d). The shed-stick is inserted

48

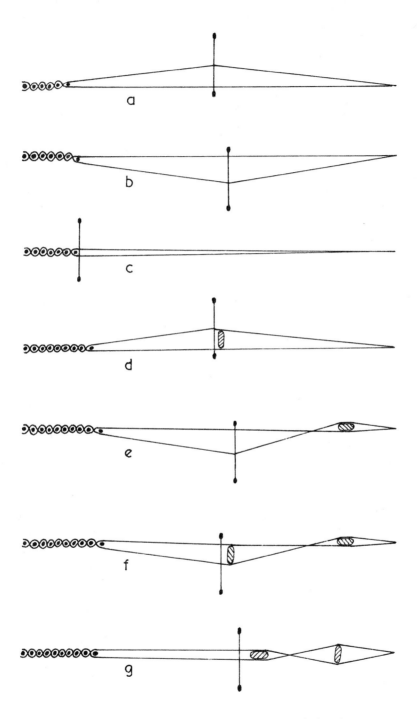

Fig 32   Shedding action of rigid heddle- and shed-stick

behind the rigid heddle and can be left in the shed that is most difficult to open (usually the raised shed). Push the stick to the back of the loom when the counter shed is opened (Fig 32e). A second shed-stick can be used for the counter shed (Fig 32f) but it must be removed before the first shed-stick can be used again. Fig 32g shows how the counter shed-stick will stop the action of the shed-stick if it is left in place.

Beating with the rigid heddle

The weft is beaten into place with the rigid heddle by pulling it to the fell of the cloth after each weft pick has been inserted. If using a wide rigid heddle hold it at both ends and keep it parallel to the front of the loom. It is very easy to pull one side slightly harder than the other (because one hand is usually stronger than the other) and if this happens the weft will begin to slope to one side (Fig 33a). Do *not* try to compensate for this by rocking the rigid heddle from side to side or the weft will become curved (Fig 33b). Pull evenly with both hands and keep

the rigid heddle at right angles to the warp. If using a narrow rigid heddle it can be held at the centre with one or both hands and the weft is less likely to become curved. Do not pull too hard or the rigid heddle itself will bow. 'Beat' with a gentle but firm pressure against the fell of the cloth until the weft has been beaten as close to the previous pick as required. With some rather resilient yarns the weft may not bed into the web of the cloth until the next pick is beaten in.

Stick-shuttles

The weft can be inserted using finger skeins, or by using *stick-shuttles*. These are usually made of wood with notches cut into each end (Fig 34a) to hold the weft thread. Stick-shuttles can be made with stiff card or plastic. When using this type of shuttle make sure there is enough weft unwound from it to complete a weft pick or the selvage will be pulled in (Fig 34b). Stick-shuttles should be slightly longer than the width of the warp.

Fixed sett

There are very few plain weave structures that

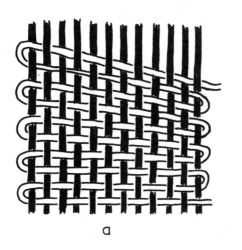 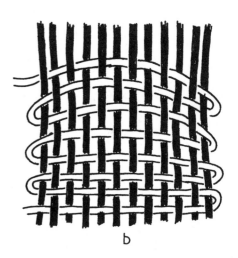

a   b

Fig 33   Sloping and curved weft

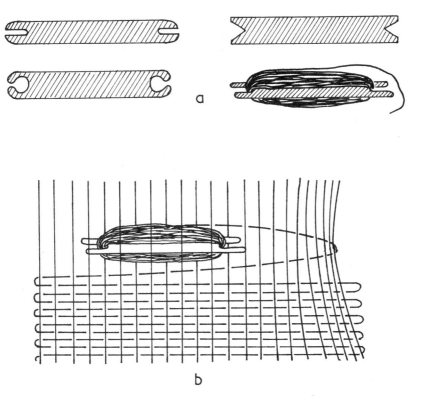

Fig 34   Stick-shuttles

cannot be woven with a rigid heddle provided that a yarn suitable to the predetermined sett of the rigid heddle is used (Chapters 4 and 5).

Wooden rigid heddles usually have a fairly small number of holes and slits and these also tend to be rather small. The metal ones usually have a sett that is more suitable for weaving a balanced plain cloth because they will accept fairly thick threads. The warp ends should pass easily through the holes and slits. Very thick threads may prevent the sheds from being opened easily or cleanly. This is because the warp ends will lie close enough to touch each other and may become matted with the friction of weaving. If this happens, the shed can be opened more easily by pulling the rigid heddle up to the fell of the cloth for beating and then either pulling up-and-away for the raised shed, or pushing down-and-away for the lowered shed. This will clear the shed as it is being opened.

The spaces around the slits and holes may occasionally need to be cleared of fluff on either side of the rigid heddle. If this is not done the warp ends will become bound together and the sheds will not open correctly. This will cause faults in the weave and may weaken or break the warp ends.

MENDING BROKEN WARP ENDS
You are unlikely to weave off any length of cloth without having at least one broken warp end. A broken end is temporarily replaced by a

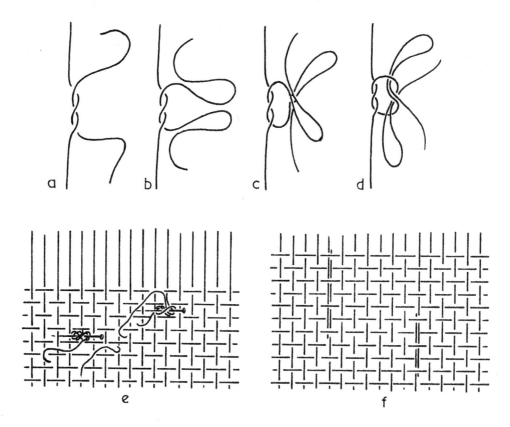

Fig 35   Mending broken warp ends

new length of thread. This is tied to the broken end, as near to the back of the loom as possible, with a *double bow knot* (Fig 35a–d) (App 3.3). The new piece of thread is entered and brought to the cloth. A pin is tacked into the cloth a couple of centimetres ($\frac{3}{4}$in) below the fell and vertically below the point of the break, and the new thread is wound around the pin. Make sure that it is the same tension as the rest of the warp. The front part of the broken thread is turned back across the web (Fig 35e). When the point at which the thread broke has been woven past, the knot at the back is undone and the original warp end is brought to the cloth and pinned in place. When the cloth is removed from the loom the mend is completed

by darning each end of the replacement thread into the cloth, to make an overlap join for a couple of centimetres (Fig 35f). The excess threads are cut off flush to the cloth face.

SIMPLE ROLLER LOOMS

Box looms and frame looms limit the length of the warp to the distance around the loom. A *roller* loom makes it possible to increase the length of the warp, without the need to make the loom larger. The warp is made and entered in the rigid heddle as previously described.

The loom has a roller fitted to each end (Fig 36a), and the warp is wound on to the back roller. The rigid heddle spreads the warp to the

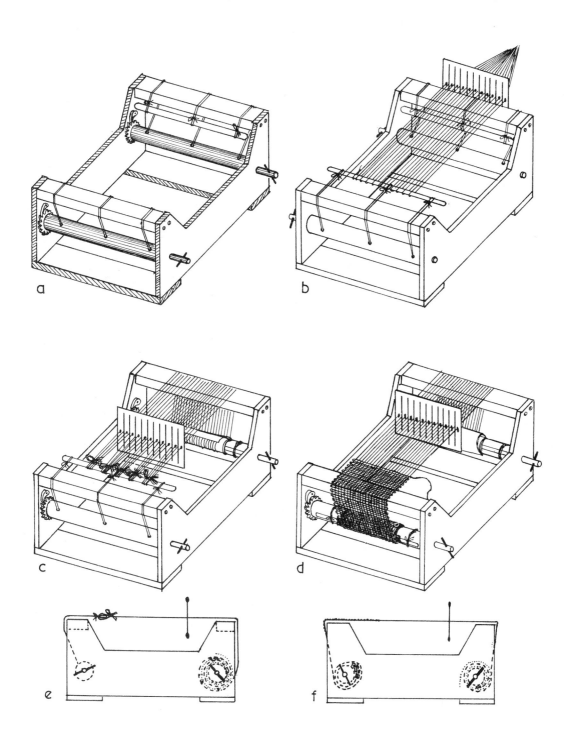

Fig 36   Simple roller loom

weaving width on the roller (Fig 36b). The warp is tied to the front roller (Fig 36c) and as the weaving progresses along the length of the warp, the cloth is wound on to the front roller (Fig 36d). A layer of stiff paper several centimetres (3–4 inches) wider than the width of the warp should be wound on to the back roller with the warp. This separates the layers and helps to keep the tension of the warp even (Fig 36e). The knots, where the warp is tied to the front roller, should be covered with sticks or stiff paper when the cloth begins to wind on to the roller. This prevents the cloth being distorted by the knots (Fig 36f).

The extra length of warp makes it possible to weave scarves, sets of table mats, cushion covers etc, as well as lengths of cloth to be used for dress fabrics or furnishings. The following two chapters give descriptions of experiments and weave structures that can be done on the rigid heddle.

4
COLOUR AND TEXTURE

In the preceding chapters we have discussed the structure of plain weave and some of the simple looms on which it can be woven. Perhaps because it is such a simple and direct weave, many people have a tendency to ignore it. This is a mistake, as many beautiful, exciting and intricate looking fabrics can be woven with it. It is the most fundamental weave and some of the more complex fabrics are simple extensions of it, or use it as the foundation structure.

YARNS

Properties of wool yarns
Because we recommend that you use wool yarns in some of the following exercises it is important that you know something about the nature and properties of wool. As we explained in Chapter 1 there is a difference between wool and hair. Hair fibres are round, smooth and generally fairly straight or slightly waved. A wool fibre is not smooth, and under magnification it looks rather like an extended pine cone. It is made up of a series of overlapping scales that grow towards the tip. These scales and the molecular structure of the fibres give wool very special properties.

We are only going to deal here with one important property, the property of felting. A badly felted cloth is harsh, matted and rather unpleasant to handle. This is usually caused by the cloth being roughly washed in water that is too hot and has too much soap. Once a cloth has been felted the process cannot be reversed. Felting,

however, is made use of in the production of woollen cloth.

Woollen spun yarns
Woollen spun yarns have the individual fibres lying laterally to the spin. They are jumbled and corkscrewed together by the spinning process and, unless highly spun, produce the soft bulky yarn that is so typical of tweed fabrics. Woollen yarns are spun 'in oil', which means that they are either spun without removing the natural oils of the fleece, or these oils are removed for dyeing and replaced for spinning. The oils serve a dual purpose. They make the spinning process easier and more efficient, and they protect and strengthen the yarn while it is being woven. Because the fibres are jumbled in spinning, they tend to give the yarn an uneven or hairy texture. The oil smoothes this texture and helps to prevent the yarn fluffing and fraying under the stresses of weaving.

Finishing of woollen yarns
The yarn is not *finished* (cleaned) until after weaving is completed. The cloth is *scoured* (washed) to remove the oil, and *fulled* (handled) to allow the yarn to expand and open up. Because of this the sett of the warp should not be too close and the weft should not be beaten too tightly. If the sett is too close there will be no room left between the threads for the yarn to *full* (expand), and the result will be a thick, heavy and

rather stiff cloth. Because the fibres in the yarn cannot spread laterally they will expand on the faces of the cloth and cause it to become much thicker than was intended. A woollen cloth should be set to allow for the lateral expansion. Until it is finished the cloth will look thin and open. The yarn and the cloth will also look dull, dirty and rather unpleasant until the oil is removed. The oil collects and holds dirt and this dulls the colour as well as flattening the texture. In order to see the true colour and texture of a woollen yarn, a short length should be washed lightly in warm soapy water. Handle the yarn gently or it will start to disintegrate and will not give a true idea of its texture. When the yarn is wet it will appear a shade or two darker than its true colour.

Worsted spun yarns

Although we have been talking about wool fibres, we have referred to woollen-spun yarns and woollen cloth. *Worsted spun* yarns are usually also made with wool. It is basically the spinning process that is different, though a different quality of wool fibre is used. This is more like hair in appearance although not in molecular structure. The fibres are usually much longer than those used in woollen yarns and the yarns are spun with the fibres lying *parallel* to each other. They bunch tightly together and produce a smooth, firm and strong yarn with a lustrous sheen. Because the yarn is smooth it does not require oil to help in weaving. Worsted yarns are supplied in skeins or wound on spools. 'Clean on cheese' is a term used to describe a woollen yarn that has been scoured and finished to eliminate these processes after weaving. A woollen yarn of this type will be plied to give it stability and strength for weaving, as are all worsted yarns. Worsted cloth is not finished in the same way as woollen cloth because the fibres are held parallel in the spin and will not full like

woollen yarns. It is still possible to felt a worsted cloth by rough treatment in washing. For more details see Chapter 9, Cloth Finishing.

COLOUR

Samplers

The following samplers cover the basic uses of colour, but need not be done consecutively. After weaving a sampler it may give rise to some ideas for further experiments. We advise you to follow these up before proceeding to the next suggested sampler. They should be kept and used for reference, and as your experience increases, so will your ability to use and develop the ideas contained in your samplers.

Calculating the sett to produce as near a balanced weave as possible is important (see Chapter 1). Balance is essential, as the colour and texture effects alter with a change in proportion of warp to weft.

Mixing colour in weaving is very different from mixing colour with paints or pigments. Observe carefully what actually happens to colour mixtures in your samplers. We suggest the use of fairly smooth woollen yarns in oil. Not only will this show the difference in colour value between a yarn in oil and one that has been scoured, but it also shows how colours 'blend' in a weave and how the close integration of wool fibres in the finishing process will increase this effect.

The following colour arrangement is suggested for this sampler, using a balanced sett and a minimum of 5cm (2in) of each colour to make the warp: black, green, turquoise, blue, purple, red, orange, yellow and white. If 5cm (2in) sections are used the warp will be 45cm (18in) wide and should be planned for at least 45cm (18in) length, plus wastage. The warp can be longer than this if you wish to experiment with a wider range of colours in the weft.

Use the same colour order for the weft as is

used in the warp. If you have made 5cm (2in) warp stripes, weave 5cm (2in) of each weft colour. In this way each new weft will produce one area of 'pure' or *self* colour and eight variations. It is unwise at this stage to be tempted into making this sampler as a stole, cot blanket or similar article. Some of the colour combinations will be pleasant, some unpleasant and some subdued but effective. By studying the results of the sampler you can select colour areas that you like and use these in your own designs. You will find that using colour combinations that please you is more likely to lead to personally satisfying results than trying to be fashionable by using popular colours that you do not really like.

Wider samplers can be made (up to the full width of your loom) by increasing the number of colours rather than the width of the warp stripes. If your loom is less than 45cm (18in) wide, two or more samplers can be woven and then placed side by side. In either case the length of the warp is calculated to equal the width of the completed sampler(s), plus extra for experiments and wastage.

Variation 1

In the above sampler we suggested using a longer warp and experimenting with a wider range of weft colours than the basic primary and secondary colours. A second sampler along the same lines will give a much wider range of colour 'blends', if the warp is (or warps are) arranged in the following way.

Use the basic black, green, blue, red, yellow, white sequence, but include as many intermediate shades of these colours as possible between the basic primary colours. Weaving the sampler with the same colour sequence in the weft will produce a vast range of colour combinations which you can use to select and plan colourways for your fabrics.

Variation 2

Use either of the above suggestions for colour warps and weave the weft colours in the same way. Plan the warp for three sections. In the first, use a heavy beat to produce a close weft sett, so that the warp only just shows. In the second, use a very light beat so that the warp colours predominate, and in the third section use very textured wefts of different colours and thicknesses and beat to produce a balanced sett (Fig 8c–e).

Variation 3

A sampler in cotton or similar smooth or shiny yarn will show the different colour effects that these yarns produce. This sampler is not an essential one, but is a useful guide, and as such need not contain as many colours as the previous samplers.

COLOUR AND WEAVE EFFECTS

The great variety of small repeating patterns caused by the interaction of colour changes in warp and weft can come as a pleasant surprise. A very large number of patterns is possible. The sampler described and illustrated in this section will suggest other possibilities. The warp should be set for a balanced plain weave. All the effects are created by the warp and weft showing equally on the face of the cloth.

Threading diagram

In paper-weaving, using black strips for warp and white strips of equal width for weft, four picks over four ends looked like Fig 37a.

Numbering the warp ends (1) for the odd ends and (2) for the even ones, it can be seen that the odd (1) ends show black when raised, while the even (2) ends are covered by the white weft. When the (2) ends are raised for the opposite shed, the (1) ends are covered by white. We use this formation as a *threading diagram* (Fig 37b).

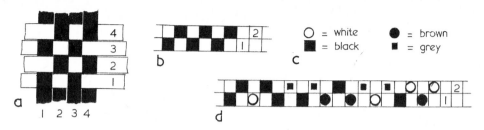

Fig 37   Simple threading diagram

When the warp is to be made in more than one colour, we can use different symbols for the extra colours in the diagram (Fig 37c–d).

Colour-and-weave sampler
The sampler illustrated (Plate 4a) was woven in black and white cotton. If the loom is wide (60cm or 24in) warp sections of 5cm (2in) are made as they show the patterns clearly. The sampler can be divided into two or more warps if the loom is narrower than this.

There are twelve sections, each of different colour orders: (1) all ends white; (2) 1 end white, 1 end black; (3) 1 end black, 1 end white; (4) 2 white, 1 black; (5) 2 white, 2 black; (6) 1 white, 2 black; (7) 3 white, 1 black; (8) 3 white, 2 black; (9) 3 white, 3 black; (10) 2 white, 3 black; (11) 1 white, 3 black; (12) all black (Fig 38).

When the basic sampler has been woven it will be as long as the warp is wide. The warp can be made longer than it is wide and the extra length of warp can be used to try two shades of a colour, or black and a colour in the weft. The patterns using black and white will be very bold. When the weft is in two shades of a colour, a colour and black or a colour and white the patterns will be

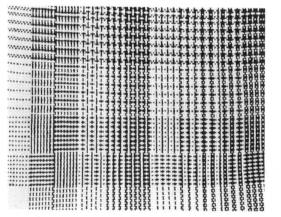

Plate 4   Colour and weave
a (left) Colour and weave sampler. b (right) Colour overcheck.

58

muted, with new interesting effects.

The weft is woven in sections that follow the colour order of the warp sections. Each 5cm (2in) square of cloth will have a different pattern. As there are twelve sections of warp order, to be woven twelve times in the identical weft order, there will be 12^2 (144) pattern areas when the sampler is finished. Some of these will be familiar. They have been a source of design for centuries.

A little time spent in studying the cause and effect in colour-and-weave will make *drafting* (the planning of a cloth) quite clear. When weaving

Because of this there will be solid white and solid black vertical lines. When the colour order in the weft is reversed, the verticals and the horizontals will also reverse (Fig 39b). This traditional pattern is called *log cabin*.

When the 2 white, 2 black picks are woven, a small 2 ends, 2 picks check pattern called *houndstooth* appears (Fig 39c) in the 2 white, 2 black warp section.

A few more *draw-downs* (diagrammatic representations of the weave structure) are given in Fig. 39d–i. The threading diagram with two sym-

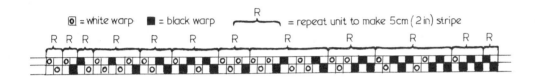

Fig 38   Warp Colour order

with a white weft for instance, a self-coloured cloth will appear where the warp is white. In the black warp area the distribution of black and white will be even (Fig 39a). The other areas will have various broken or broken and solid stripes.

The next two sections are related, as they simply reverse the colour order. Sections (2) and (3) in warp and weft form squares of horizontal and vertical stripes. When the white weft goes under the white ends and over the black ones, the white ends show and the black ends are covered, and a white horizontal stripe results. In the next pick, where the black weft goes under the black ends and over the white ends, a black horizontal line results. As the colour order in section (3) is reversed, the white weft covers its own colour in the warp, and travels under the black ends. In the second pick the black weft goes under the white ends and over the black ends of the warp.

bols, one for white and one for black, is given at the top of each. The colour order for the weft is shown vertically on the right of the draw-down. Only a few draw-downs are given, and a close study of the sampler will be of great value. Not all the possible two-colour combinations are included in this sampler. More variations will suggest themselves. Putting these down on paper is valuable practice for cloth analysis and drafting. Remember that as the warp ends raised for one shed will show their colour in the cloth, so the warp ends down in that shed will be covered by the weft and show the weft colour.

TEXTURE

Texture yarns
Plied texture yarns are often unsuitable for warps. The texture is usually created in the spinning and held with fine 'binder' threads. If the binder

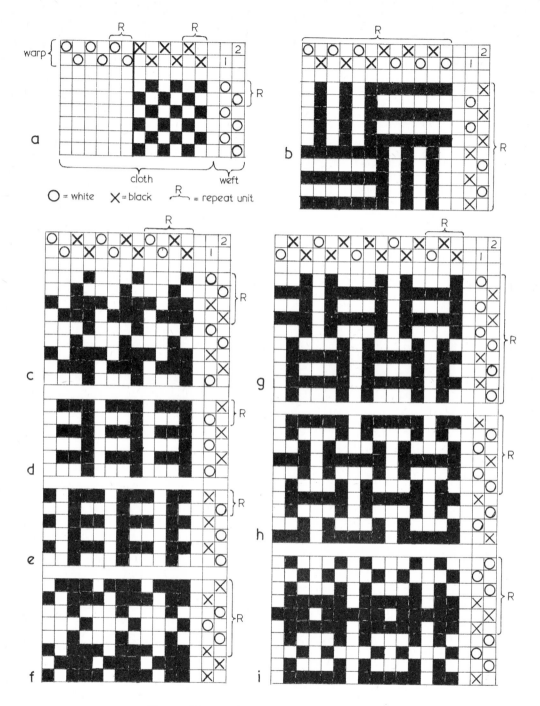

Fig 39 Colour and weave drafts and draw-downs

breaks or stretches, or the texture thread slips when friction is applied to the tensioned yarn, it will be difficult or impossible to use in a warp. The yarn can be tested by holding a short length under tension and rubbing it lightly but firmly between the nails of the finger and thumb. If the yarn slips, frays or breaks, it will not be very suitable for a warp. When you have more experience you may be able to use some of these textured yarns for special effects in warps, but until then we recommend that you only use them for weft.

The strength of a yarn is relative. It depends on the type of fibre, the amount of spin and the thickness. It is easy to forget the first two factors and rely on a medium or thick yarn being strong enough for a warp. Fine yarns can be very much stronger than a much thicker yarn of the same material if the spin is tight on the fine one and loose on the thick. The yarn should be tested for strength before making a warp. If it snaps when a strain is exerted on it, it will make a suitable warp. It is the snap break that gives the clue to the strength. It shows that it will take a certain amount of strain before breaking and providing you do not exceed that breaking strain it can be used for a warp. The yarn that does not snap but slowly pulls apart is not suitable for warp, because there is not enough spin in the yarn to hold the fibres together. This kind of yarn will be quite suitable for weft as the weft does not take the same kind of strain as the warp, and once the cloth is woven the threads support each other. This is a generalisation, and commonsense must be used when choosing yarns for a particular type of cloth. An upholstery fabric takes a different set of strains in wear from a wall hanging for instance (App 4.1).

Texture weaves

Texture is described in one dictionary as 'arrangement of threads in textile fabric, degree of openness or closeness in a surface or substance when felt or looked at'. From this definition it will be seen that all textiles are textures, though the reverse is not true. However, we tend to describe yarns and fabrics with a great variety of surface interest as being 'heavily textured', or simply 'textured', as opposed to the smoother ones which are described as 'flat' or plain. (This does not always indicate the use of plain weave, though it is possible that it is the source of this term.)

Texture samplers

It is therefore obvious that texture can be achieved and used in a wide variety of ways, and the following samplers are a guide and a foundation to build on. It would be impossible to try and enumerate all the variations.

We suggest that you make warps, each of one type of yarn, and experiment with wefts of all kinds. This should be treated as a 'limited series' of warps, using a fine smooth yarn for the first warp and increasing the thickness and surface texture of the warp yarn as the series progresses.

The warp should be approximately 10cm (4in) wide, and long enough to weave 10cm (4in) of each weft you are going to use, plus wastage.

We do not suggest a sectioned sampler like the first colour sampler, because of the technical problem of finding suitable balanced setts for a number of different yarns in the same warp. The weave *take up* (the extra length of yarn required to allow the warp and weft to bend around each other, see Fig 5) would vary with each yarn and would cause some areas to become very slack or very taut. Even if you overcame this problem, the various shrinkage rates in the finishing would almost certainly cause the sampler to become cockled and lumpy. The results could be disappointing. For these reasons we suggest making a number of warps, which can either be kept as complete strips or cut into single samples and mounted for reference.

By weaving the samplers separately, quite different fibres such as tweed yarn and silk, linen and worsted, as well as similar fibres, can be used in the warp and the weft to give a huge variety of fabric qualities and textures (Plate 5).

TEXTURE AND COLOUR

The next step is to use two or more textures or colours in contrast to each other in the same sampler. An occasional single pick of a textured or coloured weft, on a plain ground, will result in broken horizontal or *weft stripes*. By increasing the number of picks of one and decreasing the picks of the other, you can 'shade' from one texture (or colour) into another. Unbroken weft stripes can be woven by using two or more picks of each. More than two textures (colours) can be used in this way. One of the technical problems that can arise when weaving weft stripes in different yarns does not become apparent until the fabric is

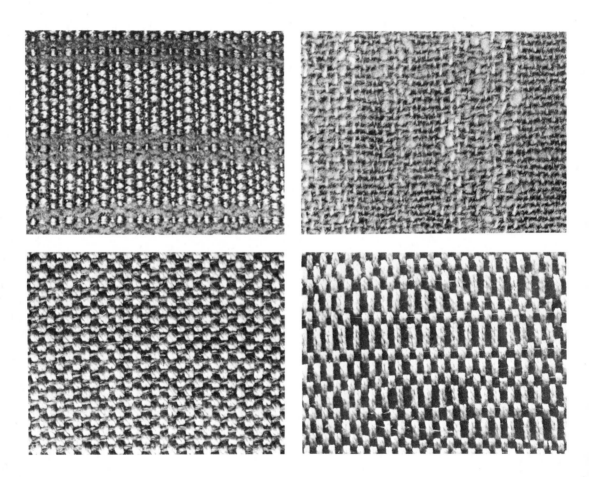

Plate 5   Plain weave
Four examples of textured plain weave

washed. If different fibre types are used together in the weft, one of the yarns may have a much greater shrinkage rate than the other. If this is so, a *seersucker* effect will be produced. This may be an accident the first time, but once discovered can be used to create a controlled design.

Similar effects can be achieved in the warp, provided you remember that:

(a) the sett of the warp must be calculated for each yarn

(b) the possibility of unintentionally or intentionally producing seersucker

(c) that to produce warp stripes, the weft should only be in one colour or texture.

Taking this idea one step further, checks and overchecks can be produced by repeating the warp sequences in the weft (Plate 4b).

Stripes and checks can be woven for all kinds of uses, from dress and furnishing fabrics to rugs and wall hangings.

The rule that vertical and horizontal stripes tend to emphasise height and breadth respectively, should be taken into consideration when planning designs for garments or household fabrics. Checks, particularly bold ones, tend to emphasise contours. Most people are aware of these points when choosing designs for clothing, but are liable to forget that they apply equally well to domestic fabrics. The small patterns of the colour and weave effects are suitable for most things. Each can be used by itself, as an all over pattern, or with others to make bigger pattern repeats.

5

FINGER MANIPULATED WEAVES

WEFT PATTERNS

The handweaver can manipulate both warp and weft to produce colour, texture and structure patterns with plain weave as the basic cloth structure. These patterns can extend all over the cloth or form only part of it. They can be used with warps of any sett, colour or texture combination, but for your early samplers we suggest the use of self-coloured warps. Suitable setts are suggested in the text. Spaced warps are suitable for many of these techniques.

Spaced warps

A *spaced warp* is made of stripes of warp with empty spaces between the stripes. On a frame loom the number of ends needed for a stripe are

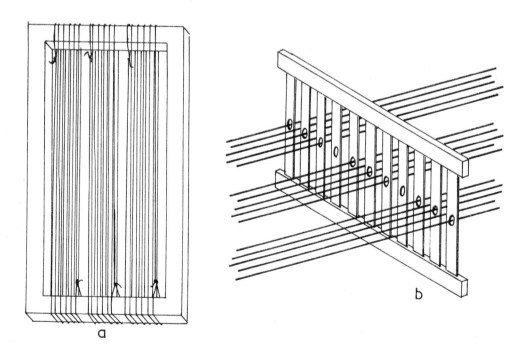

Fig 40 Spaced warps

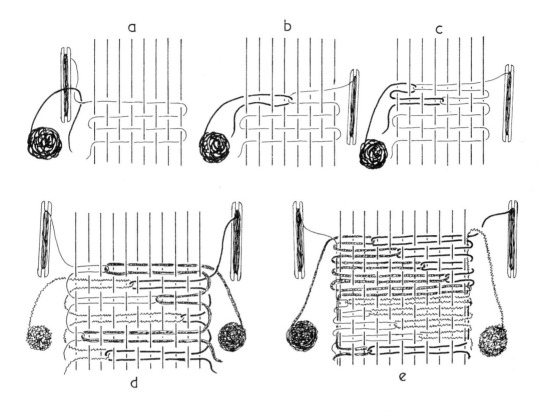

Fig 41   Linked weft and variations

spaced according to the sett and followed by a section without warp, and so on across the width of the cloth, ending with a warp stripe (Fig 40a). A rigid heddle is entered as usual for the width of each warp stripe, and empty slits and holes are left for the width of each space between the stripes (Fig 40b).

Linked weft

Two contrasting weft threads are *linked* in each shed to shade into each other or to divide the fabric into two contrasting areas. A ball of one of the yarns is placed at one side of the loom near the selvage. The other weft yarn is wound on a shuttle and woven through the shed from the opposite selvage. The shuttle picks up a loop from the free end of the contrasting yarn, and returns through the *same* shed to the selvage from which it started (Fig 41a). Pulling the weft brings the contrasting yarn into the shed to any point desired. The two wefts are interlocked and form a double-weft pick (Fig 41b). The counter-shed is woven in an identical manner, the shuttle weaving right across, picking up the contrasting weft and returning to the selvage from which it started. Again the contrast weft is pulled into the shed (Fig 41c). Care has to be taken to make sure that the selvage is not pulled in, and that long loops are not left.

Variations will easily suggest themselves. Using two shuttles, one to weave from each side of the

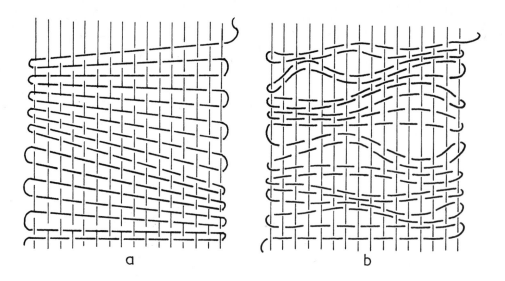

Fig 42   Angled and curved weft

web, and two contrasts, one on either side, will afford great freedom of design (Fig 41d and e).

Angled weft

Beating the weft into place with a sword-stick or rigid heddle makes it possible to place the weft at an angle. The angle can be increased in succeeding picks and then decreased until the weft is again at right angles to the warp. Regular or irregular fan shapes can pattern the whole or only part of the cloth (Fig. 42a and App 5.1).

Smaller areas can be formed by weaving a few picks at right angles to the warp; moving sections of the weft with the fingers to leave some of the warp uncovered, with the weft curving around these sections (Fig 42b).

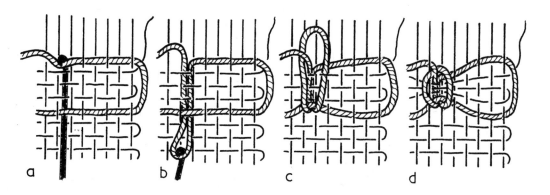

Fig 43   Distorted weft—Danish medallion

Danish medallion

A very decorative pattern, *Danish medallion* uses one pick of a group to loop around the others and distort the weft into oval sections. The medallion looks best when the ground weft and distortion weft are of contrasting colours or textures.

Weave one pick of contrast yarn, followed by several picks of ground weft. Bring the contrast weft up the selvage and into the next shed for the width of the medallion, bring it out of the shed to the surface of the cloth. Push a crochet or threading hook through the web vertically below the point where the shuttle left the shed, and below the last contrasting pick. Push the hook up to the fell of the cloth to pick up a loop of weft from the shuttle (Fig 43a). Pull the loop down underneath the web (Fig 43b) and bring it to the top. Take the shuttle through the loop and tighten (Fig 43c–d). Re-introduce the shuttle into the shed and weave the next medallion in the same way. The

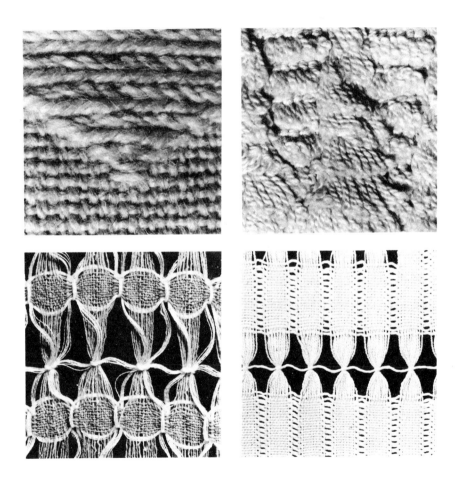

Plate 6   Finger weaves
a (above left) Soumak. b (above right) Knotted tufts. c (below left) Danish medallion.
d (below right) Wrapped warp.

67

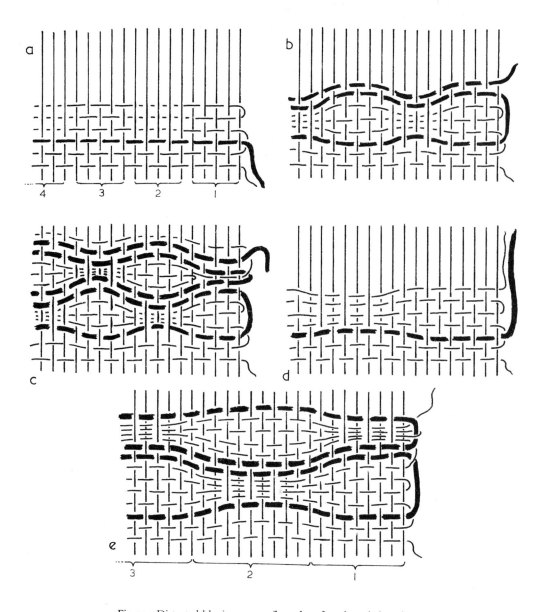

Fig 44 Distorted block weave—floated weft and corded weft

medallions can be wide or narrow, thick or thin, regular or irregular, in borders or all over. A spaced warp woven with a medallion for each section of warp, will have the appearance of bordered plain weave ovals or circles floating in open space (Plate 6c).

Distorted block weft

Another distorted weft technique uses opposing blocks of plain weave. The distortion can be emphasised by linking the blocks with two picks of a contrasting colour or texture.

For the first sample we suggest that you divide the warp into an odd number of equal width sections. These sections (*blocks*) are numbered 1, 2, 3, 4, 5 etc, and for the first band of weft the shuttle passes *through* the plain weave sheds on blocks 1, 3, 5 etc, but *under* all the warp ends in blocks 2, 4 etc (Fig 44a). The next band is woven through the shed of blocks 2, 4 etc and under blocks 1, 3, 5 etc (Fig 44b). Two picks of plain weave passing through both odd and even numbered blocks will emphasise the distortion of the weft. These two plain weave picks are woven between the first band of odd blocks and the second band of even blocks. The distortion will form oval-shaped areas in the individual blocks (Fig 44c).

The blocks can also be woven in contrasting colours, one colour for the odd numbered blocks and the second colour for the even ones.

Changing-shed cording

The weft floats formed at the back of the fabric with the above method are not always desirable and can be avoided by letting the weft cord in one of the sheds of the block not being woven. With this method, the weft passes from selvage to selvage through one of the sheds, but returns through a changing block shed.

Weave one pick of contrast weft. Change the shed and weave the first pick of block weft right across the fabric. Change the shed, weave for the width of the first block and bring the shuttle to the surface. Change the shed and weave for the width of the second block, bring the shuttle to the surface. Change the shed for each block across the width of the fabric. This second pick, in a changing shed, will weave alternate blocks but the weft passes through the same shed as in the preceding pick for the corded areas (Fig 44d). The order of one unchanging and one changing shed is followed until the first set of blocks is woven. Weave two picks of contrasting weft and follow these by weaving the opposite blocks in a

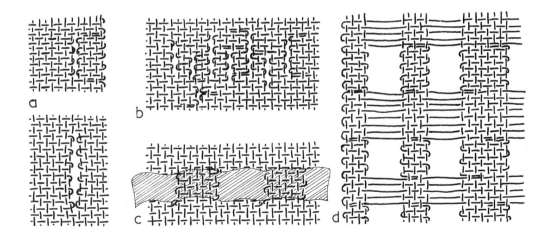

Fig 45   Slit cloth

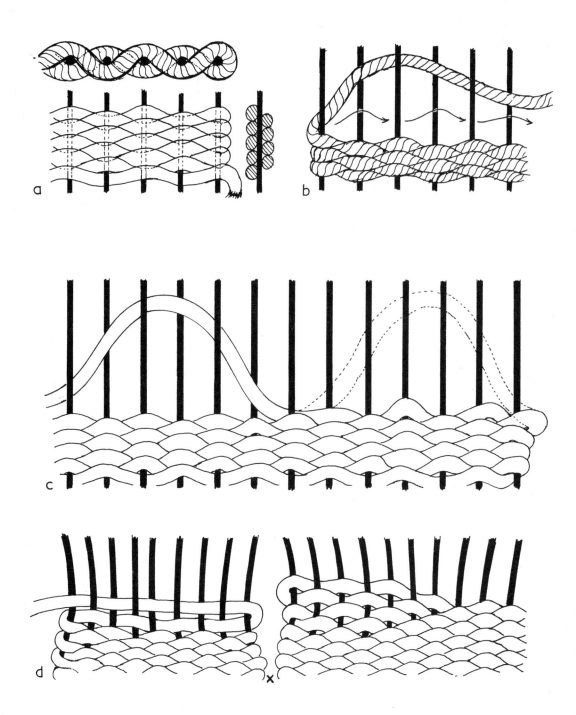

Fig 46 Tapestry—weft take-up and arcing

succession of unchanging and changing sheds. Make sure to weave in the areas that corded before, and cord in the areas that were woven before (Fig 44e and Plate 10b).

DISCONTINUOUS WEFT

Slit cloth

Separate areas woven with individual wefts will form adjoining selvages running along warp way slits. These slits can be functional, such as button-holes (Fig 45a), or purely decorative (Fig 45b). Each area has an individual weft weaving to and fro in that area only, and any two or more areas can be joined again by a common weft. The slits can allow an additional decorative weft to pass through the fabric, or permit the passage of a drawstring for a bag (Fig 45c). When each warp stripe of a spaced warp is woven in this way for a section and followed by a section of common weft passing across the fabric, an open net structure results (Fig 45d).

Tapestry

Some of the above techniques are related to *tapestry*. The most accurate definition of tapestry is a *weft-faced* weave in which one weft thread does not necessarily pass from selvage to selvage. To make the fabric weft-faced, the warp has to be set far enough apart to let the weft pack down closely to cover the warp completely. The warp should be a strong, smooth yarn such as cotton or linen, and the weft should be soft and pliable. The cloth will have warp-way ribs formed by the covering weft bending around the warp ends.

Weft take-up and arcing

Because the weft bends around the warp ends and the warp remains straight (Fig 46a), the weft take-up will be considerably greater than in a balanced cloth (see Fig 5). To allow for the take-up, the weft is *arced* (Fig 46b). The size of the arc

should be determined by experiment, as it will vary with the type of weft being used, the exact sett of the warp and the width of the area being woven. A series of small arcs as illustrated in Fig 46b will make it easier to control the weft take-up than one large arc across a wide area. If the arc is too big, the weft will loop where it turns between picks and may 'bubble' between the warp ends (Fig 46c). If the arc is too small, the weft take-up will make the warp ends converge (Fig 46d) and distort and narrow the area. This will alter the warp sett and the weft will no longer have enough room to bed down to cover the warp completely, creating gaps between unlinked areas (Fig 46d at x).

Different wefts each build up an area of the design by weaving to and fro in that area only. As shuttles are impracticable for weaving a large number of small areas, finger skeins are used (Plate 2). Each pick can be completed from selvage to selvage, taking the different weft colours in turn. On the other hand, each area can be woven independently *only* if the shape is a vertical or diminishing one (Fig 47). If underlying design areas are 'overwoven', the warp will be locked and there will be no shed available to weave the underlying area.

Slit tapestry

Where two areas meet vertically a slit (Fig 48a) will appear in the fabric unless the areas are linked. A tapestry or tapestry rug woven leaving the slits, is called a Khilim (Plate 7b). Sometimes the slits are sewn together afterwards. To avoid long slits, a design with more verticals than horizontals can be turned and woven sideways. The design will have the warp lying horizontally.

Weft links

Vertical slits can be joined during weaving by *dovetailing* or *weft links*. Dovetailing will break the

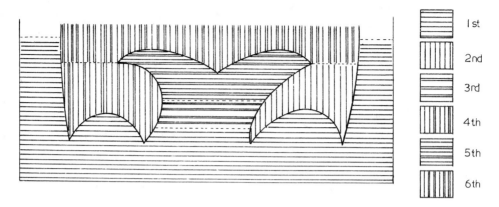

Fig 47   Weaving two-colour areas—key to weaving sequence on right

☰	1st
|||	2nd
☰	3rd
|||	4th
☰	5th
|||	6th

vertical line into a zig-zag (Fig 48b). Both the dovetail and the weft link described below are easier to weave when the two adjoining wefts travel to meet each other in one shed and to part from each other in the next (Fig 48c). It will be found that not only the links, but a change of each area is helped by following this *meet-and-part* rule of direction.

The weft link between two areas takes place once only for any two picks and lies between adjacent warp ends (Fig 48d). As its name implies,

the two adjacent weft threads turn round each other after meeting, and before parting in the next pick.

Hatching and shading
An extension of the two-pick meet-and-part technique can be used for triangular and two-pick hatching and shading. This can be done in regular or irregular interacting horizontal lines (Fig 49 and Plate 7c).

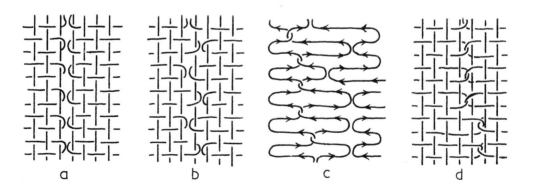

Fig 48   Slits and weft links

Plate 7   Tapestry
a (above left) Tapestry sampler. b (above right) Khilim, diagonals and curves. c (below
left) Curved weft and hatching. d (below right) Diagonals and triangles.
Samples illustrated show warp horizontal, weft vertical.

Lines and outlines

Lines and outlines present no problem when they are horizontal or diagonal (Fig 50a and b). Single warp-end outlines can be woven over a continuous background by wrapping the outline weft around the end when it is raised (Fig 50c and d). An outline between two colour areas can be woven in a figure-of-eight over two warp ends, leaving slits (Fig 50e), or weft linked (Fig 50f). It can be dovetailed into both areas using three ends, one by itself and one on either side, alternating with the area colours (Fig 50g). The outline weft can be woven round one end and weft-linked on both sides (Fig 50h). If a finer yarn than the main weft is used it can link and outline the two areas with a weft link, without using a warp end (Fig 50i and j). Because of the relatively wide setting of the warp, a really fine vertical outline is not easy to achieve. An outline from the horizontal through the diagonal to the

73

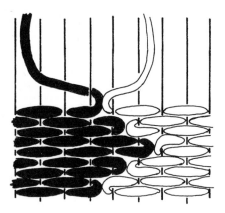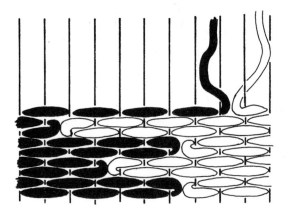

Fig 49   Weft links—hatching and shading

vertical will need more than two picks horizontally and diagonally to balance. This is because of the thickness of the vertical outline, determined by the distance between two warp ends, and the very fine line two picks will produce in the horizontal part of the line.

Diagonals

Design areas with diagonal edges are built up in steps (Plate 7d). Identical angles can be woven in various ways, from a smooth gradation (Fig 51a) to a stepped outline (Fig 51b–d). Steep angles will need more picks before each side step is taken (Fig 51e and f). A combination of varied diagonals will appear as a curve (Fig 51g and Plate 7a–c).

Curved weft

Tapestry does not always require the weft to travel at right angles to the warp. Individual areas can be rounded and the weft curved into position (Fig 52 and Plate 7c). Pressing the weft into place with the fingers or a fork allows considerable freedom. Care will have to be taken to avoid buckling or contracting the fabric. Only practice will overcome this problem, but tapestry

is a most fascinating and versatile technique to master.

Tapestry sampler

As the weft is usually wound in finger skeins, and each weft travels only a short distance through the same shed, the frame loom with shed-stick and leashes is the easiest to use. A box or roller loom can be used for small panels. A rigid heddle is suitable with fine wefts and fine warps and can be used to keep the warp ends spaced and parallel in a wider sett, when only the slits are entered and the sheds either picked up with the fingers or made with a shed-stick and leashes. We suggest that you weave a tapestry sampler, following the above descriptions. An illustration of a tapestry sampler is shown in Plate 7a.

Double weft effects

With two wefts of contrasting colours or shades in the same shed, further designs are possible. When the two colours lie parallel and in the same sequence in both sheds, the area so woven will look spotted (Fig 53a). If they change sequence, lying colour *a*, *b* in the first shed and *b*, *a* in the

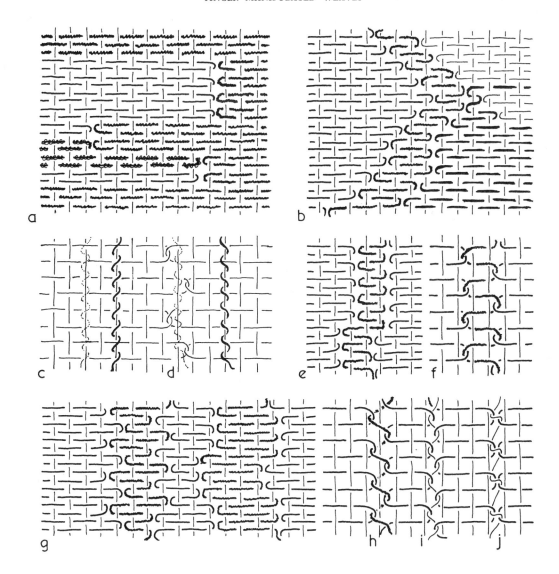

Fig 50   Lines and outlines

second, the appearance is one of horizontal stripes (Fig 53b). If they are twisted irregularly the area will be mottled (Fig 53c). If they are twisted with exactly the same number of turns, they will form diagonals (Fig 53d). Both wefts can be woven from selvage to selvage and manipulated

before they are beaten into place, producing two or more of these areas side by side.

Tapestry rugs

Tapestry rugs should always have the warp completely covered by the weft, and the weft should be beaten well enough not to slide on the warp when the rug is in use. The warp can be made of any strong smooth yarn. To get a truly weft-faced fabric, the weft must be pliable and for rugs fairly bulky. A singles or plied wool yarn is the most usual. Cotton yarn or rag strips as weft will make very useful washable rugs.

Tapestry rugs can use all the techniques in the above section as well as the stripe effects explained in the section on vertical rib in Chapter 7. Horizontal stripes, hatching and vertical stripes are all very easy and can be used for contrasting and blending areas of design. If a weft is made of fine multiple threads, very subtle colour mixtures can be used. As the warp will have to be set widely enough to accommodate a bulky weft yarn, the design will have to be bold. The vertical slits of a Khilim rug should be stitched firmly.

Expanded tapestry

All the tapestry techniques for weaving different areas of a cloth in different colours, and dovetailing or linking the individual wefts, can be used in a balanced sett. Contrasting areas of balanced plain weave will then show both warp and weft. If yarns of varying thickness are used, some areas may be weft-faced, and some areas balanced plain weave or even predominantly warp-faced. The weft can pass at right angles to the warp or be curved. Colour contrasts need not be the only ones. The fabric can be self-coloured with areas of varying textures.

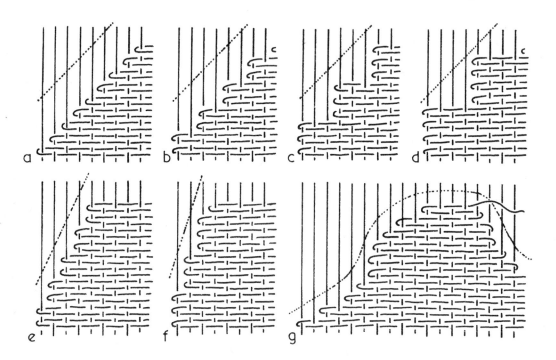

Fig 51   Diagonals—stepped outlines—curved outlines

All these techniques are suitable for fine or coarse setts in fine or bulky yarns, to produce free or formal designs for fabrics of all kinds.

RAISED AND ADDED WEFT

Inlay

A contrast yarn can be laid into the shed with the

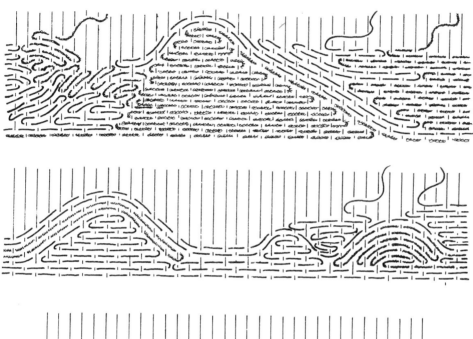

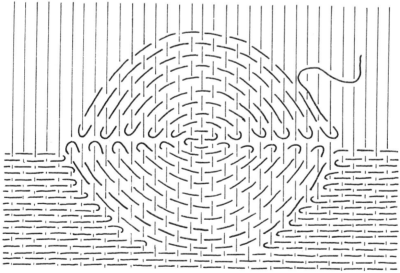

Fig 52   Curved weft

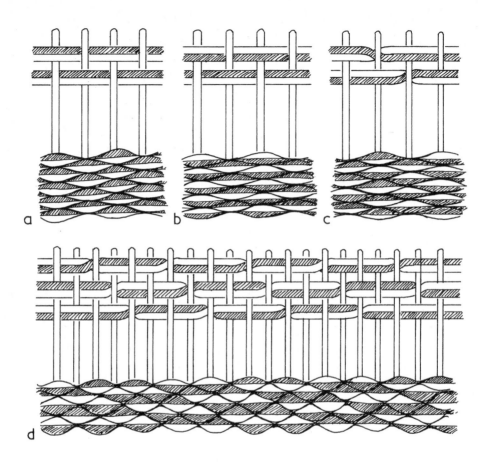

Fig 53   Double weft effects

weft of the cloth. This *inlay* can be used with almost all weaves and setts, but first experiments should be done on a self-coloured warp and weft in a balanced plain weave sett.

When a pick of the background weft has been woven, short lengths of a contrasting colour or texture are inserted into the same shed. For a flecked fabric they may be at random, or they may be used to build a pattern of colour or texture contrast. In the areas of inlay the double weft takes up more room than in the plain (single weft) areas. Because of this the inlay should be evenly distributed (Fig 54a–c) or compensating picks should be woven to balance the areas (Fig 54d).

The pattern threads can be trimmed on either side of the inlay after each pick, or carried up the cloth and inserted again in the next shed. When the pattern thread is not trimmed it will form a broken outline of edge floats to the inlay area (Fig 54e). A continuous inlay thread can be used, and as the underside of the fabric will not show the edge float, this can be used as the face of the cloth.

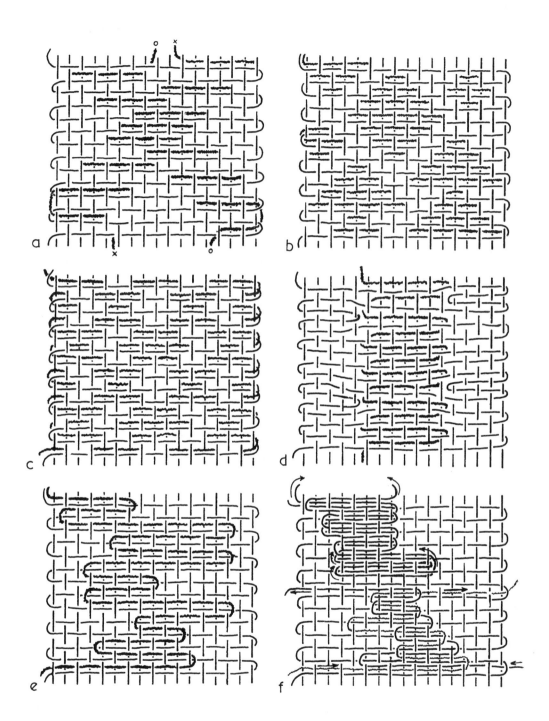

Fig 54   Inlay

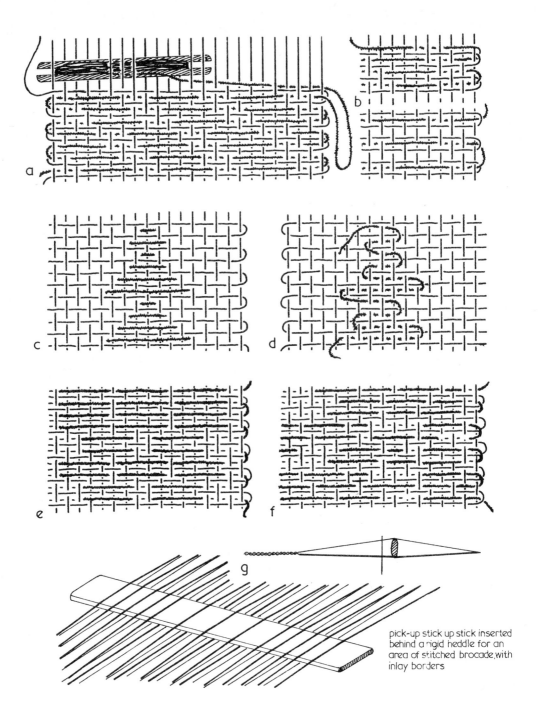

pick-up stick up stick inserted
behind a rigid heddle for an
area of stitched brocade, with
inlay borders

Fig 55   Brocade

An unbroken outline on both sides of the pattern uses two inlay threads travelling in opposite directions in each shed (Fig 54f).

Brocade

A *brocading* weft is not really woven into the cloth. The brocade floats over the surface of the web for the pattern or figure, and floats on the underside when it is to be hidden. A border of small brocade patterns running right across the cloth will avoid floats of unmanageable length. After weaving a plain heading, the pattern weft is passed in and out of the warp from back to front, and front to back on a closed shed (Fig 55a). One or two picks of background plain weave follow before the next brocading weft (Fig 55b and Plate 8c). When brocading a motif on a plain background it is better to take the pattern wefts to and fro in those areas only. In this case it is easier to weave the fabric with the underside uppermost so that the wefts can be carried up the cloth without showing the linking floats and without the need

to trim them (Fig 55c,d). Very long floats are not practical as the weft does not lie flat and is easily snagged. When the brocade area extends too far for a single float, the float is held down by a *stitching end*. The pattern weft is taken under a single warp end to hold it down. This stitching may be at regular or irregular intervals (Fig 55e,f). When the stitching is done at regular intervals, each pattern weft may employ the identical ends in each pick, forming lines running along the brocade pattern (Fig 55e and Plate 8d).

Regular stitching can be speeded up by using a *pick-up stick*. This stick is woven into the warp with the stitching ends passing over it and all other ends under it. The stick is turned on edge to give the brocading shed when the cloth is woven right side up (Fig 55g). When the brocade is woven wrong side up, the pick-up stick goes under the warp and over the stitching ends. When using a rigid heddle, the pick-up stick is inserted behind the heddle and the stitching ends must be ends that pass through slits.

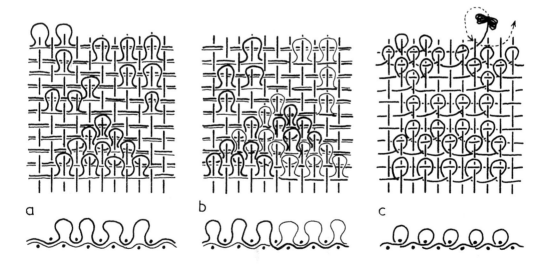

a   b   c

Fig 56 Pulled and wrapped loops

Pulled loops

Pulling the weft into loops on the surface is the simplest method of getting a deep soft texture. This can be used with any yarn and sett, either for decoration on a fine dress fabric, or for a deep texture on a heavy rug.

To keep the fabric at an even width and of firm construction, two wefts should be used in a shed. Only one of these will be used for loops at any given time. The first weft is woven from selvage to selvage and beaten into place. The second weft follows in the same shed but is not beaten at first. Loops are pulled to the surface where the weft passes over a warp end, starting from the selvage at the side where the shuttle entered the shed (Fig 56a). The shed is closed to hold the loops in place, before the pick is beaten in. Both wefts can be used for looping if it is remembered that one weft has to travel straight in the shed while the other is providing the loops (Fig 56b). The loops can cover the whole surface of the fabric or only parts of the surface, and can be of varying lengths.

Wrapped loops

Wrapped loops are easier to control for length and are firmer than pulled loops (Plate 16b). They take rather longer to weave as the weft has to be carried round each raised end (Fig 56c). The pulled loops have a tendency to ease through to the back when weaving. This is much less likely to happen in wrapping.

Soumak

Soumak is much flatter and firmer than either of the above loop techniques. Traditionally soumak is wrapped on a closed warp. The basic ground weave is plain. Either one or two picks of ground weft are woven between rows of soumak.

The soumak weft passes over a group of warp ends, back under part of that group and forward over the same number as before. For example, the soumak weft is passed over four ends, back under two ends, over four ends, back under two ends etc. The number of ends it passes over and under can be varied, as can the thickness of the soumak weft. As the floats lie at a slightly inclined angle pointing upwards from right to left when weaving from left to right, and the opposite way when weaving from right to left, any two rows of soumak look like a single chain stitch. This type of soumak is called *non-locking* (Fig 57a). A *locking* soumak is formed by bringing the weft under the forward float on the back movement before pushing this against the fell of the cloth (Fig 57b). This can be used for the formation and variations of diagonals (Fig 57c). If several rows are woven with the locking movement only, the final appearance of the fabric will be the same as the non-locking, as long as the rows start from opposing sides.

Open shed soumak

Soumak can also be woven on an open shed. The fabric gains in firmness and the back floats are eliminated by making the back movement in the open shed (Fig 58a). The surface floats can also be pulled to form loops (Fig 58b). These loops can be cut later to form a pile (Fig 58c).

As the ground weft weaves from selvage to selvage, any number of soumak wefts of different colours or textures can be used for the surface texture in each pattern pick. Design in colour and shape will be free from the need to interlock verticals. The soumak can be used to give contrast textures on a plain weave (Plate 6c) or tapestry ground. Compensating picks will have to be woven in the ground areas.

Cut floats

A pile fabric of simple construction uses two picks of pile weft in each shed, with one pick of

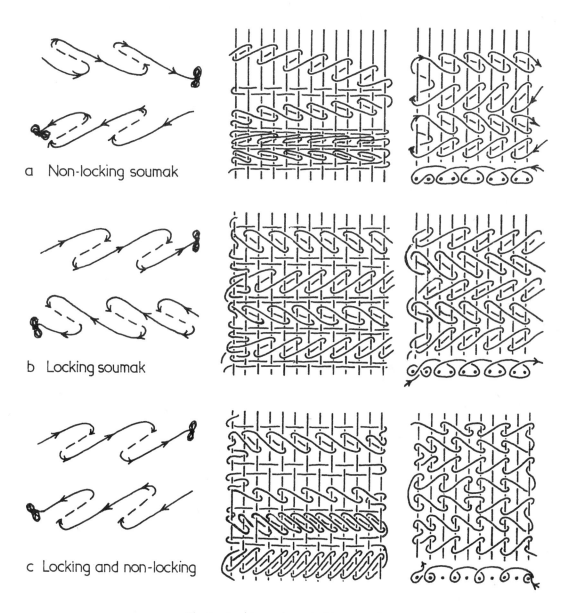

a   Non-locking soumak

b   Locking soumak

c   Locking and non-locking

Fig 57   Locking and non-locking soumak

ground weft (Fig 59). The ground weft is woven first and beaten into place. The first pile pick is woven into the same shed for a short distance only (under at least two raised ends) and brought to the surface. The weft floats over the top for a distance before re-entering the shed. This sequence is followed for the width required, either right across the fabric, or for a selected area only. The

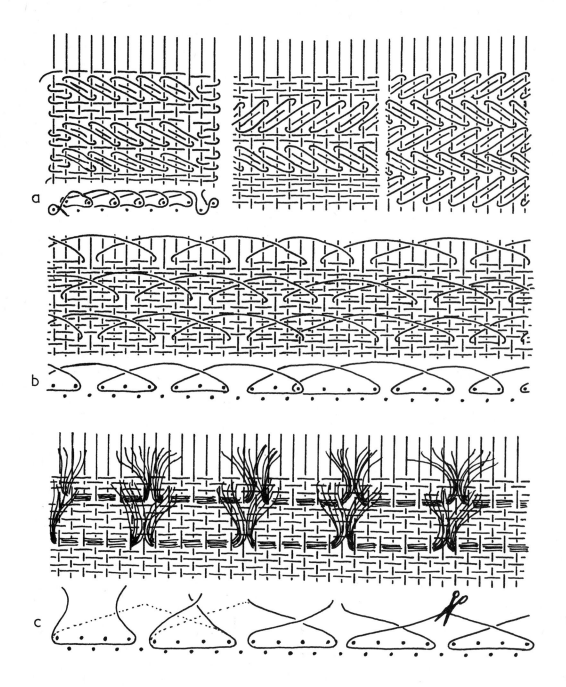

Fig 58 Open-shed Soumak

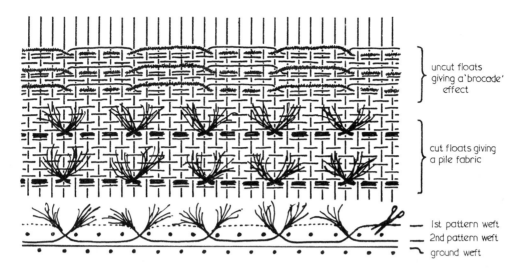

uncut floats
giving a 'brocade'
effect

cut floats giving
a pile fabric

— 1st pattern weft
— 2nd pattern weft
~ ground weft

Fig 59   Cut floats

second pile weft travels in the shed where the first floats, and floats where the first weft passes inside the shed. A regular shift to left or right will produce a fabric with diagonal ridges. The weft floats can be cut while weaving, with exception of the last few rows at the fell of the cloth. Cutting is easier on the loom while the cloth is under tension. For a deep pile, the floats can be pulled to form loops before the pile weft is beaten into place. Small colour areas can have short lengths of yarn placed for that area only.

When the pile does not extend the full width of the fabric, the ground weft may have to be woven with compensating picks to avoid build-up.

Knotted pile (Ghiordes knot)
The majority of *knotted pile* rugs are woven on a plain tapestry ground. The pile can be cut or uncut. The knot most often used is the *Ghiordes knot*. In the cut version each knot is one design unit. To some extent the length of the tufts (pile) produced will determine the number of ground

picks to be woven between succeeding rows of knotting. The shorter the tufts the fewer the number of ground weave picks if the ground is not to show between the pile. When the tufts are very long the resulting fabric will be very definitely one-directional, the pile lying towards the weaver. At least two ground picks should be woven between rows of knots. The selvage and any untufted areas will have to be built up in tapestry weave to compensate for the thickness of the tufts.

The knots can be made from continuous yarn or pre-cut lengths. If a very even pile is required it is better to cut the yarn before knotting. Even lengths are best achieved by winding the yarn round a grooved stick and cutting along the groove. Each tuft is made from a number of threads, according to the thickness of pile wanted. The tuft is made by placing the bundle of threads across two warp ends, taking them to the back and bringing them to the front between the two ends underneath the float. Pulling towards the

85

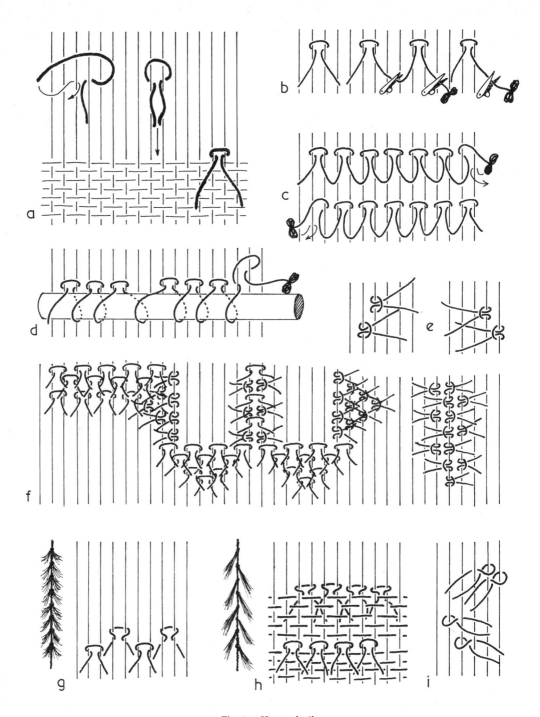

Fig 60   Knotted pile

fell of the cloth tightens and finishes the knot (Fig 60a). When using uncut yarn for the knots, take the yarn down between two ends, underneath one end, and bring to the surface. Take it back over both ends and the cut end of the tufting yarn, behind the other end and bring it to the surface between the two ends *under* the float (Fig 60b). The length is adjusted from the uncut side, the knot is pulled tight and the uncut end of the yarn is cut to correspond to the length of the cut end.

Loop pile

When weaving an area of one colour or when the pile is to be left uncut, the knotting can be continuous (Fig 60c). The loops between one knot and the next are left at the required length, to remain as loops or to be cut later. For a very even pile the loops can be made round a stick, which is withdrawn after the row is finished (Fig 60d). This method is fast and accurate, but limits the design. When each knot is made individually, it can form a single design unit, changing colour for each knot. When the knots are made continuously, this freedom does not apply.

Vertical lines and selvage knots

The direction of the tufting can be modified by forming the knot around a single warp end (Fig 60e). As this knot has less horizontal width than the conventional one, it is useful for fine vertical design units as well as for a change in direction to right or left (Fig 60f). It is impracticable to knot right up to the selvage and single warp-end knots, used near each edge, can give extra cover to the ground weave.

Double-faced pile

When a pile rug is woven on a vertical frame loom, it can be tufted on the reverse face as

well as on the surface. The rug will be reversible and can have different designs on the two sides. If only every second pair of ends is used for the surface knots, the frame can be turned and knots for the reverse formed around the other pairs (Fig 60g). With a little practice the reverse knots can be done without turning the frame, but it is not easy to tighten the knots correctly. If close tufting is required and therefore every pair of ends is used for the surface pile, only half the amount of tapestry weave is woven after a row of surface knots. The loom is turned for the reverse knots and followed by the second half of tapestry before the next surface pile (Fig 60h). The two sides do not need to have the same length or density of pile.

Sehna knot

A closer pile of slightly less firmness uses the *Sehna knot*. As in the Ghiordes, the knot is made round two warp ends, but every end is involved in two knots. The Sehna knot looks like an open-ended figure-of-eight with one warp end encircled by the weft. The weft crosses between the two warp ends, and one end of the weft passes over the other. The other end of the weft passes under the warp end before coming back to the surface. The tufts (pile) can slope to right or left (Fig 60i).

Sett for weft-faced plain weave

As the basic structure is the same as tapestry, the warp yarn and setting must take account of this. Tapestry and tapestry rugs use a weft-faced plain weave. The warp yarn should be strong and smooth, and the weft rather soft and bulky. The sett is found by winding one thread of warp yarn and two threads of the weft yarn round a stick. These should not overlap, but must be firmly pushed together. For accuracy, wind at least 5cm (2in). The number of warp threads wound will show the number of ends needed per 5cm (2in) of warp.

For rugs, a simple frame loom is all that is required. It has the advantage of keeping the whole rug in view during weaving. As most of the time taken is spent in knotting, speed is hardly impaired by this simple loom.

It is useful to remember that all the above techniques can add texture to tapestries and, in fine yarns, decorations to dress fabrics etc (Plate 6b). Detail and intricacy of design depend on the sett of the warp. The closer the warp is set and the finer the weft yarn is, the closer the tufts will be. Not only spun yarns of every kind, but unspun fibres can also be used for pile fabrics.

LACE-EFFECT WEAVES

Lace weaves on a plain weave setting will show best with a balanced plain weave sett, either right across the width of the fabric or in the individual stripes of a spaced warp. Most of these woven laces depend on the distortion or twisting of the warp ends to give an open but stable fabric.

Spanish lace

Spanish lace uses long and short picks to create a delicate openwork fabric in plain weave. The warp sett can be close or wide, even or spaced. A balanced plain cloth setting is the most suitable for a first sampler. We suggest a warp with a multiple of sixteen ends, as this will allow for a great number of various regular groupings across the width of the fabric.

Taking the group of sixteen ends as a design unit, for example, pass the weft under four ends through the shed, bring the shuttle to the surface and change the shed. Return the weft through the counter-shed under four ends and bring to the surface. Change shed again, and pass the weft into the shed under eight ends, change shed and return in the counter-shed under four ends etc.

Small slits will be left between groups of eight ends. The longer weft picks will slope down from the right to the left when weaving from right to left, and slope down from the left to the right when weaving from left to right (Fig 61a).

The lengths of the slits can be increased by weaving a number of picks into the same unit area before moving to the next. The unit areas can also be varied in width (Plate 8a).

Spanish lace can be woven right across the web, in both directions or, if an odd number of plain weave picks is woven between pattern picks, from one direction only (Fig 61b). Areas of lace on a plain ground require corresponding picks in the plain weave areas. When the lace is woven on a spaced warp, the weft passing from one group to the next will show as diagonal links (Fig 61c). Pulling the short picks tight will distort the warp and open the lace effect of the weave (Fig 61d). Staggering the groups will form a network of lace (Fig 61e).

Wrapped ends

A lace effect is produced when the weft is coiled firmly around groups of ends, pulling these together and leaving spaces between wrapped groups. At least two picks of plain weave are woven between wrapped bands. The wrapping is done on a closed shed, coiling the weft around a group of warp ends in a spiral from the fell of the cloth to the height required, then returning to the fell of the cloth. The wrapping weft passes diagonally across the gap and coils around the next group (Fig 62a). When the wrapping does not extend from selvage to selvage, compensating picks will have to be woven in the plain weave areas. After two or more picks of plain weave, wrapping can start again, using identical groups as before (Fig 62b), or new groupings (Fig 62c).

If a clove-hitch is used (Fig 62d), a firmer fabric structure will be produced, which will hold even

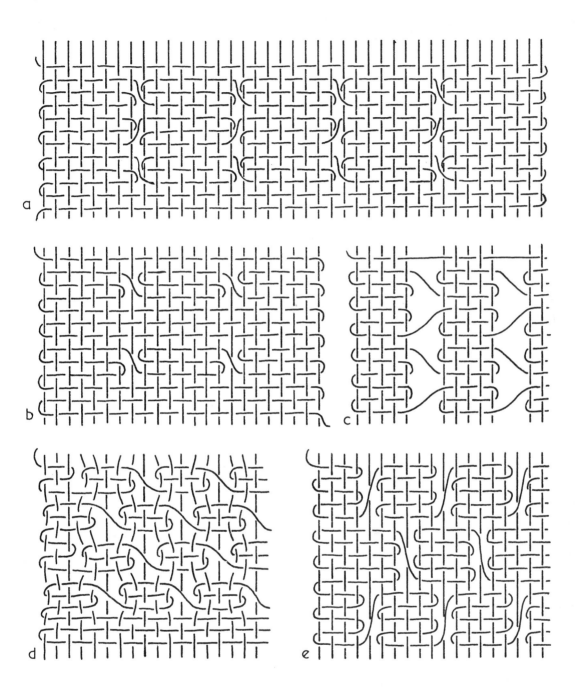

Fig 61   Spanish lace

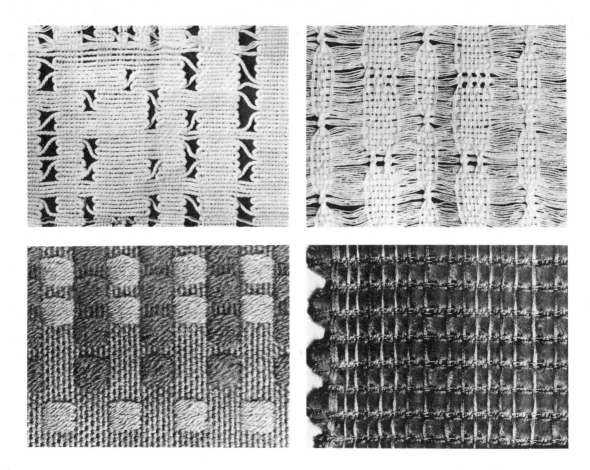

Plate 8 Finger weaves
a (above left) Spanish lace. b (above right) Leno. c (below left) Two-block brocade.
d (below right) Stitched brocade.

slippery yarns securely (Plate 6d).

Wrapping on an open shed to produce a delicate lace of grouped ends and one weft thread crossing over one warp end in the gap formed, can be done as follows:

Open the shed and insert the weft up to the area intended for lace. The pattern is started by weaving under three ends in the same shed, bringing the shuttle to the surface, taking it back over three ends (Fig 62e) and back into the shed

under six ends (Fig 62f). Pull the weft to tighten the backstitch, which will pull the first three ends together. Repeat the sequence across the lace area. The warp ends between the wrapped raised ends are not encircled, but are pulled together with the wrapped ends. The end between each group is not affected. The weft passing over this end forms a cross motif in the gap (Fig 62g). Plain weave is woven for a number of picks before wrapping again.

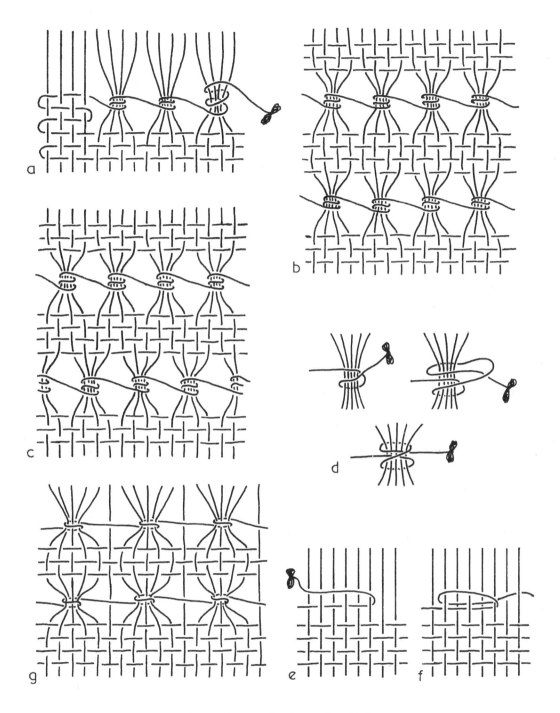

Fig 62   Wrapped ends and clove-hitch

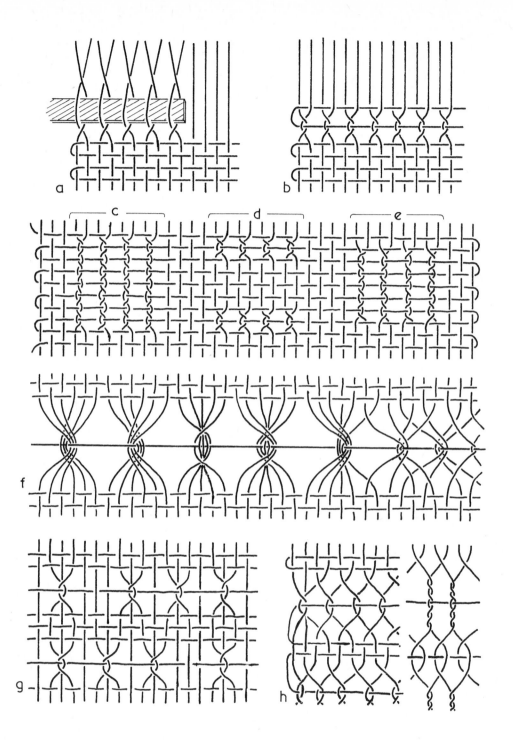

Fig 63   Leno

Leno (finger manipulated)

A very open sett of warp and weft to produce an open plain weave can be unstable, or *sleazy*, because the weft may shift on the warp. The weft threads can however be locked into an open position by twisting two or more warp ends around each other, with the weft passing through the centre of the twist. This *leno* weave can be done on any setting, but a very open sett makes best use of its characteristics. The crossed shed can be picked up on a pick-up stick. For a two-end cross, open the shed, push a raised end over the lowered end to its right and pull up the lowered end, placing it over the pick-up stick (Fig 63a). These two ends will now cross each other at the fell of the cloth and again past the stick. Proceed in this way across the width of the warp. Turn the pick-up stick on end and pass the shuttle through the shed created by the stick. Withdraw the stick and beat the weft into place. One pick of plain weave into the opposite shed will complete the leno cross (Fig 63b). The ends can be crossed again for the next pick, or a band of plain weave can be woven between leno picks (Fig 63c, d and Plate 8b). The leno twist can be left or right handed (Fig 63e). The leno can also be formed on groups of ends on an open or closed shed (Fig 63f, g). When the first end crosses the fourth, the third end crosses the sixth and the fifth end crosses the eighth, and so on across the warp, a triple twist produces a lace of interlocking ovals (Fig 63h).

Leno can be woven on any of the simple looms, provided that the warp is not under high tension to begin with. If large areas of leno are required, a roller loom makes it possible to release the rapidly increasing tension (formed by the crossing and twisting of the warp threads) making it easier to weave the leno design.

All the lace weaves can be picked up with the fingers and a stick-shuttle. When using fine yarns, a pick-up stick will be of help. All the techniques may be combined, simplified or elaborated. Their structure is most suited to strong smooth yarns.

ADDED WARP

Warp brocade

Warp brocade works on the same principle as weft brocade. The pattern threads pass under the cloth when they are to be hidden, and over the cloth where they are to form the pattern. The ground cloth is quite independent of the pattern, and the pattern threads could be pulled out of the cloth leaving the plain cloth structure undisturbed.

The ground warp can be any sett. The brocading threads are supplementary ends of contrasting colour or texture wound on to the warp roller with the ground warp, or left hanging to the back of the loom and tensioned with weights (Fig 64a, b). On a frame loom they are tied to the top and bottom of the frame where required. When a rigid heddle is used, the brocading ends must pass through slits only. The brocade warp can be added after the ground warp has been tied in place, or after a section of plain or other weave has been woven. The added warp is threaded through the slits of the rigid heddle where required and pinned to the fabric (Fig 35e). When the fabric is completed, the ends of the added warp can be darned to the back of the cloth.

When the brocading ends are to float at the back of the fabric, a shed-stick is placed under the ground warp and over the brocading ends (Fig 64c). When the brocade is to form a pattern on the surface of the cloth, the shed-stick passes over the ground warp and under the brocading ends (Fig 64d). With two shed-sticks used at the same time, some pattern threads can pass underneath, while some float on the surface of the cloth (Fig 64e). Patterns are produced by raising the brocade warp for several successive picks, and

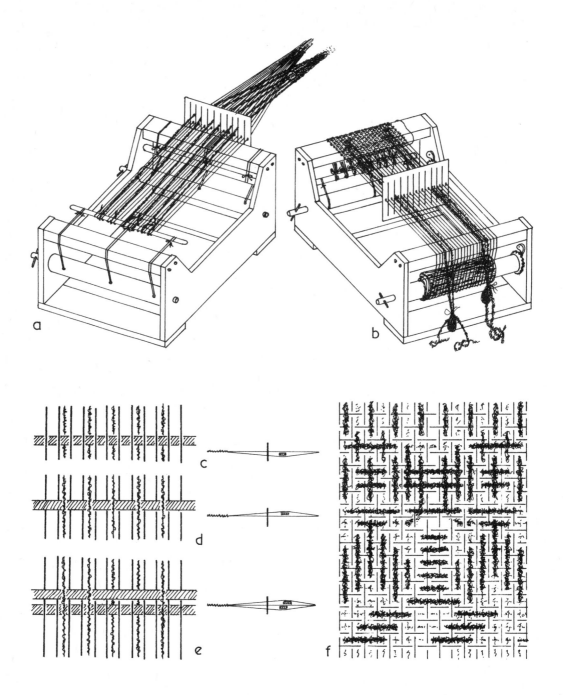

Fig 64   Warp brocade

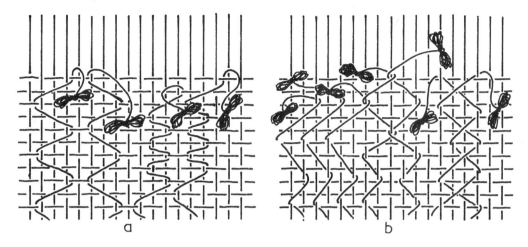

Fig 65 Overlay

then 'dropping' the brocade warp to the back of the cloth. Long brocade stripes can be 'stitched' by going under one pick only before being brought back to the surface. The warp-way brocade can be joined by a weft-way brocade to form a double brocade fabric, bound into the ground cloth (Fig 64f).

Overlay

In an *overlay* weave each pattern thread is wound in a finger skein and lies on the woven cloth while the ground cloth is being woven. Each pattern weft is taken up the warp at intervals and,

according to the pattern, bound into the cloth by a weft pick (Fig 65a), or a warp end (Fig 65b).

Combination of techniques

The combination of overlay weaves with leno or lace over a plain ground, or in fact the combination of any of the above techniques, can lead to innumerable designs for every kind of fabric.

All the techniques written about so far can be woven on simple frame looms, box looms and roller looms. They can also be woven on the two- and four-shaft looms described in Chapter 6.

6
TWO- AND FOUR-SHAFT LOOMS

SHEDDING ACTIONS

Shafts (harnesses)

All the looms discussed so far have been two-shed looms. A loom with *shafts* introduces a new principle: movable heddles on shafts. A shaft loom can have two shafts producing two sheds, or more than two shafts and therefore more than two sheds.

The shaft supporting the heddles can be a frame, and is based on the same principle as a rigid heddle. The frame may be a complete four-sided frame (Fig 66a), or two *shaft-sticks* (Fig 66b). When the warp ends are entered through the heddles on the shafts, these can be raised or lowered to open the sheds. If the shaft is pulled up, the warp ends entered into the heddles on that shaft rise, and the loom has a *rising shed* (Fig 66c). If the shaft sinks, lowering the ends, the loom has a *sinking shed* (Fig 66d). If it sinks and the opposite shaft rises, the shed is *counter-balanced* (Fig 66e).

Whether a loom has a rising, sinking or counter-balanced shed, the weave structure will be exactly the same. As the heddles on the shafts are movable the e/cm (epi) of the warp can be altered to suit the yarn being used (Fig 66a, b).

This book does not include more than four-shaft techniques. An understanding of these will make it possible to use up to sixteen shafts if so desired. Three shafts are used for some special weaves such as two-by-one twills (App 6.1).

In a four-shaft loom, sheds can be obtained by raising one, two or three shafts (rising shed), lowering one, two or three shafts (sinking shed), or raising some and lowering the others (counter-balanced shed).

TABLE LOOMS

Two-shaft shedding action

In a two-shaft table loom the shafts are usually linked over a roller. The sheds are obtained by turning the roller backwards for the shed, and forwards for the counter-shed (Fig 67).

Four-shaft shedding action

Most four-shaft table looms have a rising shed. The shafts are usually activated by side levers, connected over pulleys to the top of the shafts. As each lever only lifts one shaft, all the sheds can be obtained by using one, two or three levers. By numbering the shafts from 1 to 4, starting from the front of the loom, the position of each shaft in the loom can be indicated by its number. The fourteen sheds of a four-shaft loom can then be described as in Fig 68.

FLOOR LOOMS

Floor looms have foot pedals instead of hand levers to activate the shafts. The hands are left free to throw and catch the shuttle, and beat the weft into place with the batten.

Two-shaft floor looms

Two-shaft foot looms can be either vertical or horizontal. In either case the shed will usually

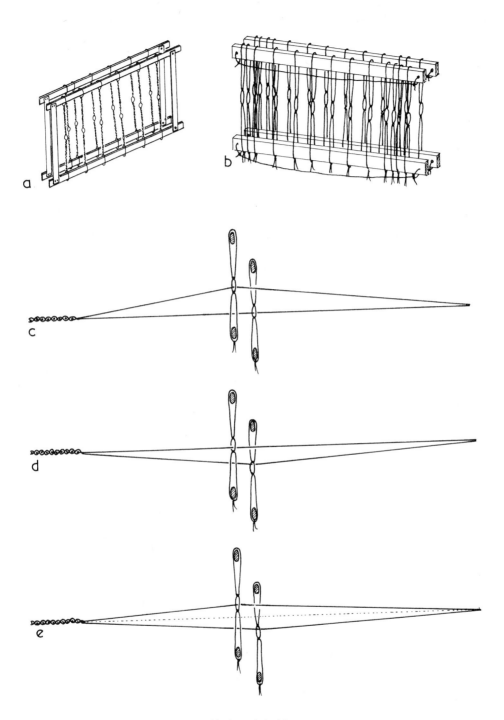

Fig 66   Shafts and shedding actions

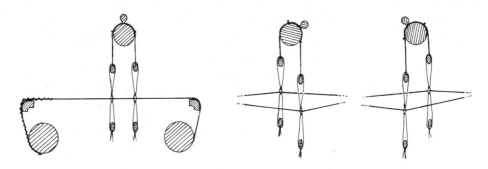

Fig 67   Two-shaft table loom—shedding action

be counter-balanced. A vertical two-shaft loom of strong construction is especially advantageous for the weaving of rugs and tapestries. The shafts move in horizontal grooves and are activated by hinged arms connected to a large roller pulley. The pulley is turned by a cord connected to two foot pedals (Fig 69). The two-shaft horizontal floor loom has the two shafts linked over a roller in the same way as the two-shaft table loom. One shaft is tied from its bottom centre to one foot pedal, and the other shaft is tied in the same way to the other pedal. When a pedal is depressed the shaft tied to it is pulled down, and the other one rises.

Four-shaft floor looms

Four-shaft foot looms have balanced, rising or sinking sheds. Balanced shedding actions are the most usual and most advantageous. They may be either counter-balanced or counter-march.

Counter-balanced loom (balanced sheds)

A counter-balanced loom couples the shafts in such a way that the sinking shafts balance the rising shafts (Fig 70a,b). The six two-by-two (two shafts up, two shafts down) sheds are therefore the only truly balanced sheds, and are the easiest to obtain with this action (Fig 70c–h). These looms are usually supplied with six pedals,

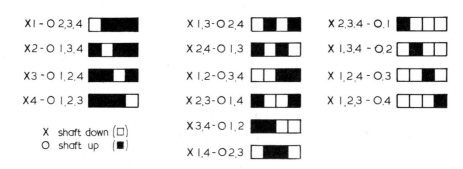

Fig 68   The fourteen sheds of a four-shaft loom

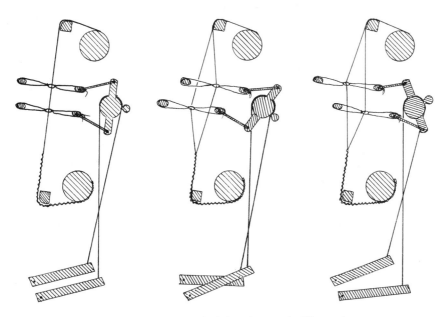

Fig 69   Vertical two-shaft floor loom—shedding action

each to be connected to the bottom of two of the shafts. Depressing a pedal will lower two shafts. This direct tie between shafts and pedals makes it almost impossible to keep the shafts level, as all but the centre ties will be at an angle.

Lamms

To centralise the pull on the shafts, *lamms* (pivoted levers) are needed (Fig 71a).

Counter-balanced loom (balanced and unbalanced sheds)

Each shaft is tied from the centre to a lamm, and the pedals are connected by ties to the lamms. Tying each pedal to two lamms limits the shedding action to the two-by-two sheds (Fig 71b, b1). We therefore suggest a modified pedal tie-up (Fig 71c, c1).

By the use of one or two pedals at a time, all fourteen sheds can be used. The two-by-two sheds (Fig 70c–h) will be deeper than the three-by-

one sheds (Fig 71d–k), but all should be usable.

Two pedals (A and B) are tied to two lamms each, and the remaining four pedals are tied to one lamm each (Fig 71c). Depressing a pedal with one tie will pull down the shaft it is connected to, and raise the other three shafts (Fig 71h–k). Depressing one of the pedals with two ties will lower the corresponding shafts and raise the others (Fig 70c, d). Depressing two of the single-tie pedals will also raise two and lower the opposite two shafts (Fig. 70e–h). Depressing a single-tie pedal with a double-tie pedal will lower three shafts, leaving only one shaft up if the three ties are three different ones (Fig 71d–g). The tie-up can be shown in diagrammatic form (Fig 71b1, c1).

Counter-march loom

The *counter-march* loom uses two lamms for each shaft. One lamm for raising the shaft, the other

99

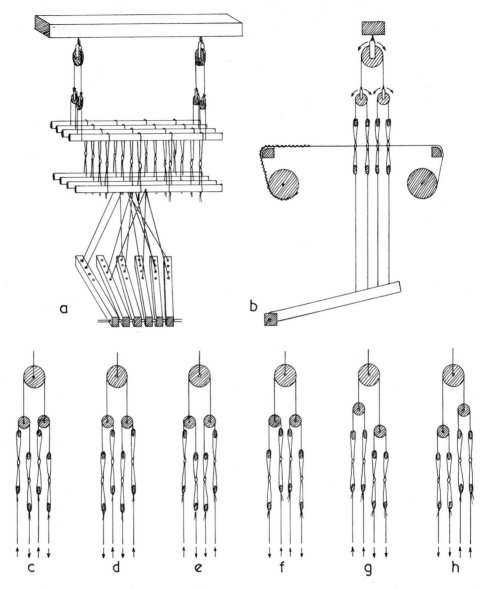

Fig 70   Counter-balanced loom—balanced sheds (direct tie)

for lowering the shaft. For each shed all shafts have to be activated, either being raised or lowered. Each shaft is balanced by its two lamms. All sheds are therefore level and equally deep.

The two sets of lamms are usually hung from two side pivots (Fig 72a), one set above the other, or both sets may be placed on one pivot. The lower lamms are usually a little longer than the other set and are connected via jacks (pivotal levers) in a castle (supporting frame) at the top of the loom, to the top of each shaft (Fig 72b). They provide the rising (O) action. The higher set of lamms are connected to the bottom of each

shaft and provide the sinking (X) action.

Most counter-march looms are supplied with six pedals. Therefore the usual tie-up of each pedal with four ties (Fig 72d), only provides for six sheds at a time (Fig 72e). The pedals will have to

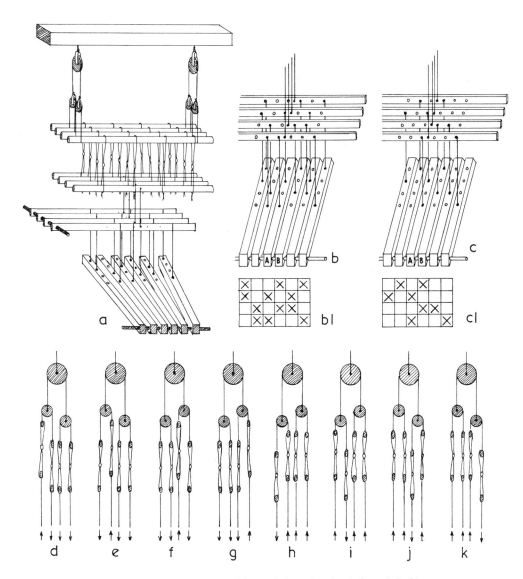

Fig 71   Counter-balanced loom (balanced and unbalanced sheds)

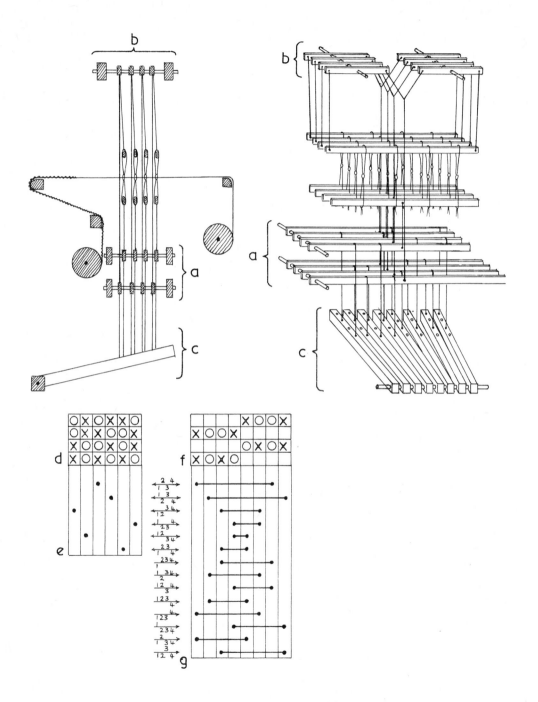

Fig 72　Counter-march loom. 6 pedal and 8 pedal (Universal) tie-up

be re-tied every time a different set of sheds is required. It is, however, easy to make two more pedals from pieces of wood to match those already in the loom. This simple addition makes it possible to use all fourteen sheds (Fig 72g) without re-tying the lamms to the pedals (Fig 72c). Both feet are needed for shedding, each shed requiring two pedals.

Using the eight-pedal tie-up provides a truly universal shedding action. In Fig 72d and f, O represents the rising ties and X the sinking ties. Each pedal only has two ties, and therefore each foot controls four pedals and all four possible movements of two shafts. By using both feet, it is possible to raise and lower any combination of four shafts and obtain all fourteen sheds (Fig 72g).

Mounting ties

All ties should be made with double cords (Fig 73a, b). Connections are made with an adjustable *snitch knot* (larkshead) (Fig 73c), and the cords are attached to the loom parts with a *hitch knot* (Fig 73d).

Batten and reed

When shafts are used for the shedding action, a *batten* and *reed* are needed for beating the weft into place. The batten, a frame holding a reed, is

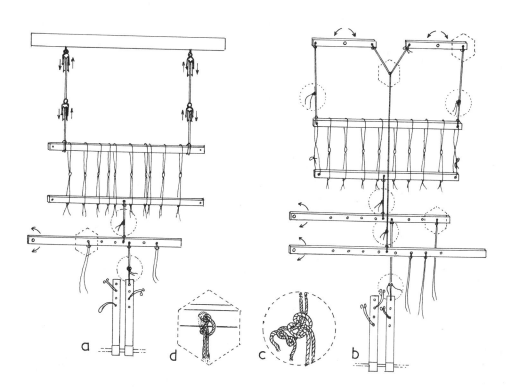

Fig 73 Mounting ties — for the sake of clarity only one shaft is shown

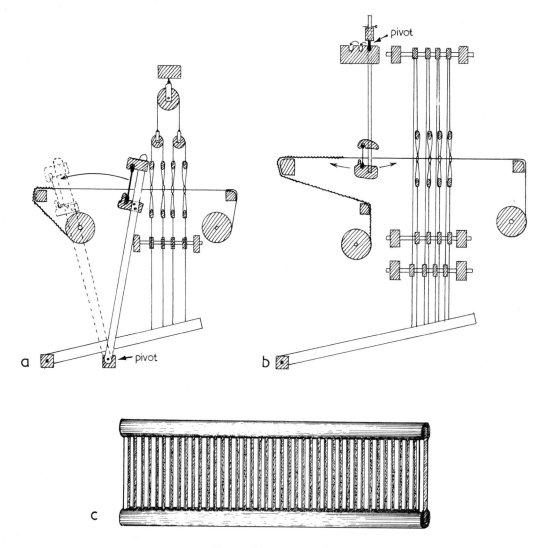

Fig 74   Batten and reed

usually pivoted from the side members of the loom. The pivot allows the batten to swing up to the fell of the cloth.

When the batten is pivoted from the base of the loom, it is called an under-slung batten. In most floor looms the batten is hung from the top side members of the main framework. The over-slung batten rests on wooden or metal pegs at the top, allowing it to swing freely (Fig 74a, b).

The reed is like a closed comb through which the warp ends are threaded after they have been entered through the heddles (Fig 74c). The teeth of a reed are at regular intervals. The unit spaces between teeth are called *dents*. Different reeds can be defined by the number of dents per centimetre (d/cm), dents per inch (dpi) or dents per decimetre (d/10cm).

MODIFIED SIMPLE WARPING

Raddle

Making a warp for a shaft loom is similar to the method of simple warping described in Chapter 2, but with an important modification. The warp has to be spread to the weaving width as it is rolled on to the loom. This is done with a *raddle* (Fig 75c). The raddle is like a large comb with a removable cap (Fig 75a), with teeth at regular intervals (Fig 75b). The warp is spread in groups of threads usually equal to the e/cm (or half or quarter the epi) of the sett.

Raddles can be bought, but are easy to improvise with a strip of wood and some flat headed nails. The nails are spaced 1cm (½in) apart, and to avoid splitting the wood they can be staggered. The 'cap' for the home-made raddle is made, with a length of string wound around each nail across the width of the raddle, after the warp has been spread (Fig 75d).

Planning the warp

The details needed for making a warp are the length, width and e/cm (epi). The warp length must be greater than the cloth length to allow for *wastage*, and the length and width should be slightly increased to allow for take-up and shrinkage. The wastage is the extra length required for tying on to the loom, plus the length at the end of the warp (the distance from the

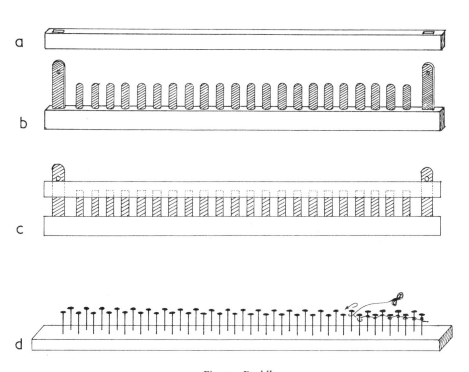

Fig 75   Raddle

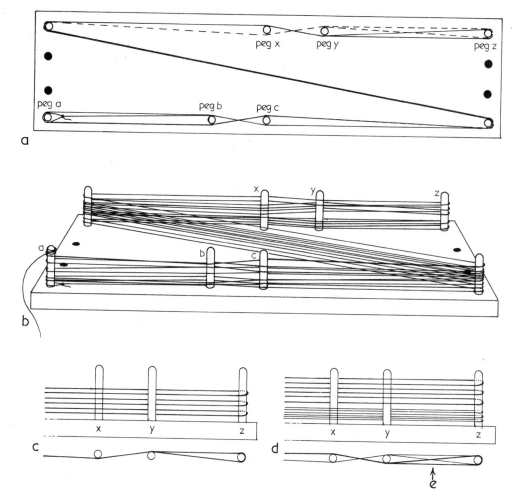

Fig 76   Raddle-cross

back apron-stick through the heddles and reed) that cannot be woven.

The take-up is the extra length and width needed to compensate for the bending of the threads over and under each other (Fig 5, Chapter 1). The thicker the threads are, and the more bending they have to do, the greater the amount of take-up that has to be allowed for. Take-up is dependent on two factors, the tension of the warp during weaving and the type of yarn being used. The higher the warp tension, the more the threads will relax and shorten when taken from the loom with the tension removed. The threads will tend to revert to their former unstretched length and may contract even more when the fabric is washed.

Washing the fabric may also cause the yarn to shrink. The amount of shrinkage will depend on the type of yarn being used and the washing conditions (see 'Cloth finishing', p170).

This is one of the instances where sampling is invaluable for discovering the characteristics of both yarn and weave.

Raddle-cross

A *raddle-cross* is made at one end of the warp so that the correct sequence of thread-groups can be spread in the raddle. The raddle-cross is made of groups of ends to equal the e/cm (epi) while winding the warp. If you are working in inch units, use the raddle-cross to divide the warp into half-inch groups. Inch groups are too bulky to wind smoothly on to the loom. Some raddles are divided into quarter-inches, and if one of this type is being used, the warp should be grouped in quarter-inch units.

The raddle-cross requires the use of two extra pegs on the warping board, but otherwise the warp is made in exactly the same way as described in Chapter 3, in the section on simple warping (pp34–43). The singles-cross is made between pegs *b* and *c* (Fig 76a, b). The length of the warp is determined by the number of pegs used along the length of the board. As the number of pegs used will depend on your requirements, we will refer to the raddle-cross pegs as *x*, *y* and *z* (Fig 76a, b). The raddle-cross is made between pegs *x* and *y* and a loop is formed between pegs *y* and *z* (Fig 76c). Remember that each thread turns around peg *z* and is the beginning of the next warp end from that peg. The width of the warp is counted in e/cm ($\frac{1}{2}$ epi) groups by passing all the threads for the first centimetre ($\frac{1}{2}$in) of warp in front of peg *x* and behind peg *y* (Fig 76c), and the next group behind peg *x* and in front of peg *y* (Fig 76d). All the threads will turn around peg *z* and this will form a 'double' cross between pegs *y* and *z* as soon as the second group is started (Fig 76e). This must not be confused with

the raddle-cross. The 'double' cross is formed by the end loop groups passing alternately behind and in front of peg y.

Tying up the warp

When the correct number of groups has been made, the warp is tied up to secure *both* of the crosses. The single-end cross is tied with a long tie string (Fig 77a) and the raddle-cross is secured in the same way (Fig 77b). A firm tie is made through the loop at peg *a* and around the whole of the warp past peg *c* (Fig 77c). Further ties around the whole warp are made, at intervals of approximately one metre (one yard) along its length, to keep it tidy. The end loop around peg *z* is secured with two ties (Fig 77c). Make sure that it is the complete loop that is tied, and not part of the 'double' cross. Check with Fig 77c that all the ties are securely in place before removing the warp from the board. The warp is chained from the singles-cross so that the raddle-cross is at the open end of the chain, ready to be spread in the raddle (see Fig 26 for chaining).

Spreading the warp

The warp is laid over the raddle with the raddle-cross towards you. A pair of cross-sticks is placed in the raddle-cross and the ends of the sticks are tied together. A piece of card covering the section of the raddle under the unspread warp will prevent the teeth snagging the warp threads and the ends falling into the wrong dents (Fig 78a).

Place a stick through the end loop. Tie a string from one end of the stick to the other, to prevent the warp loop from slipping off. This end-stick should be wider than your warp, but not wider than the roller on the loom. Remove the ties holding the end loop and the raddle-cross. Measure half the width of your warp from the centre of the raddle to find the dent from which to start spreading. Spread the warp by placing the

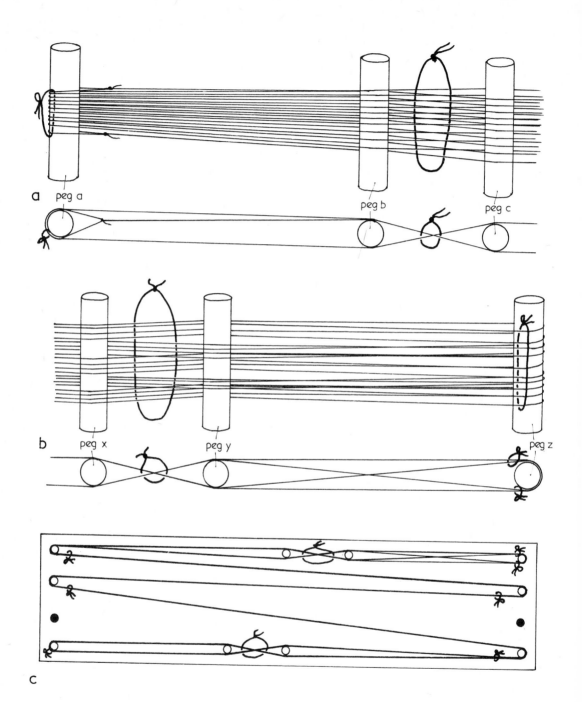

peg a

peg b

peg c

a

peg x

peg y

peg z

b

c

Fig 77   Tying up the warp

raddle-cross groups into the dents between the teeth of the raddle (Fig 78b).

It is important to make sure that the groups are taken from the cross in the correct sequence and that the *whole* group is put into one dent. More than one group can be placed in one dent without harm, but a *split* group will snag during rolling on.

When the entire warp has been spread, check that it has been spread to the correct width and is placed with its centre in the centre of the raddle. Firmly tie the cap into place on both sides of the warp (Fig 78c and Fig 80a). If a wooden raddle cap is being used, check periodically that it has not warped. A warped or bowed cap may not sit correctly across the top of the raddle teeth to seal the dents off from each other. It may therefore allow the groups to jump across the top of the teeth and upset the thread sequence. If the cap is slightly warped or bowed, the method of tying a string from tooth to tooth used on the home-made raddle, described earlier, can be used in conjunction wth the cap. The warp is now ready to be wound on to the back roller of the loom.

MULTIPLE WARPING

The requirements for making any warp for any loom are the same. The sett of the yarn being used has to be found; the width of the cloth has to be decided; and the length of the warp has to be calculated to include take-up, loom wastage and cloth shrinkage.

To make a reasonably long warp with the simple warping method can take considerable time. Making the warp with a *unit* group of threads (*multiple warping*), follows the same principle, but makes the process faster. The warp ends are kept in sequence by a single-end cross at one end of the warp and a raddle-group cross at the other as before. When warping with one thread, the single-end cross is made by crossing alternate ends between two pegs. In multiple warping the singles-cross has to be found, keeping the threads of each group in their correct sequence. The cross can be picked up between the fore-finger and thumb of one hand by weaving the forefinger over one end, under one end etc, and the thumb under one end, over the next etc. The cross will form between the forefinger and thumb, and can be transferred to the pegs on the warping board or warping mill.

As the two triangular openings on either side of a single-end cross are identical with the two sheds of a plain weave, the picking-up of the cross can be speeded up by using a *frame shaft* with heddles. This can be made from a small frame with heddles tied into place (Fig 79a). The warp threads pass through the frame shaft on their way from the spool rack to the pegs on the warping board or warping mill. The warp threads are entered alternately through a heddle and through the space between that heddle and the next. When the threads are lifted, those passing through the heddle eyes will remain stationary, and those passing through the spaces will rise. This up movement forms the shed for the forefinger. Pulling the threads down leaves the entered threads stationary as before, but lowers those in the spaces. This forms the counter-shed for the thumb (Plate 9a).

Calling the three pegs at the singles-cross end of the warp *a*, *b* and *c*, and the three pegs at the raddle-cross end of the warp *x*, *y* and *z*, the singles-cross is made between pegs *b* and *c*, and the unit groups form the raddle-cross between pegs *x* and *y*. A split half-cross forms between pegs *a* and *b*. This can be ignored, as it fulfils no function (Fig 79b).

When planning a warp, it is useful to relate the number of threads to be used in warping to the e/cm (epi). The groups of the cross between pegs *x* and *y* will therefore be convenient units for spreading the warp in the raddle.

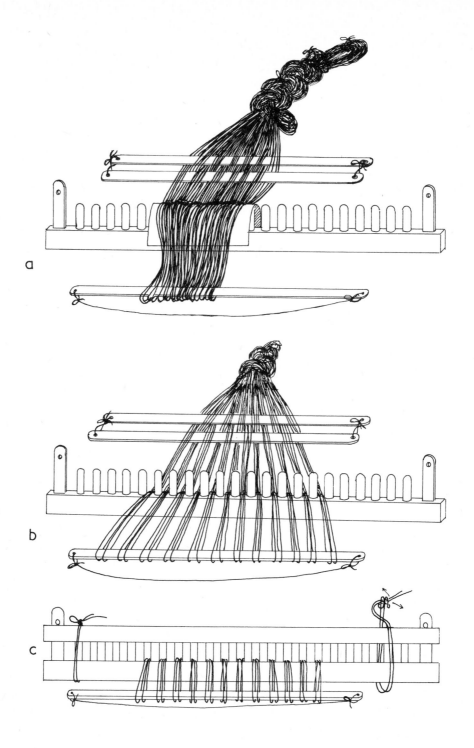

a

b

c

Fig 78   Spreading the warp from the raddle-cross

When the warp threads have been passed from the spool rack to the frame shaft and entered, they are knotted together and looped around peg *a*. The frame shaft is taped or clamped vertically to the top of a chairback or other convenient structure.

Stand with the spoolrack to the right and the warping board or mill to the left. Hold the mill steady with a foot or knee (clamp the board to the table). Gather the warp threads in the right hand, hold them under tension and lift. The threads between the heddles will rise, forming the first shed on the left of the frame shaft. Pass the forefinger of the left hand into this shed. Lower the right hand and insert the thumb of the left hand into the counter-shed. The cross now lies between the forefinger and thumb of the left hand and can be pushed along towards the pegs (Plate 9a). Peg *b* takes the place of the forefinger, peg *c* takes the place of the thumb (Plate 9b), and the cross lies in its correct position between these two pegs. Gather the threads into your hand on the left of the frame shaft and pass these down the board or mill to peg *x*. Take all the threads over peg *x*,

under pegs *y* and *z*, around peg *z*, over peg *y* and under peg *x*, making a group cross (Plate 9c). This multiple-cross could be made with two end pegs only, but the loop formed between pegs *y* and *z* makes it easier to count and tie the cross. Guide the threads back as far as peg *c*. Hold under tension at the right of the frame shaft, lift the threads, and insert the forefinger of the left hand into the shed. Lower the threads and insert the thumb into the counter-shed. Turn the left hand holding the cross clockwise, turning the whole group of threads. The tip of the forefinger will meet peg *c*, the tip of the thumb will meet peg *b* (Plate 9d) and the pegs can now take the place of the fingers as before. All threads are turned around peg *a* before the downward course starts again from the beginning.

The lift-up, pull-down sequence for shed and counter-shed always applies when going down the board or mill, and also applies for an even number of threads when returning. When an odd number of threads is used when making the warp, the shedding order is reversed on the return to pull-down, lift-up. This is easy to remember:

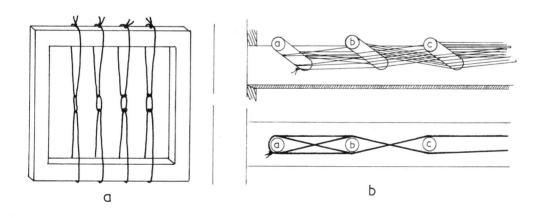

a   b

Fig 79 Multiple warping—heddle frame and split half-cross

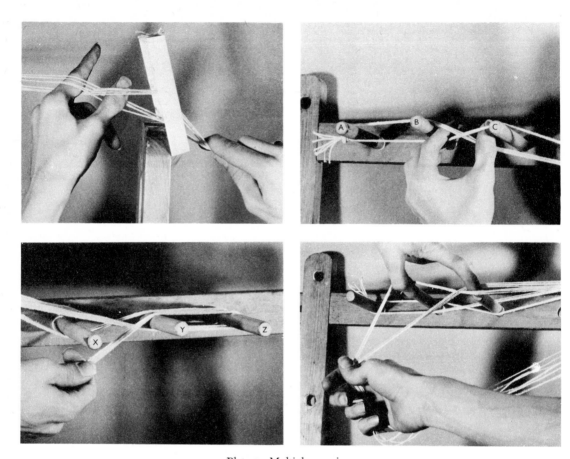

Plate 9   Multiple warping
a (above left) Picking up the singles-cross on the finger and thumb. b (above right)
Transferring the singles-cross to the pegs. c (below left) Making the multiple cross.
d (below right) Transferring the singles-cross on the return.

People have ups-and-downs, but odd people have ups-and-downs, and downs-and-ups (App 6.2).

When the number of raddle-cross units equals the required width of the cloth, the warp is tied and chained in exactly the same way as the warp made by the previous method. It is spread as before, with one or more thread groups in each dent of the raddle, according to the number of threads used when warping and the e/cm (epi) of the sett. Never split individual groups (App 6.3).

Dressing the loom
Tie the raddle to the back bar of the loom with the end-stick at the warp roller (Fig 80a, b). Make sure that the centre of the warp is lined up with the centre of the loom. Clear a path for the warp-chain through the centre of the loom to the front, by moving the heddles on the shafts to each side. An under-slung batten should be rested against the front bar. Pass the warp-chain through the loom to the front, undoing some of the chain.

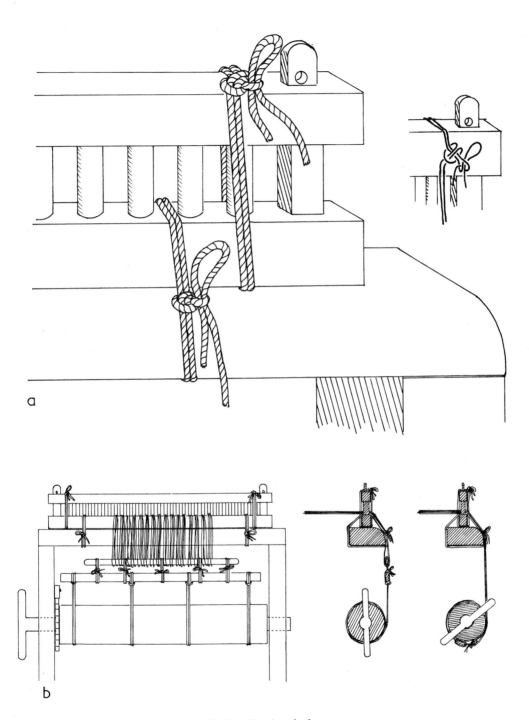

Fig 80   Dressing the loom

Take a firm hold on the warp at a point where it has not been disturbed, or at the first holding tie to be exposed, and give several firm tugs to straighten the warp threads. The end-stick will be pulled against the raddle and so spread the warp to its full width. Tie the end-stick firmly to the back *apron-stick* (Fig 80b). The *aprons* are lengths of cloth (or long cords) attached to the front and back rollers. Each has a stick attached to the free end. Tie the end-stick firmly to the back apron-stick. Several ties of strong string or loom cord at regular intervals will be necessary to prevent the stick from bowing.

With a small table loom it is easier for two people to wind the warp on, one to hold the loom steady and turn the back roller, the other to hold the warp under tension and make sure that the warp threads do not snag as they pass through the raddle.

To maintain an even tension across the width of the warp, do not wind on too much warp at a time. When the hand holding the warp comes too close to the raddle, the outside threads will be at an acute angle and at high tension, with the threads becoming progressively slacker towards the centre. The wider the warp the further the hand holding it should be from the raddle. Dividing the warp in the centre and holding one half in each hand will reduce the angles.

If you are winding on by yourself, secure the loom to prevent it from sliding. Take the warp back over the top of the loom so that it now passes from the raddle forward, through the centre and over the top, to the back of the loom. Standing at the back of the loom, hold the warp firmly in one hand, give it several firm tugs to straighten the threads, and wind on to the back roller with the other hand. Keep the warp under a firm and even tension while rolling.

Watch that the warp divides easily where the teeth of the raddle pass through it, and clear any tangles before the teeth can break any threads.

To clear the raddle groups, place the tips of the fingers of one hand *between* the groups at the raddle, keeping the warp under tension with the other hand. Draw the fingers gently through the warp. If the warp is very 'sticky' (a tweed yarn for example) it should be cleared in this way across the full width before each turn of the roller. Never 'comb' the warp in such a way that the raddle-groups are split. This can cause uneven tension of individual warp ends.

Wind the warp in short sections, one full turn of the roller at most, before moving the hand to grasp the warp further along. Each time the hand is moved give a sharp tug to straighten the threads.

A correctly made warp with an even tension should have no loose or tight threads when winding on. A thread that appears to be loose may be broken, so check this and mend if necessary. If there is no break, hold the warp further along and give it several sharp tugs. If the thread still appears loose, re-tension it gently. It is very easy to pull a single thread tighter than the rest of the warp and so cause uneven tension. This will give trouble when weaving. A very tight thread has probably been caught into the wrong group in the raddle while winding. It may have travelled quite a distance before becoming noticeable. Unwind the warp until the caught thread can be released, and clear the warp groups as before.

Warp-sticks

Warp-sticks are placed in between layers of warp as the warp is being wound on to the roller. They provide a smooth base and keep the tension even by keeping the warp roll firm as its diameter increases. When the apron has been wound on and the warp has reached the roller, the knots need to be covered with two or three flat sticks to present a flat surface to the warp (Fig 81a). The

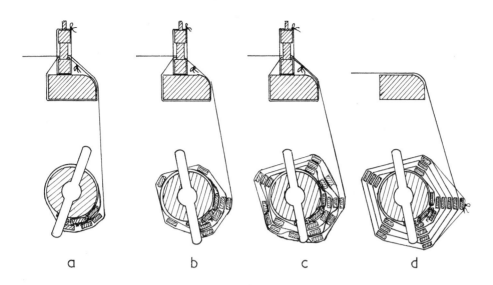

Fig 81   Warp sticks

warp-sticks must be at least 10cm (4in) longer than the width of the warp so that they project at least 5cm (2in) on each side of the warp roll. Wind two or three layers of warp around the roller and then 'quarter' the roller with four more warp-sticks by placing them between the warp and the warp roll after each quarter turn of the roller (Fig 81b). Wind approximately three more turns before quartering the roller again with a further four sticks. Make sure that the sticks are lying *parallel* to the roller and that they are placed *directly* above the previous sticks in the lower layers. If the sticks are not placed directly above each other, they will be pressed into the under layers of warp by the pressure of the upper layers (Fig 81c). This can seriously damage a yarn by permanently stretching it and making it weak at these points.

If there are not enough warp-sticks available, sheets of strong paper can be used instead. These should be wound in to form a continuous separating layer between the warp layers. If using paper in place of sticks, wind the warp at a lower tension and make doubly sure that the tension is even. High tension will tend to make the paper sheets crinkle and buckle, and will cause uneven tension between the layers. It is advisable to use a warp-stick at the point where the warp leaves the roller when the entire warp has been wound on. This stick will be pushed back as each layer is unwound during weaving and helps to ensure a smooth even tension as the warp leaves the roller.

Remove the holding ties as you reach them. Wind the warp on until there is only enough left in front of the raddle for threading. Do not cut the singles-cross ties yet. The unwound warp should reach from the back roller, through the shafts, to just in front of the batten. The raddle can be left in place during entering, but if it has to be removed, tie a stick across the outside of the warp roll to keep the threads in position and lying parallel (Fig 81d).

Insert the cross-sticks into the singles-cross and

tie them together at their ends, leaving a space of approximately 2cm (¾in) between the sticks. Do not undo the cross-ties *until* the cross-sticks have been inserted and *tied* together. Divide the warp from the centre of the raddle and tie each half with a firm bow-knot. Cut open the end loop (Fig 82a). If the warp has a lot of join-knots at this end, cut the warp a little shorter to remove the knots.

Take each tied bunch of warp threads through to the front, between the side of the loom and the heddles (Fig 82b). Tie each group to the front bar with a double length of string, a hitch-knot holding the warp threads (Fig 82c), and a bow-knot around the front bar (Fig 82d). These groups should be tied with enough tension to hold the cross-sticks up, but the hitch-knot should not be so tight as to make it difficult to withdraw a warp end from the group. The firm

bow-knots around the two bunches are removed and the warp is ready for threading.

DRAFTING
Planning the threading order and the shedding sequence is called *drafting*. The warp ends will have to be entered into the heddles on the shafts in the order determined by the draft.

A full draft contains three elements: the *threading diagram*, the *shedding order* and the *draw-down* (a diagram of the interaction of warp and weft).

Threading diagrams
A threading diagram is a condensed 'picture' of the actual position of the threaded heddles on the shafts (Fig 83).

The position can be marked in several ways. This book uses numbers in four horizontal

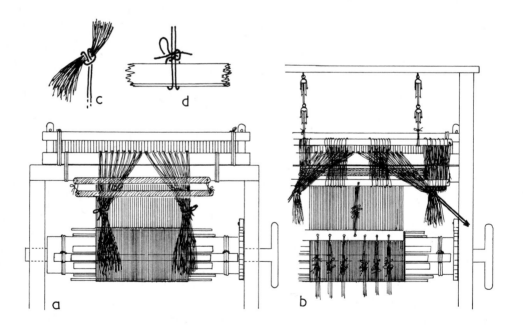

Fig 82 Securing the warp prior to threading

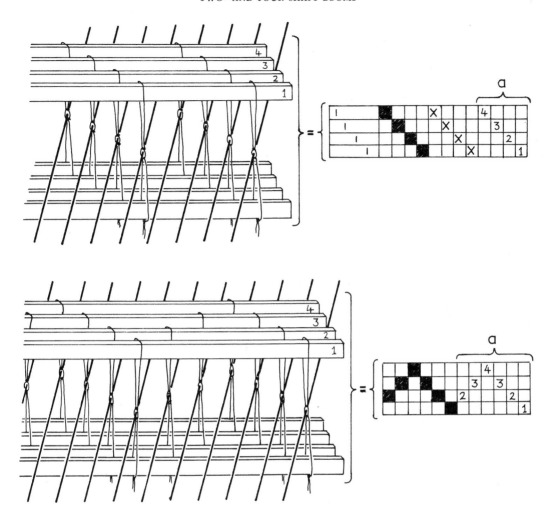

Fig 83   Drafting—threading diagrams

staves of squared paper (Fig 83 at a). Shafts are numbered from the front to the back of the loom. In the diagrams each horizontal stave represents one shaft, also numbered from front (bottom) to back (top). The position of the number on the stave gives the position of the heddle on the shaft. The threading diagram can be read from left to right, or right to left. Each heddle is threaded in order of the diagram with an end taken in sequence from the cross. No threading diagram is needed for a two-shaft loom, as the sequence is simply 1-2-1-2- etc.

Shedding order

The shedding order for a two-shaft loom needs no diagram, as there are only two sheds, the shed and counter-shed, to follow each other.

The shedding diagram for a four-shaft loom

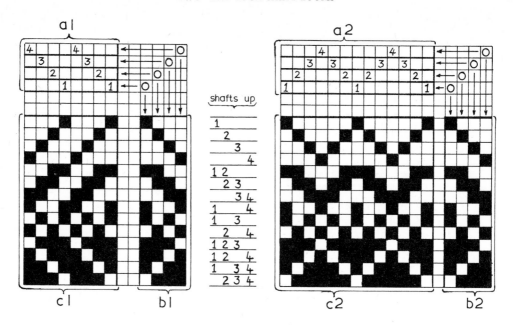

Fig 84   Drafting—draw-down

shows each shed in one horizontal line of four squares for each shed (Fig 84a1, a2). As succeeding picks build up the cloth along the warp, succeeding sheds are shown vertically (Fig 84b1, b2). A black square represents warp *over* weft. Therefore, black squares (or *X*'s) represent shaft(s) up, white squares represent shaft(s) down. A four-shaft loom has fourteen sheds, and all fourteen sheds are shown in Fig 84 at b1 and b2.

Draw-down

A diagram of the interaction of warp and weft is called a draw-down. This is a correct diagrammatic but flat representation of the weave. It may not look like the final cloth, as it ignores the three-dimensional nature of yarn, the varying relationship between warp and weft, and the effects of colour. A balanced cloth will relate more closely to the appearance of the draw-down than an unbalanced or distorted weave.

Again, each pick is drawn horizontally and succeeding picks follow vertically, according to the shedding order at the right. Black squares represent warp over weft (shafts up) and white squares represent weft over warp (shafts down). When, according to the shedding action, a shaft is up, all ends entered on that shaft will be up and therefore over the weft. The position of these ends can be read from the threading diagram above the draw-down (Fig 84c1). When the threading diagram is a *straight entry* (Fig 84a1), the draw-down will look like the mirror image of the shedding order. When the threading follows a different order (Fig 84a2), the fourteen sheds (Fig 84b2) will produce a different interaction of warp and weft, as shown in the draw-down (Fig 84c2).

DRESSING THE LOOM

Entering

Threading or *entering* is done from the centre of the loom to each side, to keep the warp centred and the shafts balanced. Before entering, make sure that there are enough heddles on the shafts for the number of threads in the warp. Remember that the heddles on all shafts are included in these calculations.

Divide the heddles at the centre of the shafts into two equal groups. If the shafts have a central lifting tie, it will be easy to find and keep the centre. Otherwise the heddles should be counted and the centre heddle on each shaft marked with a piece of coloured thread. Remember to re-mark the centre if any heddles are added or removed (App 6.4).

In a two-shaft loom, thread a heddle on shaft 1; follow by threading a heddle on shaft 2 etc. Remember that if the first thread from the centre to the left was on shaft 1, the first thread to the right of the centre must be on shaft 2, or there will be a double end running through the centre of the cloth.

In a four-shaft loom the warp ends are threaded through the heddles on the shafts according to the threading diagram. Read the diagram from left to right when entering from the centre to the right, and from right to left when entering from the centre to the left. When the threading asks for an unequal number of ends on the different shafts, make sure before starting that you have the right number of heddles on each shaft.

Remember that the numbered threading diagram is a condensed picture of the position of the entered heddles on the shafts.

The threads are selected from the order of the cross held by the cross-sticks, and they pass through the centre eyes of the heddles. If you are using large-eyed string heddles it will be easy enough to thread with the fingers, but if the heddles have small eyes, a threading hook will make threading easier (Fig 85a). Mistakes made while warping will show up in the cross as double or treble ends passing over and under the cross-sticks together (Fig 85b). It is too late to correct a mistake of this kind, but as the threads are unlikely to be twisted more than once or twice around each other, they should not create great difficulties in weaving.

Checking small groups of threads regularly as threading proceeds is essential to avoid having to re-enter large sections of warp. Each checked group can be tied together with a slip thumb-knot (overhand slip knot) to prevent the warp threads from tangling or from getting out of order (Fig 28).

Selvage

When weaving plain weave only, the weft turns correctly around the selvage thread and no special provision has to be made for it. Some of the four-shaft weaves will leave the selvage end up or down for two or more consecutive picks, allowing the weft to pull back into the cloth for a distance on one or both sides of the cloth. Thought should be given to the formation of a correct selvage. The purpose of the fabric to be woven will determine the importance of the selvage. In a furnishing fabric when the selvage will be turned under, and in a dress fabric when the selvage may be cut away, it is more important to prevent distortion of the fabric at the edges, than to get a perfect looking selvage. Tugging the weft tight after each pick does more harm than leaving small loops protruding from the selvage. Fabrics that are intended for use with the selvage showing, such as curtains or rugs, need more care. But for all fabrics it is an advantage to have selvages that prevent the weft from being pulled back into the cloth, whatever the shedding sequence.

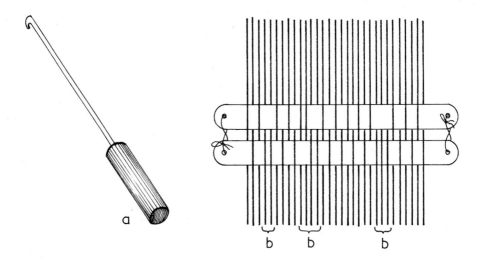

Fig 85 Entering—threading hook and mistakes in the cross

Catch thread

The simplest way to prevent picks pulling back, is to use a *catch thread*. The last two ends at either edge can be used as one double end. These double ends are not entered into a heddle, but pass straight through a dent of the reed. Whatever the sett of the cloth, the double catch thread should have the last dent to itself. It is tied with the last group of entered warp ends to the front apron-stick in the normal way and at the same tension as all the other ends.

As the catch thread is not held by the eye of a heddle, it can easily be moved up or down, independently from the shaft action. The shuttle entering the shed presses the catch thread down and passes over it. The hand, ready to receive the shuttle after it passes through the shed, lifts the catch thread, and the weft passes under it. As the catch thread is working quite independently from the shedding action, with the weft going over it when entering the shed, and under it when leaving the shed, a perfect selvage is possible, even when weaving several picks into the same shed.

Sleying

When all the warp ends have been entered through the heddles, they are entered through the reed. This is called *denting*, or *sleying*. The choice of reed will depend on the sett of the warp and the reeds available. It is not always advisable to select a reed that has the same number of dents as the e/cm (epi), particularly when using a close sett. Double denting is a common practice with close setts or textured yarns. The fewer the teeth there are the more room the threads have to move past each other when changing shed. Treble or even quadruple denting may produce vertical 'break lines' in the cloth while it is on the loom, but washing the fabric will usually remove these, allowing the threads to move into their correct positions.

A few differently dented reeds will give a wide variety of possible warp setts. For example, a four dents per centimetre (4 d/cm) reed can be used to give the following warp settings: 1, 2, 4, 6, 8, 10 e/cm etc. Threading one warp end through one dent and leaving the next three dents empty before threading the next warp end, will give a 1 e/cm sett. Threading one end through one dent and two ends through the next dent etc, will give a 6 e/cm sett. Threading 2-3-2-3 etc gives a 10 e/cm sett. The nearest equivalents of different counts of reed in centimetres and inches are: 3 d/cm = 8 dpi, 4 d/cm = 10 dpi, 5 d/cm = 12 dpi, 6 d/cm = 15 dpi, 8 d/cm = 20 dpi. Sometimes reed counts are expressed in dents per decimetre (10cm or 4in) (App 6.5).

to the front apron-stick. This can be done as described earlier (Fig 31). A self-adjusting tie is useful for a wider warp. A strong, smooth string is cut into 50cm (20in) lengths. Each length is attached by a hitch-knot to the apron-stick (Fig 87a). Cut a string for each 2 to 3cm (1in) section, for the width of the warp. These string ties will serve several succeeding warps.

Make the tie-on by straightening a group of warp ends, by running the fingers of one hand

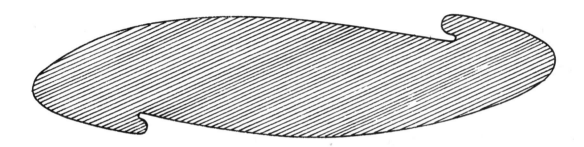

Fig 86   Reed hook

A reed hook, also known as a 'fish' hook (Fig 86), is used for denting. It can be used with the hook uppermost or with the hook on the underside. Again, starting from the centre, the ends are drawn through the dents in the reed according to the sett of the cloth. Make sure that the ends do not cross each other between the heddles and the reed. They must be taken in the same sequence as the order on the shafts. Check in groups that the right number of ends has been entered into the correct number of dents and in the correct order. Tie off into groups. Remove the raddle, or the stick tied across the top of the warp roll, and the cross-sticks before tying on.

Tie-on

When all ends have been entered, the warp is tied

through the threads, while the other hand gathers the whole group and holds it under tension. Tie the group with a slip thumb-knot (Fig 87b and Fig 28a). Turn the knot down through the centre of the group (Fig 87c). Make a snitch-knot (larkshead) in the loop thus formed and pass the two ends of one of the string ties through this (Fig 87d). Pull on the string to tighten (Fig 87e). It is of help to include the same number of ends in each group, and to keep the groups fairly small, in any case not more than 3cm (1in) wide.

When all warp end groups have been attached to the string ties, equalise the tension by rolling the cloth roller forward a short distance, leaving sufficient length of string protruding from the snitch-knot (larkshead) to tie a half bow or bow

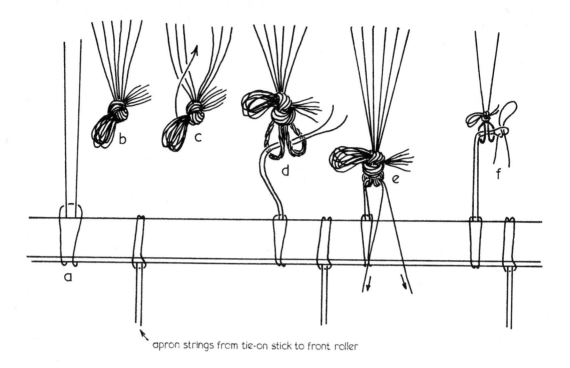

apron strings from tie-on stick to front roller

Fig 87   Tie-on

knot (Fig 87f). It is essential that all ends are tensioned as evenly as possible before this final knot.

Before weaving, check for mistakes in the threading or sleying by opening the sheds to be used. Threads that have been crossed between heddles and reed will not open and can be seen lying together in the centre of the shed. An end not entered into a heddle will stay stationary and not take part in the shedding action. An end entered into the top half of a string heddle instead of the eye will rise higher than the other ends. An end entered into the bottom loop of the heddle will not rise at all. Mistakes in sleying will show as thick lines when too many ends have been entered into a dent, or thin areas when dents have been missed. When all mistakes have been cor-

rected (there need not be any if all checking has been done carefully throughout!) and the warp re-tensioned and re-tied, weaving can start.

Weaving

To spread the tied groups and eliminate the gaps between them, and to test the tension and correctness of threading, a *heading* of a few picks of a thick yarn of contrasting colour to the warp is woven. A stick-shuttle will suffice for this. With fine yarns and a wide cloth, stick-shuttles will be slow and cumbersome to use throughout. *Boat* or *roller* shuttles can be thrown through the open shed from selvage to selvage in a smooth even rhythm (App 6.6). Bobbins of yarn are wound by hand, or preferably by a *bobbin winder* or hand-drill, on a paper, cardboard or wooden

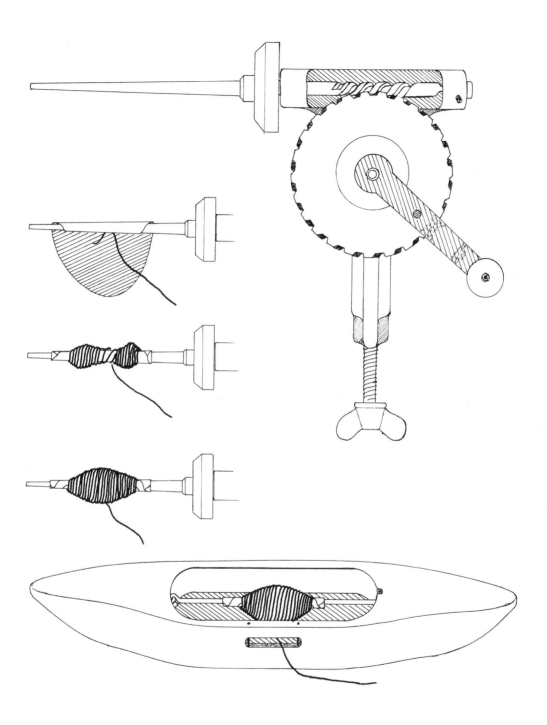

Fig 88 Bobbin winder—making a bobbin-boat shuttle

core to fit the centre spindle of the shuttle (Fig 88). The yarn should not be wound to the edge of the bobbin core. The completed bobbin should be firm and slim enough to rotate easily on the spindle inside the shuttle.

When weaving, the shuttle is held in the palm of the hand, the tip is introduced into the shed, passing over the catch thread. It is propelled through the shed by a flick of the wrist, and caught by the other hand after passing under the raised catch thread. Placing the thumb on the bobbin for a moment to stop it rotating and releasing the weft, slightly pull to place the weft around the catch thread at the other edge.

Releasing the bobbin before beating the weft into place with the batten, will provide the slack needed for the take-up of the weft as it bends over and under the warp ends. Change the shed, and bring the batten forward again to clear it. This is particularly important, when using a hairy yarn, as it separates the threads. On a floor loom the feet change the shed as soon as the shuttle has been caught and while the free hand is swinging the batten. For this reason a floor loom is faster than a table loom. The weaver soon establishes a smooth rhythm of: throw, beat and change shed, beat again, throw, beat and change shed, beat again and so on.

7

BASIC TWO- AND FOUR-SHAFT WEAVES

PLAIN WEAVE ON TWO AND FOUR SHAFTS

Plain weave and all its variations can be woven on two-shaft or four-shaft looms. As the shed and counter-shed of the plain weave let the weft pass under–over alternate warp ends in the shed, and over–under in the counter-shed, plain weave needs only the two sheds of a two-shaft loom. The four-shaft loom can be used to produce plain weave on a variety of entries. This makes it possible to weave plain weave in combination with more complex structures.

When a shaft is raised (or lowered) all ends entered through the heddles on that shaft will rise (or sink). One, two or three shafts of a four-shaft loom can rise (or sink) simultaneously, lifting (or lowering) all ends entered on these shafts.

All warp ends can be divided alternately into odd and even ends. The rule for a plain weave entry is then: odd and even ends must never share a shaft if the plain weave shed and counter-shed are to be available (Fig 89a–d).

The most usual draft when only plain weave is required is a straight entry (Fig 89a). The warp ends are entered in regular order for four ends, using all four shafts for a four-end repeat. The two odd shafts carry all the odd ends, the two even shafts carry all the even ends. Raising the odd shafts will open the shed, and raising the even shafts will open the counter-shed.

Not all plain-weave drafts are straight entries. All drafts repeating on all four shafts with four ends will work as a plain entry *if* the shedding action is adapted accordingly (Fig 89b). Both

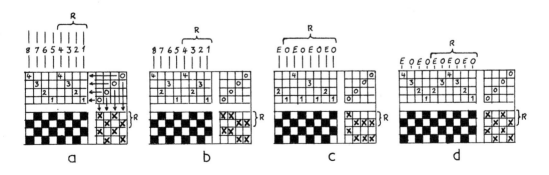

Fig 89   Plain-weave drafts

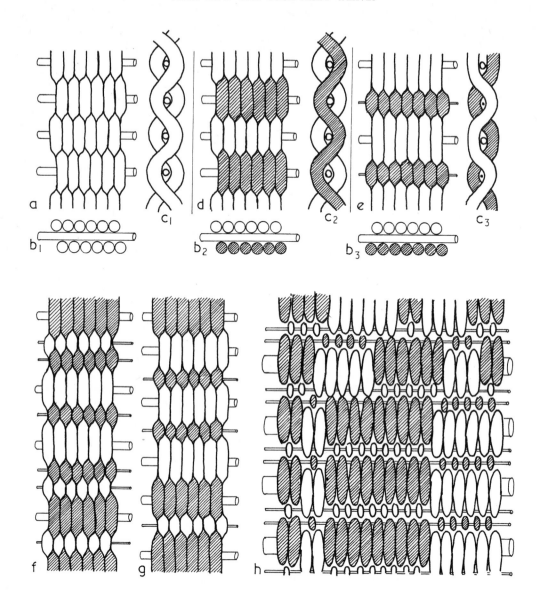

Fig 90   Warp-face weaves

drafts in Fig 89a and b raise two shafts alternately.

A draft with all odd ends on *one* shaft and all even ends distributed on the other three shafts will use one shaft for the shed and three shafts for the counter-shed (Fig 89c). If the ends are entered on odd and even shafts alternately, but not in a straight entry, the shedding action of odd shafts against even shafts will give plain weave (Fig 89d).

Many weaves need a plain weave ground. Many use plain weave picks in combination with pattern picks, and some benefit by having plain weave headings or borders.

STRAIGHT ENTRY WEAVES

All fabrics described in this book so far can be woven on two shafts, or with any of the entries giving plain weave on four shafts. Plain weave itself has many variations caused by different setts of warp and weft.

Horizontal rib (warp-faced plain weave)

In a balanced plain weave the warp and weft show equally. When the warp is set closely enough to cover the weft, a warp-faced fabric results (Fig 90a). The close sett of the warp prevents the weft from bending over and under the warp ends, and therefore the weft lies straight between two layers of warp (Fig 90b1–3). The warp ends bend over the weft (Fig 90c1–3) forming horizontal ribs. Colour and design depend almost entirely on the way the warp is made.

In theory the warp should have four times as many ends as a balanced plain cloth to cover the weft entirely. It will be found in practice that this setting makes the shed difficult to open and that two or three times the number of ends will usually be enough to give the desired effect. A smooth strong yarn such as cotton, linen or silk can be set more closely than a hairy or loosely twisted yarn such as wool, worsted or mohair. Warp-faced plain weave fabrics are firm but flexible. A single-coloured warp can produce only a plain-coloured fabric, but the ribbed structure gives light and shade. The thicker the weft and the closer the beat the deeper the rib will be. A striped warp will produce bold stripes along the length of the fabric when two or more ends are used together. The Nova Scotia Drugget, a carpet of homespun warp and rag or thick wool weft, is a typical and effective example of this. Making the warp in two colours, one end

colour *a*, one end colour *b*, (end-by-end), and weaving with a thick weft will show horizontal stripes (Fig 90d).

Repp

If two wefts are used alternately, one thick, one fine, a deeply ribbed fabric, *repp*, is woven (Fig 90e).

An end-by-end warp (made of alternating colours) woven as a repp, produces a fabric of one colour on one side and the other colour on the reverse. One colour of the warp lies over the thick weft in the first shed and dominates the other colour passing over the fine weft in the other shed. The colours can be interchanged by throwing either two fine picks or two thick picks in succession. The former separates the change of colour by two fine lines (Fig 90f), in the latter this break is eliminated (Fig 90g).

Warp-faced pick-up weave

The colour effect of the reversible repp can be used for a 'free' pick-up design (Plate 14a).

If all the odd ends are dark and all the even ends are light, the first shed *a* is used for the dark areas and the counter-shed *b* for the light areas of the design, when the thick weft is woven. The thick weft travels from selvage to selvage in a *changing* shed.

To weave the changing shed design in Fig 91, the thick weft travels in *a*-shed to the first *x*. The shuttle is brought to the surface, the shed is changed and the thick weft re-introduced. The weft is taken through the *b*-shed for the next part of the design and brought to the surface again at the next *x*. The shed is changed for the subsequent part of the design and the shuttle is re-introduced into *a*-shed. This sequence is continued following the design from one selvage to the other. Two picks of fine weft (sheds *a* and *b*) are woven before the next design pick of thick weft.

Fig 91   Changing shed design

A certain boldness of design is required, as the unit of change along the length of fabric depends on the width of the rib formed by the thick weft, and the change across can be as fine as the width of one warp end (Fig 90h).

Solid-block log cabin

A warp in alternating sections of one dark end, one light end and one light end, one dark end (as for log cabin, part of the plain weave colour and weave sampler), can be woven as solid colour

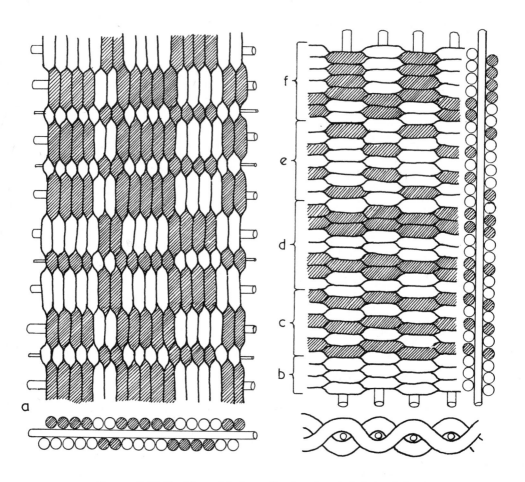

Fig 92   Solid-block log-cabin (warp-faced) and vertical rib (weft-faced)

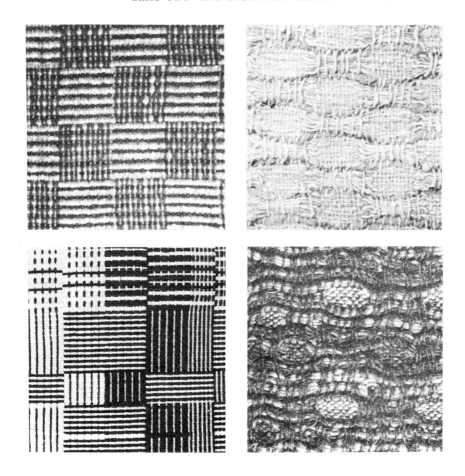

Plate 10   Two- and four-block weaves
a (above left) Two-block log-cabin. b (above right) Two-block distorted weft.
c (below left) Four-block log-cabin. d (below right) Four-block distorted weft.

blocks. One set of blocks will appear when the weft is in the order of one fine pick, one thick pick. The other set of blocks uses the reverse of this order—one thick pick, one fine pick, using two picks of thick weft for the change (Fig 92a and Plate 10a).

Warp-faced plain weave fabrics are useful for furnishing fabrics, table mats and wall hangings. A very thick weft is used for rugs. The pick-up repp adds the element of two-colour free design.

Vertical rib (weft-faced plain weave)

In a weft-faced plain weave the weft covers the warp completely. The warp ends lie straight and the weft bends round the warp. The warp has to be made of a strongly twisted smooth yarn. It should be set wide enough apart to allow the weft to bend sufficiently to cover the ends (Fig 92b and see Tapestry, pp71–8).

To find the appropriate sett, wind one thread of warp yarn and two threads of weft yarn round a stick. These should not overlap, but must be firmly pushed together. For accuracy wind at least 5cm (2in). The number of warp threads wound will show the number of ends needed per 5cm (2in) of warp. The spaces between the warp ends will then be wide enough to allow two weft threads (two picks) to pack closely to cover the warp (Fig 46a). The fabric will have warp-way ribs and can be self-coloured or patterned.

Colour and pattern depend entirely on the weft. Horizontal stripes are the easiest to weave. At least two picks of a colour are required to show as a continuous horizontal line (Fig 92c). Any number of picks can be woven to thicken the line (Fig 92d). One pick of a contrasting colour will cover every second end, and will appear as small dots when used on a plain ground (Fig 92e). If two colours are used in alternating sheds, the colours will show as vertical stripes (Fig 92f and Plate 14b). Tapestry and all the raised and added weft techniques (Chapter 5) can be woven on two-shaft and four-shaft looms. The batten cannot be used for beating when the weft is curved or when individual design areas are being woven.

Table mats and shoulder bags, cushions and rugs can be made in this strong simple weave. Fine strong yarns make very good furnishing fabrics.

FOUR-SHAFT WEAVES
Colour and weave sampler
A sampler of colour and weave effects on a straight entry can be woven to provide an insight into the fourteen-shed action of a four-shaft loom. You can use either cotton or wool in two contrasting colours or shades. As the number of intersections of warp and weft, in the weaves suggested, will be fewer than in a balanced plain weave, the sett of the warp will have to be closer to give a balance of warp and weft.

To find the sett to be used, wind the warp yarn around a stick for 5cm (2in) with the threads just touching. Two-thirds of the total number of turns of the yarn equals the number of ends needed for 5cm (2in) of warp sett.

Each colour section of warp should be at least 5cm (2in) wide, a total of 30cm (12in) wide. The warp should be at least 180cm (2yards) long.

Follow the colour order in Fig 93a when making the warp, and thread the warp in a straight entry (Fig 93b).

Follow the shedding sequence in Fig 94a–t for weaving. As the entry consists of a straight draft, the threading draft is only shown in Fig 93b. The number and position of each shaft for the shedding action is shown as a direct tie-up above the shedding diagrams (Fig 94H). In the shedding diagram, the black squares represent shafts to be raised, and white squares

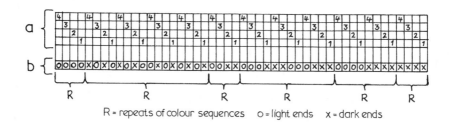

R = repeats of colour sequences   o = light ends   x = dark ends

Fig 93   Draft and colour order for four-shaft colour-and-weave sampler

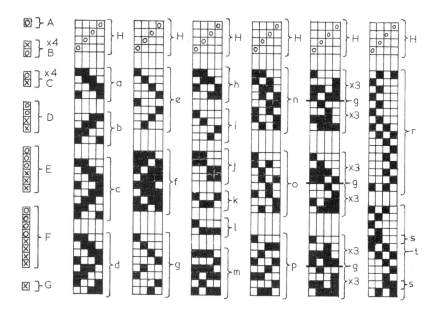

Fig 94   Shedding diagrams for colour and weave samples

represent shafts to be lowered. One complete repeat is bracketed for each weave, and the sequence for that weave should be repeated, for at least 5cm (2in) of woven cloth.

The weft could be one colour only (Fig 94A and G), but many interesting effects are caused by the interaction of colour sequences in warp and weft (Fig 94B–F). As there are practical limitations to the length of a sample warp, we suggest a few variations and leave further selection to you.

TWILL

Right-handed and left-handed twill

The most familiar characteristic of a *twill* weave is its diagonal construction. In the two-by-two (2/2) twill (Fig 94a, b), the weft passes under two ends and over two ends, shifting by one end in succeeding picks. The weave requires four picks for a complete repeat. The diagonal can run

from right to left, or left to right (Fig 94a, b). Weave 5cm (2in) of cloth in each colour order for the weft (Fig 94A–G) for one of the twills (Fig 94a), and one colour only (Fig 94G) for the other (Fig 94b).

Reverse-twill

Combining the shedding order for the two opposing diagonals in an eight-pick repeat forms a return or *reverse-twill* (Fig 94c). At each point of turn one warp end floats over three weft picks.

The example given turns the diagonal after every fourth pick, but the turn can be made after fewer or more picks at regular or irregular intervals.

The warp float at the point of turn can be avoided if the opposing diagonal is started from the opposite shed (Fig 94d). This changes the reverse-twill and its continuous vertical zigzag

Plate 11   Twill weave
a (above left) Point return. b (above right) Herringbone return. c (below left)
Combined point and herringbone returns. d (below right) Mock satin

into a *herringbone* (Plate 11c).

A three-by-one twill can be woven as weft-faced (1/3) or warp-faced (3/1). The weft travels over three ends and under one end for the weft-faced twill (Fig 94e), and over one end, under three ends for the warp-faced twill (Fig 94f), shifting by one end in each succeeding pick (Plate 11a). Using one colour for the weft of the weft-faced, and the other colour for the warp-faced twill (Fig 94A and G) will show their effect.

The three-by-one twill can also be woven as a herringbone by starting the reverse diagonal with the opposite shed (Fig 94g and Plate 11b).

Breaking the order of the four pick repeat will also break up the diagonal of the twill, producing a *broken twill* (Fig 94h).

The three-by-one (1/3) weft-faced twill, broken in a similar manner (Fig 94i), shows a *mock sateen* on the face of the cloth and a *mock satin* (Plate 11d) on the reverse (App 7.1).

MISCELLANEOUS WEAVES

Two-shed weaves

For a *basket weave* two picks are woven into the same shed, followed by two picks in the opposite shed (Fig 94j). When using two opposing two-by-two sheds with one pick in each shed only, the weft will beat down closely, forming ribs of weft running warp way (Fig 94k). A more deeply ribbed structure uses a one-by-three shed, followed by its opposite three-by-one shed (Fig 94l). As the three warp ends working together will move towards each other, and different combinations of one-by-three sheds will bunch a different group of three ends, a combination of two different groups will cause the warp ends to bend from side to side for a *distorted warp* effect (Fig 94m). This becomes more evident when the fabric has been taken off the loom and the warp is no longer under tension.

Combination weaves

The plain weave and twill sheds can be used in combination to give a less bulky but firmer construction than the twill by itself. The diagonal becomes steeper. Both the two-by-two and three-by-one twills can be woven this way (Fig 94n and o).

The two twills can also be combined in various ways. In the example given (Fig 94p), the order is so arranged as to lift any one or two shafts for one pick only. Try using the four picks of each weave in different combinations and note the differing results.

Two layers of cloth, lying on top of each other, can be woven. Any two shafts can weave the top layer while the other two shafts weave the bottom layer. There are therefore six combinations, any two shafts for the top against the opposite two shafts for the bottom (Fig 94q). Using this shedding sequence will produce double-cloth ribs. The construction will be most

easily seen and understood if the weft is in two colours, two picks of one colour followed by two picks of the other colour (Fig 94D). Repeating one of the groups of four picks will produce two separate fabrics.

A Bedford cord uses two shafts only for a surface of plain weave (cord), with the four-shaft plain weave sheds between each cord. The ends on the two shafts not involved in the cord, float at the back (Fig 94r). This straight entry cord runs across the width of the fabric. The cord can be padded (stuffed) with a thick weft. After the first group of cording picks have been woven, both shafts weaving that cord are raised, and the padding (stuffer) yarn is woven into the shed between the woven cord and the floating ends (Fig 94t at s). The two four-shaft plain weave picks follow. The next padding weft is introduced after the second group of cording picks has been completed, by raising the two shafts which have woven that cord, and passing the padding weft through the resulting shed. The cords, and/or the plain weave areas between cords, can be extended or varied by the number of picks used.

Even though the weaves suggested for this sampler cover only a very small part of those possible on a straight entry, you will find that many more complicated structures are based on these. If you have any warp left, experiment with some different combinations of the fourteen sheds available, as well as with different colour combinations and colour sequences.

POINT-TWILL

When weaving twill on a straight entry, the diagonal can be reversed by reversing the shedding action. The twill then forms zigzags along the length of the fabric. To reverse the diagonal across the width, the threading draft has to be changed, reversing the direction of the threading at every turning point (Fig 95a). Weaving a

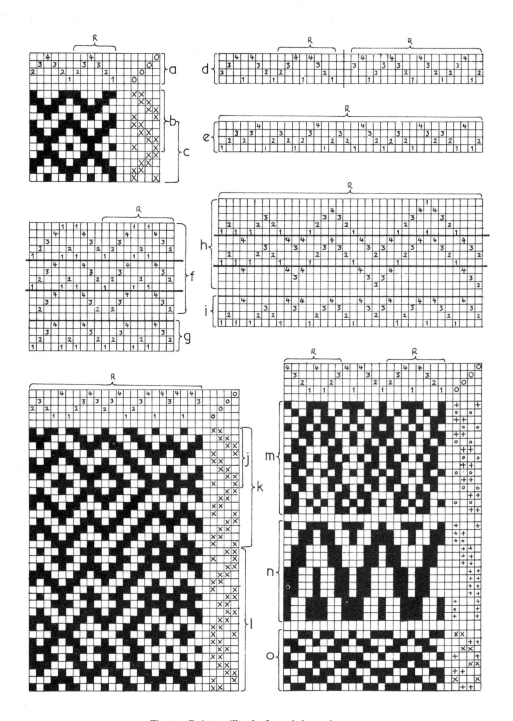

Fig 95 Point twill—drafts and draw-downs.

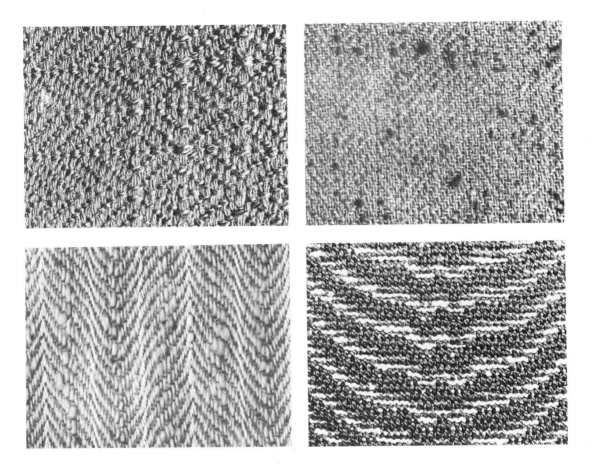

Plate 12   Twill weaves
a (above left) Straight return and point return. b (above right) Point herringbone.
c (below left) Crammed and spaced point twill. d (below right) Extended point twill.

point-twill with the straight shedding sequence of the 2/2 twill (Fig 95b), forms the zigzag across the cloth. In this case the weft will have three-end floats in two of the picks. Weaving the point-twill in the reverse-twill shedding order forms diamonds (Fig 95c).

The turn in the threading can be made at any point, after long or short intervals, in regular or irregular steps (Fig 95d and e). When designing a threading diagram for a point-twill with long diagonals, it is useful to write it initially on more than four staves of squared paper, using only the four numbers of the four shafts (Fig 95f). Isolating four staves completes the threading draft (Fig 95g). A point twill of constantly increasing or decreasing diagonals can first be written showing the diagonal in full (Fig 95h), and can then be condensed into a threading draft for the four shafts (Fig 95i).

The point-twills turn the diagonals across the

width of the cloth when they are woven in the straight twill shedding sequence (Fig 95b and j). They will turn in on themselves, forming diamonds, with a reverse-twill shedding sequence (Fig 95c and k; Plates 12a and 13d).

An irregular point-twill, woven with an equally irregular reverse-twill shedding sequence, will build a complicated pattern of long and short diagonals, and large and small diamonds (Fig 95k and l and Plate 13b). Long warp floats occur when the turn is made after only one or two picks. A pattern like this is therefore more stable if woven as a combination weave (twill and plain weave) (Fig 95m).

The combination weave makes it possible to repeat any one of the twill sheds to build up different patterns. The plain-weave shed and counter-shed are woven alternately after each pattern pick. The plain weave supplies the firm ground weave of the fabric and the twill picks form the pattern. Weaving the plain-weave picks with one colour and the pattern picks in a contrasting colour or shade will show the twill weft as a contrast pattern (Fig 95n). A section of the full draw-down and shedding sequence is shown in Fig 95m, pattern picks only are shown in Fig 95n.

Another way of avoiding long warp floats when weaving a pattern on point-twill and at the same time adding colour contrast to show the pattern, uses weaving on *opposites*. Each 2/2 shed in one colour is followed by the opposite 2/2 shed in the other colour (Fig 95o). The colour patterns reverse on the back of the fabric.

Just as the herringbone on a straight entry avoids the float at the point of reverse, the point-twill entry can be changed into a herringbone turn. The opposing straight entries are used for the diagonals. Each diagonal starts with an end on the opposite shaft to the last end of the other diagonal (Fig 96a–d). The diagonals can be short (Fig 96a and c) or long (Fig 96b and d) and consist of an even number of ends (Fig 96a and b) or an uneven number of ends (Fig 96c and d). The 2/2 twill shedding sequence is followed (Plate 12b). Using the reverse-twill or herringbone shedding sequence forms staggered diamonds. Plain weave is unobtainable on this threading, as odd and even ends share odd and even shafts (Fig 96e).

Extended twill

The pattern units of the 2/2 twill are produced by each warp end floating over two weft picks, and each weft thread floating over two warp ends. The intersections of the warp and weft advance in succeeding picks. Any two succeeding warp ends, entered on two shafts, therefore form

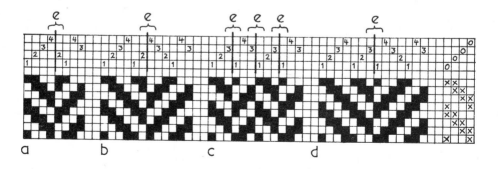

Fig 96 Herringbone drafts and draw-downs

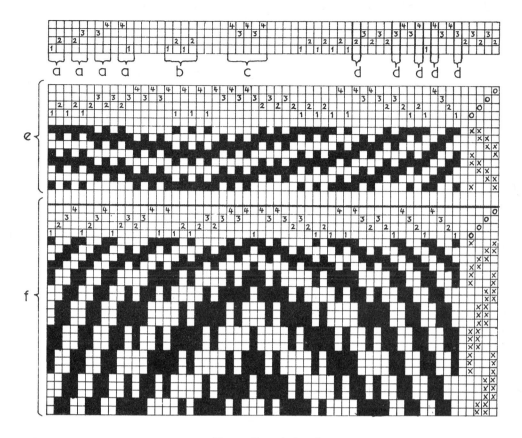

Fig 97　Extended twill

a *block* (Fig 97a). This block can be extended by repeating the threading on these two shafts (Fig 97b and c). All adjoining blocks will have one thread in common (Fig 97d). Each end is involved in two blocks.

Extending the twill in this way makes it possible to have diagonals of varying width and angle. These can have the appearance of curves (Fig 97e). Ovals and circles can be designed and woven by extending the twill shedding action and reversing the twill. When several pattern picks follow each other in identical sheds (Fig 97f), these patterns have to be woven in one of the *combination weaves*. The alternate weft can be woven in plain weave

or in opposites (Plate 12d). Because the pattern weft floats, or 'shoots', over the warp in the extended blocks, these pattern weaves have acquired the name *overshots* (App 7.2).

A long tradition of using the extended twills for pattern weaving has led to the development of many named drafts and different methods of weaving them. The weaver who wishes to use traditional overshots will find pattern books easily available. We hope that our explanation of the structure of the overshot weave will lead you to design your own drafts. Exciting colours and interesting yarns can give highly individual and modern results.

137

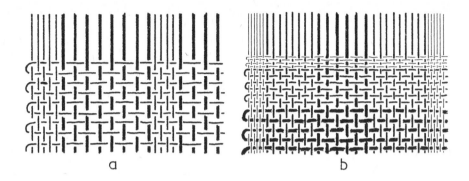

Fig 98   Crammed warp

CRAMMED AND GROUPED THREADS

Crammed warp

A warp can vary from one sett to another across the width of the cloth. A close sett causes more take-up of warp than a wide sett, and with warp stripes of varying sett this will have to be taken into consideration. When the stripes are of regular width and of regular spacing across the width, the closer warp sett (crammed ends) will determine the sett of the cloth. The weft will not beat in closely, causing an open weave in the more open warp sett. This can be used to great effect when a very lightweight or open fabric is wanted (Fig 98a).

Different thicknesses of yarn need different setts to produce a balanced cloth. A striped warp, of a different yarn for each stripe, can be balanced by giving each stripe its own balanced sett (Fig 98b). As the sett changes across the warp, the weft floats change in length. A twill woven on a straight entry and a crammed and spaced warp will appear as a wavy instead of a straight diagonal (Plates 12c and 13a).

Grouped warp and weft

Grouping warp ends in twos, threes or fours right across the width of the warp, and weaving two, three or four picks into each shed, produces a basket weave. When using two shafts, the number of ends to work together for the basket weave are entered on one shaft, and the same number of ends follow on the other shaft (Fig 99a–c).

A two-end basket weave can be woven on a four-shaft straight entry by weaving two of the 2/2 sheds in opposition (Fig 99d). A three-end three-pick basket weave needs a draft of three ends on two shafts, and three ends on the other two shafts (Fig 99e). Each group of three ends forms a small two-shaft block. Plain weave can be woven on these drafts (Fig 99f). A four-end, four-pick basket weave can be woven on the draft shown in Fig 99g1.

Grouped and crammed threads in warp and weft form textures, stripes and checks, which can give an appearance of great complexity in spite of the simple structures.

BLOCK DRAFTING

Two-block opposites

As a plain weave needs only two shafts, two plain weave entries (each on two shafts only) (Fig 99g2) can be placed in blocks, side by side, across the

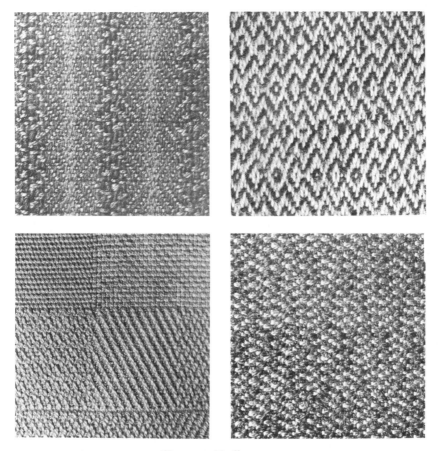

Plate 13   Twill weaves
a (above left) Crammed and spaced point return herringbone. b (above right)
Increasing/decreasing point return twill. c (below left) Two four-end repeat blocks.
d (below right) Point twill with regular changing weft colours.

width of the warp. When the plain weave rule of odd and even ends not sharing a shaft is observed, plain weave can be woven right across the fabric for a stable ground weave, making it possible to repeat pattern sheds for several picks. The blocks can be woven independently of each other (Fig 99h).

A plain weave structure, combined with a pattern (brocade) weft passing under one block and over the other, will give weft-float stripes or checks (Fig 99i and j). As the weft-floats are only held at the intersection with the cloth, they will spread to cover the underlying plain weave (Fig 99k). The four picks of each shedding sequence can be repeated for any number of picks, and each block can vary in width from two warp ends to any multiple of two (Fig 99l). The full draw-down (Fig 99h–j) gives a correct but extended picture of the interaction of warp and weft. The appearance of the fabric will differ considerably from this (Fig 99k and Plate 8c).

The plain weave weft for one block can provide

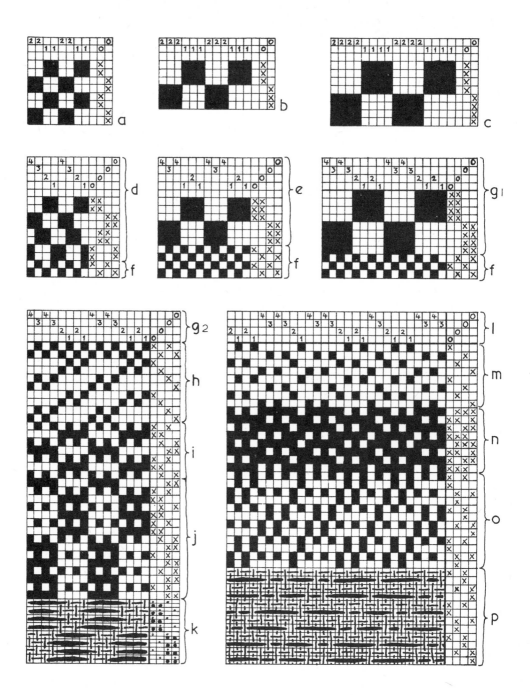

Fig 99   Block drafting—two block opposites

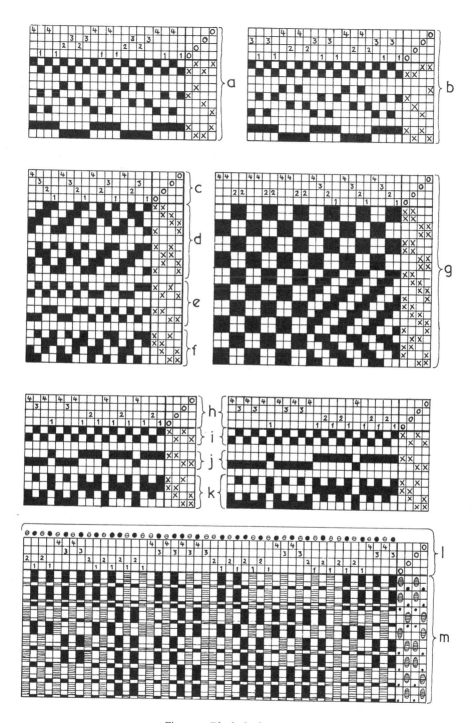

Fig 100   Block drafting

Plate 14   Rib weave, Block weave
a (above left) Horizontal rib. b (above right) Vertical rib. c (below left) Bronson
weave. d (below right) Two-block stitched brocade.

the floats for the other and vice versa. A stable fabric of underlying plain weave covered with ribs of weft in one or two colours is produced (Fig 99m). Weaving with the weft floats passing at the back of the fabric (Fig 99n) produces a cord with warp-way ribs (the same weave as the last, but upside down).

A combination weave of plain cloth and block floats is used to weave *corduroy* (Fig 99o and p). The floats can be cut to produce a pile on the surface of the cloth, provided they are bound into the cloth under at least two ends.

The use of shafts 1 and 2 for one block, and shafts 3 and 4 for the other block, is not the only way to divide the shafts for a two-block entry. One block can use shafts 2 and 3, and the other block shafts 1 and 4. Or the blocks can be entered on shafts 1 and 3 and shafts 2 and 4 (Fig 100a and b).

When no plain weave is required across the fabric because each block-weave is stable by itself,

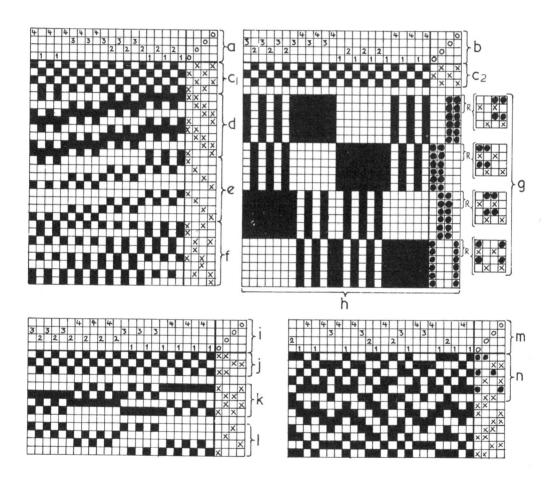

Fig 101 Block drafting—four blocks

the plain weave entry rule can be ignored (Fig 100c). In the draft shown in Fig 100c, weaving twill in one area weaves broken ground in the other, and vice versa (Fig 100d). Weaving plain weave in one, weaves a two-by-two weave in the other (Fig 100e), or the broken ground can be woven in both areas (Fig 100f and Plate 13c). A straight entry in one block, and a two-shaft, two-end entry for the other block, can be woven as a two-end basket weave across the whole cloth, or a twill in the straight entry block with the two-end basket weave in the other block (Fig 100g).

A two-block draft, requiring more than two shafts for the draft of each block, will have one or two shafts working in both blocks (Fig 100h). These shared ends are used as stitching ends for long floats (Fig 100j). A combination weave of plain weave picks (Fig 100i) and pattern picks (Fig 100j), will be of firm construction and can be very decorative (Fig 100k and Plate 14d).

Two colours changing order will weave two colour blocks on two shafts (log-cabin). Two colours changing order in a two-block entry on four shafts provide four colour blocks (Fig 100l). Each block uses two opposing sheds for one repeat. Two wefts, one thick and one fine, or one light and one dark, are needed. The threading and colour blocks can follow each other in any order (Fig 100m and Plate 10c).

Four blocks
On four shafts, only two blocks of plain weave can be woven, each block independently of the other. If more than two blocks are threaded side by side, each shaft will take part in more than one block. We have already referred to the four blocks of weft floats used to form the pattern of an extended twill or overshot, each block being threaded on two shafts. Blocks entered with odd and even ends on odd and even shafts throughout, make a ground cloth of plain weave possible.

The blocks can follow each other in twill order (Fig 101a), or in two sets of opposites (Fig 101b). A combination weave of plain weave (Fig 101c) and pattern sheds (Fig 101d and e) allows for the repeat of pattern picks to build a block pattern (Fig 101f and g). In the draw-down (Fig 101h) only pattern picks are shown. A four-block corduroy on a four-block twill draft has long weft floats and a firm ground cloth (Fig 101f). The floats can be cut to form tufting.

In Fig 101i, shafts 1 and 2 carry the odd ends and shafts 3 and 4 the even ends. The plain weave shedding sequence uses shafts 1 and 2 for the shed and shafts 3 and 4 for the counter-shed (Fig 101j), and the pattern sheds change accordingly (Fig 101k and l).

A combination of two two-block entries (Fig 101m) can exclude plain weave. When the individual blocks are not extended too much, or include stitching ends, the blocks can be woven in two-shed opposites with two or more contrasting wefts (Fig 101n).

Distorted weft
Both two-block and four-block entries can be woven to distort the weft (Plate 10b and d). A two-block distorted weft, weaves plain weave in one block, letting the weft float behind the other. When the first unit of the block has been completed, one or two picks of plain weave will beat down into the unwoven block and bend up over the other block. The second block unit is woven and followed by one or two picks of plain weave in a similar manner (Fig 102a). The weft can cord in a shed instead of floating at the back of the fabric (Fig 102b).

The four twill blocks of an extended twill or overshot can be used to weave four blocks of distorted weft (Fig 102c). While one block is weaving plain weave (Fig 102d) the opposite block will have the weft floating at the back

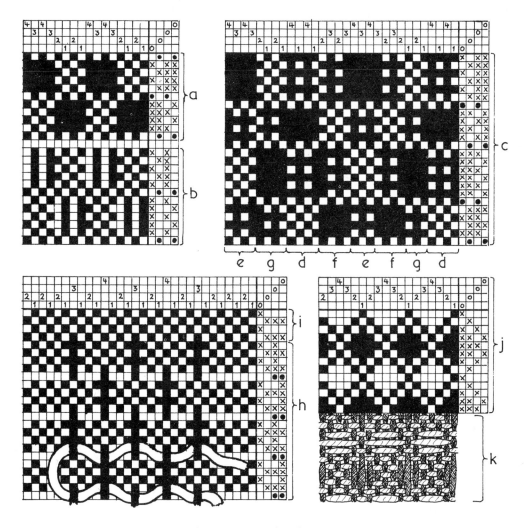

Fig 102   Distorted weft weaves

(Fig 102f), and the other two blocks will cord one weft pick and float the next alternately (Fig 102e and g; Plate 10d).

A distorted weft float on the surface of a plain weave cloth (Plate 16c) uses three shafts to weave the ground cloth while the ends on the fourth shaft float on the surface. The distorting weft travels under the floating ends of the first and second section. At the point of intersection both sets of floating ends pass over two picks, one of the ground picks and the distorting pattern pick. The shaft carrying the floating ends for the first section takes part in weaving the second section, and the second set of ends are floated (Fig 102h). The shafts not involved in the pattern floats can be used on their own to weave plain weave borders or stripes. Plain weave can be woven across the full width of the fabric (Fig 102i).

Waffle weave

All the distorted weft techniques curve or bend the weft in pockets, cords or floats, distorting the fabric. The *waffle weave* does not curve the weft, but forms the deepest distortion. The weft moves from weft-faced picks through plain weave to warp-faced picks on a point-twill draft (Fig 102j). The centre of the weft ridge on one side of the cloth is the warp ridge on the other side (Fig 102k).

Distorted warp

Grouping warp ends by weaving ribs of 3/1, 1/3 on a straight entry and breaking the grouping with a different set of three-by-one groups (Fig 94m), makes the warp ends bend for a distorted warp effect. Various extended and

When the units are small and evenly distributed, the texture is particularly suitable for cottons and linens. All odd ends are entered on one shaft, alternating with ends on one of the other shafts for each block (Fig 103a). One block is used for plain weave borders (Fig 103b), the others (Fig 103c and d) alternate for the texture spots. The texture groups can be separated by entering the plain weave block between texture blocks (Fig 103e).

When no plain weave borders are required (Fig 104a1, a2), all three blocks can be used for texture spots (Fig 104b). Any two blocks can be woven together (Fig 104c). This combination of two blocks causes floats of twice the one-block length. By using one two-end group of the third block between adjoining blocks (Fig 104a2), stitching ends can be provided. Weaving single blocks with this entry provides texture spots of varying width.

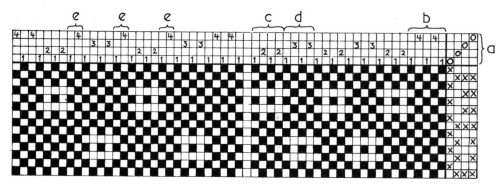

Fig 103   Huckaback

point-twills (Figs 95–97) will weave interesting warp distortions.

Huckaback

A structure of small warp and weft floats in combination with plain weave produces a textured fabric, *huckaback* (useful as towelling).

The grouping of warp and weft floats causes the fabric to bunch in spots. It is usually woven on a balanced plain weave sett.

Lace weave

Lace cannot be woven on a four-shaft loom, but a lace-like structure of warp and weft floats and

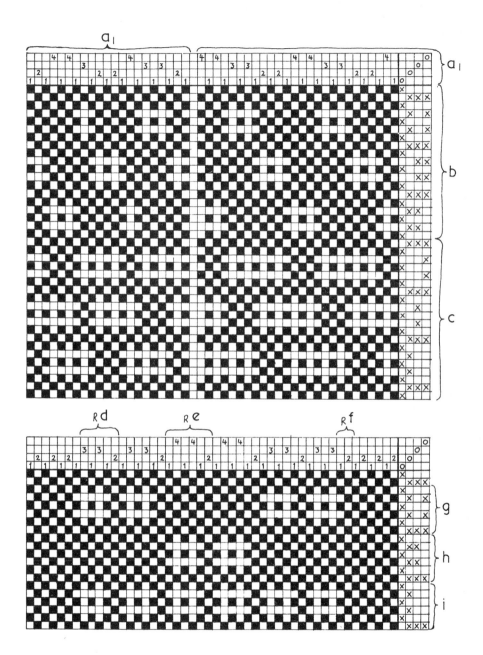

Fig 104 Lace weaves

distortions, usually called a Bronson lace, uses a structure similar to huckaback. The floats are set in groups for each block, to cause an opening of the weave in contrast to plain weave areas. The draft contains three blocks. Two blocks weave pattern (Fig 104d and e) and one block weaves plain weave (Fig 104f). Each block can weave lace by itself (Fig 104g and h), or both blocks can be woven simultaneously (Fig 104i and Plate 14c). The blocks can be repeated both in the threading draft and shedding sequence. Plain weave takes part throughout, and this makes it possible to weave plain weave borders around the pattern areas. Different arrangements of the pattern blocks with each other and in combination with the plain weave block make it possible to weave attractive designs.

All the four-shaft techniques described can be carried out in different yarns and setts for different fabrics (App 7.3). These only represent a small number of the weaves and techniques possible. We hope that the explanations of the underlying principles will help you to design your own pattern weaves.

8
DOUBLE WEAVES

DOUBLE WEFT-FACED

Two-shaft pick-up weave

A weft-faced fabric with two contrasting colours, one for the surface and the other for the reverse of the fabric, can be woven on a two-shaft loom with a counter-balanced shed. The sett of the warp has twice as many ends as the sett for a weft-faced fabric. Only half the ends are entered on shafts 1 and 2 alternately. Each entered end is followed by an end passing between heddles without being threaded. These unentered ends do not rise or sink, but form a 'core' at the centre of each shed and counter-shed, producing *split sheds* (Fig 105 a and b). The weft for the surface is taken through the space between the raised ends and the core, and the weft for the reverse is passed through the other half of the split shed, below the core and over the lowered ends. The core ends hold the two wefts apart and ensure that they will stay on top of each other when beaten into place. Both the shed and counter-shed are woven in this way, each with both wefts, one weft over the core, the other under. When using more than one colour for each face, all the weft-faced and tapestry techniques can be used for two contrasting faces. The resulting fabric is not a double-cloth (two complete cloths on top of each other), but a solid cloth with two faces.

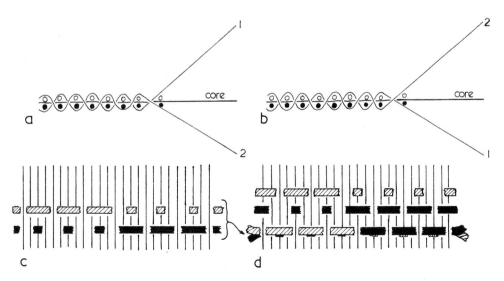

Fig 105 Double weft-faced cloth—two-shaft pick-up weave

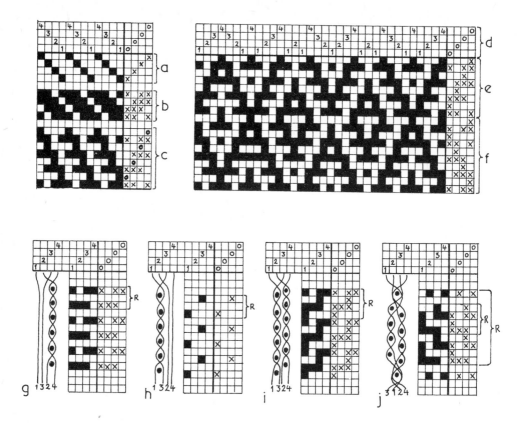

Fig 106 Double faced twill and double plain cloth

The two contrasting wefts can interchange positions in each pick for a free pick-up design. The shuttle carries the weft over the core where the colour is to show on the surface, and passes under the core in the same shed where the colour is to go to the reverse. The contrast weft is taken under the core where the first weft passed over, and over where the first passed under (Fig105c). The second pick for each colour is woven in a similar way (Fig 105d). Each weft takes part in each pick and travels from selvage to selvage.

Double-faced three-by-one-twill

The simplest of the double weft-faced fabrics is based on the two three-by-one twills (1/3, 3/1) on a four-shaft draft. A combination weave of the weft-faced (Fig 106a) and warp-faced (Fig 106b) twill woven with two contrasting wefts (Fig 106c) will have a weft-faced twill of one colour on the surface and a weft-faced twill of the contrasting colour on the reverse.

The small overshot patterns suitable for three-by-one shedding (Fig 106d) can be woven in the same way. Remember that the warp end up can be balanced by an equal weave of warp end down. You will find it easy to combine the two weaves into one double-faced fabric (Fig 106e and f).

Depending on yarn and sett these fabrics are

suitable for fine and coarse cloths, from silks to heavy woollen rugs. In dress and coat fabrics the reverse face can provide a smooth backing.

DOUBLE-CLOTH

Double plain cloth

Two layers of plain cloth, one on top of the other, can be woven on four shafts. Only two shafts are needed for each layer of cloth. The warp has to be made with twice the number of ends of the sett suitable for the yarn being used. The warp is made, and the loom is dressed, exactly as for a single fabric. Separation into two layers does not occur till the cloth is actually being woven.

As an example, consider weaving two balanced plain cloths, the top cloth to be woven with the ends entered on shafts 1 and 3, and the bottom cloth with the ends on shafts 2 and 4. If the two cloths are to have different coloured warps as well as wefts, the warp for a straight entry will have to be made with alternating ends of the two colours.

Following the shedding order for the bottom

fabric only (Fig 106g) will let the ends for the top fabric float over the surface. Weaving the sequence for the top fabric by itself (Fig 106h) leaves the bottom ends floating. Combining the two shedding sequences (Fig 106i) and weaving with two wefts, one for the surface cloth and the other for the reverse, will produce both cloths.

When plain weave patterns and stripes are to match exactly for two articles or strips of cloth, the weaving of both at the same time can ensure this.

Double plain-cloth ribs

The two layers of cloth can be joined at intervals to form double plain-cloth ribs (Fig 106j) by lifting the two shafts weaving the bottom fabric to the top for one pick.

The ribs can be separated by flat areas woven with the two four-shaft plain weave picks (Fig 107a). Ribs can also be produced by interchanging the two fabrics. The two shafts that wove the first bottom fabric are used for the top fabric of the second rib and vice versa (Fig 107b).

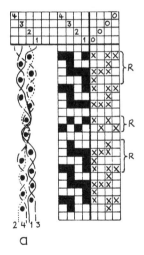
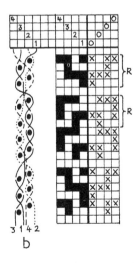
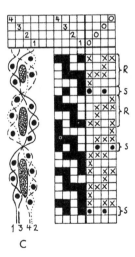

Fig 107   Double plain cloth ribs

The ribs can be raised, stuffed, with a thick weft passing between the two layers of cloth. This stuffer yarn is woven into the rib by lifting both shafts of the top fabric for the stuffer shed before weaving the next rib (Fig 107c).

Double-width cloth

The two plain weave cloths lying on top of each other can be joined at one selvage to produce a double-width fabric. The two layers will unfold when the cloth is taken off the loom.

When weaving a double-width cloth, consideration has to be given to the order of the ends at the joined edge. The face of the top fabric (Fig 108a and c) corresponds to the underside of the bottom fabric (Fig 108b and c).

Warp up in the top fabric corresponds to warp down in the bottom fabric.

The fabric will be open on the right when the shuttle starts from the right, and open on the left when the shuttle starts from the left. Both follow the identical shedding sequence (Fig 108d and e). All the plain weave techniques can be used to pattern the double-width cloth. It is not easy to use the discontinuous weft techniques as the bottom layer is not visible while weaving. When the pattern on the bottom layer is to be identical with the pattern on the top layer it can be controlled unseen by following the design on the top.

Tubular cloth

A simple change in the shedding sequence (Fig 108f) produces a tubular cloth. The weft travels through the bottom shed, top shed, bottom counter-shed and top counter-shed in that order. As the two fabrics can be combined by weaving four-shaft plain cloth, a hem of plain cloth, followed by tubular cloth, will weave a bag or cushion cover with only one open edge.

DOUBLE REPP

Two-by-two shaft combinations

Any two shafts can be used to weave one of the layers of a double plain cloth, while the opposite two shafts are used for the other layer:

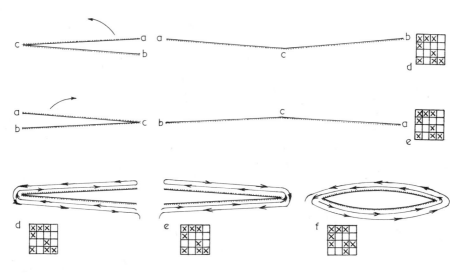

Fig 108 Double-width and tubular cloth

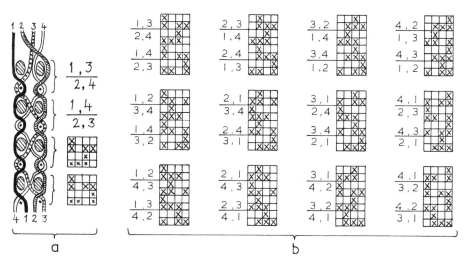

Fig 109   Double repp—notation

Top fabric	1, 3	1, 2	1, 4	2, 3	2, 4	3, 4
Bottom fabric	2, 4	3, 4	2, 3	1, 4	1, 3	1, 2

Different combinations of these pairs, woven as a double repp, will produce an interlocking double rib. For example, one of the combinations uses shafts 1 and 3 for the top, and shafts 2 and 4 for the bottom rib. Shafts 1 and 4 are used for the top, with shafts 2 and 3 for the bottom of the alternate rib (Fig 109a). Each rib can be padded by lifting the shafts of the top fabric and throwing a stuffer weft before weaving the next rib.

Four-block double repp

A two-shaft repp weave can have contrasting faces (a warp of two alternating colours) because

the warp ends passing over a thick weft dominate with their colour the warp ends of the other colour passing over the fine weft. The two colours can be interchanged by throwing two thick picks following each other. Using a log-cabin warp makes it possible to weave a two-block pattern. Combining this technique with the double repp, leads to the design of a reversible double repp with four colour changes or four pattern blocks (Plate 15b).

For example, if four colours are used in the warp in a regular order of four ends, and entered on a straight draft, each shaft will carry one colour. To produce an area of the colour on shaft 1 on the surface, and shaft 2 on the reverse, the two opposing repp ribs are woven in the order shown below in Fig 109a.

top ribs	1,3	1,4	(	rising shed	1, 134, 3, 123 : 1, 134, 4, 124
bottom ribs	2,4	2,3	or :	sinking shed	234, 2, 124, 4 : 234, 2, 123, 3.

Fig 109a

End up on the surface is followed by end down on the reverse, shaft 1 up for the first surface pick is followed by shaft 2 down for the reverse. The double repp is woven with two thick picks (one for the top, the other for the reverse), followed by two fine picks.

The full shedding sequence (Fig 109a) reads: shaft 1 up, thick weft; shaft 2 down (1, 3 and 4 up), thick weft; 3 up, fine weft; 4 down (1, 2 and 3 up), fine weft; 1 up, thick weft; 2 down (1, 3 and 4 up), thick weft; 4 up, fine weft; 3 down (1, 2 and 4 up), fine weft.

In both ribs the ends on shaft 1 pass over the thick weft on the surface, determining the colour of the surface, and the ends on shaft 2 cover the other thick weft on the reverse, determining the colour of the reverse. Shafts 3 and 4 interchange from front to reverse and interlock the fabric.

The ribs can be thickened by using a stuffer yarn as before: lifting the two shafts that have woven the rib (1 and 3) for the stuffer shed before weaving the opposite rib, and shedding for the second stuffer pick in a similar manner (1 and 4) after weaving the opposing rib.

There are 12 different possible combinations of ribs (Fig 109b):

Top ribs	1, 3/1, 4	2, 3/2, 4	3, 2/3, 4	4, 2/4, 3
Bottom	2, 4/2, 3	1, 4/1, 3	1, 4/1, 2	1, 3/1, 2
	1, 2/1, 4	2, 1/2, 4	3, 1/3, 4	4, 1/4, 3
	3, 4/3, 2	3, 4/3, 1	2, 4/2, 1	2, 3/2, 1
	1, 2/1, 3	2, 1/2, 3	3, 1/3, 2	4, 1/4, 2
	4, 3/4, 2	4, 3/4, 1	4, 2/4, 1	3, 2/3, 1

Because of the repp structure and the different combinations for the ribs, it is possible to use each shaft for one unit of a colour pattern. Any one of four pattern units can be woven on the surface with any one of the remaining three on the reverse.

Double repp sampler

For a sampler you could use two-ply rug yarn or a thick cotton in two colours. Make the warp with three times the number of ends needed for a balanced plain weave sett. Repeat each four-end colour order twelve times (Fig 110a). Use two thick (sixfold) wefts, one of each colour, and one fine neutral or black yarn for both fine picks. At the beginning, follow the shedding sequence given (Fig 110b). Experiment with all the other possible combinations, and remember that each rib combination can be woven for any number of repeats. A change in the colour of the weft will also change the appearance of the pattern. Try the effect of different thicknesses of weft as well as the use of stuffer yarns.

When planning a warp for the double repp cloth, the sett should have at least twice the number of ends as a balanced plain weave. The closer the warp is set, the more definite the pattern units will be. An open sett will show more of the weft colour. For different weft colour only, the warp can be set for a weft-faced fabric. For a truly warp-faced fabric four times the balanced sett is needed.

The colour order for warping can be read from a block design, as each unit of the pattern block is the horizontal colour order on one shaft (Fig 110c). If the horizontal change is complicated, four warps can be made, one for each shaft, and married on the loom (App 8.1).

Only four vertical changes of pattern unit are possible (the number of shafts, eg pattern units). Any number of changes of colour can be warped for each shaft. Pattern units set in the warp can be woven to different patterns by combining the blocks in different orders, or using only two or three. Any block can be woven to any desired length.

Double-repp fabrics do not drape easily, but are very sturdy, without long floats and offer a wide range of design possibilities. Bold colour blocks or subtle colour changes are possible. They are particularly suitable for reversible rugs, furnishing fabrics and table mats.

Articles can be designed with one self-coloured and one patterned face.

PICK-UP POCKET CLOTH

Changing-shed pocket cloth

A pocket cloth is a double cloth in which the two fabrics interchange positions horizontally and vertically. The name is very descriptive, as the resulting fabric is formed of closed pockets. The horizontal interchange presents no problems (see 'Double plain-cloth ribs', p151). The vertical interchange has to be picked up, unless more shafts are available (outside the scope of this book).

For example, a one-by-one warp of alternating colours or shades is made with twice the number of ends needed for a balanced plain cloth. A straight entry will have all the ends of one colour on one pair of shafts, and all the ends of the other colour on the other two shafts (Fig 111a). Two shuttles are needed, one for each colour. The simplest method of weaving uses each shuttle to pick up the shed for its own cloth by passing from selvage to selvage through a changing shed (Fig 111f).

At x in Fig 111 the shuttle leaves the shed and is brought to the surface. It enters at the same point after the shed has been changed. Both picks of one colour can be followed by both picks of the other (Fig 111b and c, d and e) or the shed of the first can be followed by the shed of the second colour, and the counter-shed of the first by the counter-shed of the other (Fig 111b and d, c and e; and Plate 15a).

Split-shed pocket cloth

Both counter-balanced and counter-march looms make it possible to produce a split-shed. The

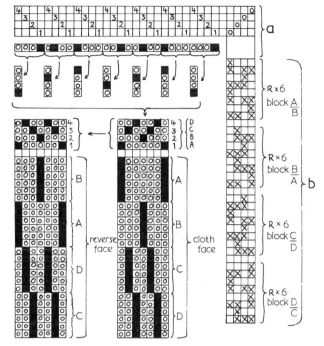

N B Reverse face shows inverted pattern as would appear if the cloth were turned over

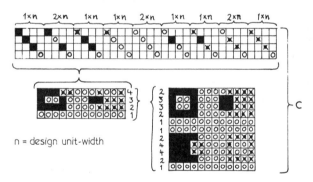

n = design unit-width

Fig 110 Double repp—block drafting and notation

counter-march action will automatically produce a split-shed if the eight-pedal universal tie-up is used. Depressing one pedal only will raise one shaft and lower one shaft, leaving the

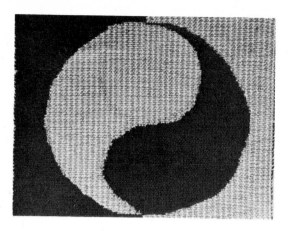

Plate 15   Double cloth weave
a (left) Pick-up pocket cloth. b (right) Double weft rib.

ends on the other two shafts inactive in the centre. The pedal with the rising tie for shaft 1 and the sinking tie for shaft 3 produces the split-shed for one colour, and the pedal with the rising tie for shaft 3 and the sinking tie for shaft 1 produces the counter-shed for the same colour. The two split-sheds for the other colour are produced by alternating the pedal with shaft 2

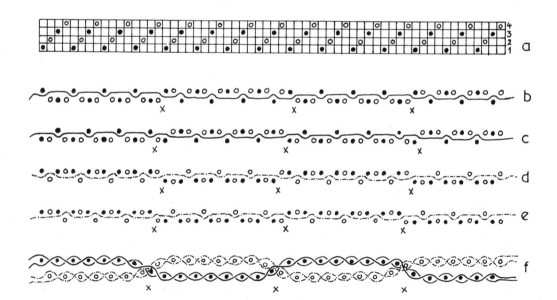

Fig 111   Pick-up pocket cloth

156

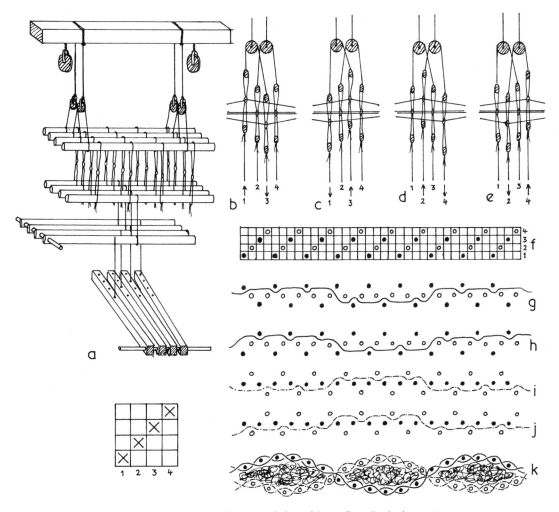

Fig 112 Special tie-up of counter-balanced loom for split-shed weaving

rising and shaft 4 sinking, and the pedal with shaft 4 rising and shaft 2 sinking.

The counter-balanced loom will require some adjustments. The top roller or pulleys will have to be disconnected or rendered inactive by tying or wedging in the neutral position. The shafts are linked 1 to 3 and 2 to 4 over the lower pulleys or horses (Fig 112a). When shaft 1 is lowered,

shaft 3 rises, and 2 and 4 will remain inactive. Sinking shaft 3 will raise shaft 1. Raising shaft 2 will sink shaft 4 and vice versa, while shafts 1 and 3 remain inactive. This system produces the split-shed (Fig 112b–e).

With light ends on the even shafts (Fig 112f), lifting shaft 1 and lowering shaft 3 produces the split-shed for the dark weft (Fig 112b and g).

Lifting shaft 3 and lowering shaft 1 produces the counter-shed (Fig 112c and h). Lifting shaft 2 and lowering shaft 4 produces the shed for the light weft (Fig 112d and i), lifting 4 and lowering 2 produces the counter-shed (Fig 112e and j).

The weft is taken under the raised ends and over the inactive ends in the centre of the shed, when it is to weave on the surface. It passes between the inactive ends (of the opposite colour) and the lowered ends, when it is to weave on the reverse (Fig 112g-j).

Pocket cloth is suitable for formal, geometric or freely abstracted designs. According to yarns and sett, it can be used for wall hangings, rugs, furnishings, table mats, bedspreads and, with patience, even for coat and dress fabrics.

The pockets can be padded before each horizontal change to produce quilting (Fig 112k).

9
TECHNIQUE AND DESIGN

YARN

Un-spun and spun yarns

Continuous filaments, whether silk or man-made, need not be spun. Single strands or bundles of strands can be used as yarns with or without a twist. When a bundle of filaments is twisted together it is described as *thrown*.

Fibres and short filaments are spun into yarn. The continuous yarn formed by the joining of the fibres is a *singles* yarn. Singles are joined, twisted around each other, for *plied* yarns. Two singles make a 2-ply yarn, three singles a 3-ply etc. When the singles are not twisted together the resulting yarn is a *multiple* yarn. Plied yarns are sometimes re-plied, letting two or more yarns twist around each other (App 9.1).

Yarns can be spun, and plied, in either direction, receiving an S-twist (clockwise) or Z-twist (anti-clockwise) (Fig 113a and b). The angle of the S or Z will give an indication of the tightness of the twist (Fig 113 c-e).

Yarn sizes

The size of a yarn is called its *count*. The count for most spun yarns is based on the number of unit lengths to a *fixed weight* eg 1lb.

Because of the early isolated development of the manufacture of wool in the British Isles, quite

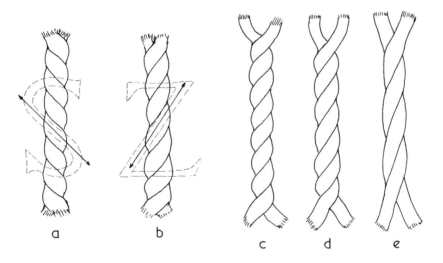

Fig 113   'S' and 'Z' twists

distinct systems of count are still in use. Yarn suppliers in the United States will usually supply details of length of yarn per lb.

In the fixed weight system, the number of the count gives the number of unit lengths in 1lb. A Galashiels *cut* has a unit length of 200yd. A singles No 1 yarn is 200yd long, weighing 1lb. A singles No 2 yarn has twice 200yd = 400yd per 1lb. It is finer, and therefore longer for the same weight. A 2-ply No 1 (2/1s) is two singles plied together, and is therefore twice as thick as 1s and half the length per 1lb. It follows that the higher the count number of the yarn, the finer the yarn is and the longer it is per 1lb. A plied yarn is as many times heavier than the number of singles used in the ply. A 4-ply/3-cut (4/3s) = 3 times 200, divided by 4 = 150 yards per 1lb.

Fixed weight system

A table for the most common *fixed weight* counts is as follows and shows yardage per 1lb of No 1 yarn:

Woollen	Galashiels	*cut*	200 yd
	Yorkshire	*skein*	256 yd
	West of England	*hank*	320 yd
Worsted		*hank*	560 yd
Linen		*lea*	300 yd
Silk	cotton spun	*hank*	840 yd
Cotton		*hank*	840 yd
Man-made	cotton spun	*hank*	840 yd

It must be remembered that there can be considerable variation in the actual length per lb in the fixed weight system. When yarns are packaged or stored in damp conditions, the more water absorbent the fibre is, the shorter the yarn will be per lb.

A singles yarn has one number only, indicating the count. A plied yarn gives the count of the singles component and the number plied. A 4s cotton has 4 times 840yd in 1lb. A 2/4s cotton

has 4 times 840, divided by 2 = 1680yd per 1lb.

Spun silk counts give the number of components used in the ply, and the count of the *resulting* yarn. A 4/40s spun silk is a 4-ply yarn of a resulting 40s count, or 40 times 840yd per lb, composed of four strands, each of a 160s count.

Fixed length system

Continuous filament yarns use a *fixed length* system.

Continuous filament

Thrown silk and man-made (rayon, nylon etc) *denier* = weight in grammes of 9000 metres; eg a 30 denier yarn will have 9000m for every 30g, or 10 g of 30 denier yarn will measure 3000m.

The Tex System

Tex is an international system for all fibres. It has a fixed length count of—*weight in grammes of 1000 metres*. For plied yarns, the Tex system gives the resulting count first (R), followed by the number of components in the ply.

Two singles of 12 count (each of a 1000m weighing 12g) plied together make a yarn of resulting R24 Tex/2 count (1000m weighing 24g). A Tex count with a multiplication sign indicates the size of the singles components with the number plied after the sign. Two singles of 12 count plied together with a resultant R24 Tex/2 count may be written: Tex 12×2.

With the *fixed weight* system the count number rises as the yarn gets *finer*.

With the *fixed length* system the count number rises as the yarn gets *thicker*. When you have to find the count of a yarn, wind a skein of known length, calculate the total length of the wound yarn by counting the turns in the skein and weigh it. This will give a close approximation of length-to-weight to calculate the count of your yarn.

Knowing the count of a yarn is necessary to

calculate the quantities needed for the warp and weft of a fabric. The number of ends in a warp multiplied by their length will give the total length of yarn needed for a warp. A balanced cloth will need as much yarn for the weft as for the warp (slightly less, because of loom wastage in the warp). It is good practice to buy rather more yarn than your calculations suggest. Re-ordering may be difficult or in the case of coloured yarns show slight variations caused by a new dye-lot. Building up a store of yarn, however little of each, will encourage experiments and sampling, as well as suggesting new combinations.

SETT

The sett of a cloth is the number of warp ends and weft picks in a unit square of cloth. Two yarns of the same fibre and count can differ from each other, one being hard and smooth with a tight spin, the other soft and loosely spun. They will produce completely different cloths with identical setts, as the soft yarn will compact more than the hard one. Variations of sett in an identical yarn can change the whole character of a fabric. The difference of tension and beat used by different weavers can produce different fabrics with the same yarns and warp sett. Making samplers and keeping samples and records of everything woven will provide the best text book. (We have never met a weaver who really does keep samples of *everything*.)

There is however a practical rule which makes it possible to find satisfactory setts for most yarns and techniques. These setts can be adjusted to the weaver's taste and requirements in the light of growing experience.

The width of a cloth is the sum of the width of all the warp ends, plus the width of the intersections of a weft thread with the warp (Fig 114a).

Each warp end occupies the width of its own diameter. Each weft pick requires the width of its yarn diameter between warp ends for the number of intersections of warp and weft in the cloth. Winding both warp and weft around a stick, with as many warp threads as there are ends between intersections, and a weft thread or threads for the intersection, will have as many turns of the warp yarn as are required for the sett. For easy calculation, the yarns are wound for a unit width (2cm, or 1in; 5cm, or 2in) and will indicate the number of warp ends needed in that unit width.

Balanced sett

In a balanced sett, warp and weft have an equal distribution. The number of ends equals the number of picks in a unit square of cloth. The warp has to be set with spaces equal to the weft yarn diameter to allow for the interlacing of warp and weft. In a plain-weave fabric, the weft intersects the warp between alternate warp ends. When the warp and weft are to be the same yarn, winding the yarn on a stick with the turns just touching for a unit width, will supply twice the number of ends needed for the sett because half the turns represent the weft intersections (Fig 114b). When two different yarns are to be used, one for warp and one for weft, two threads are wound, one of each yarn. The number of turns of the warp yarn only will give the number of ends needed for the unit width (Fig 114c). The diameter of the weft yarn will space the warp yarn to give the correct sett required for the interlacing of warp and weft.

In a two-by-two twill weave, the weft interlaces after every two ends. The balanced sett is found by winding the yarn on a stick as before, and using two-thirds of the number of ends wound, when the weft is to be the same yarn as the warp. One-third of the yarn turns represent weft intersections with a width of the weft

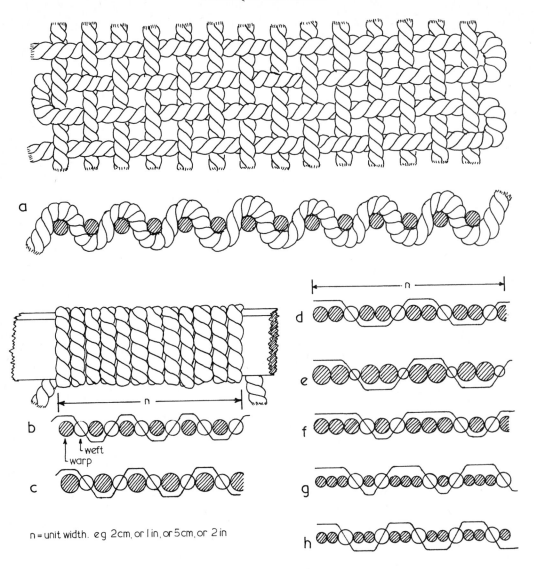

n = unit width. eg 2cm, or 1 in, or 5cm, or 2 in

Fig 114 Warp sett

diameter (Fig 114d). When the warp and weft are to be different yarns, two threads of warp yarn and one thread of the weft yarn are wound together. The number of warp turns will be the number of ends for the sett of the unit width

wound on the stick (Fig 114e).

The balanced sett for a three-by-one twill is the same as for the two-by-two twill, as the number of intersections in a unit width is the same (Fig 114d and f). When a combination weave of plain weave and twill, or extended twill, is to be used, the sett should be balanced for the plain-weave ground cloth, as this will have the maximum intersections.

A great number of fabric structures are based on the twills and their setts can be determined in a similar way. When the structure has a different number of intersections for each pick of a pattern repeat, the average number of intersections can easily be calculated and used as the basis for finding the sett.

To obtain a truly balanced sett for a balanced cloth, remember that the warp and weft will have to be yarns of similar diameter to give an equal distribution of warp and weft in the cloth.

Unbalanced sett

The sett for a stable weave of widely differing yarns in warp and weft, and both warp and weft showing in the cloth, is found exactly like the sett for the balanced cloth. When both warp and weft yarns are wound for the required number of ends and intersections, they will take up the width of their own diameters, and the number of warp ends will be correct for the sett and the spaces will be the right width for the interlacing weft (Fig 114c, e, g and h).

For a weft-faced fabric, the warp ends have to be spaced far enough apart for the weft of two or more picks to compact into the spaces to form a continuous cover for the warp ends. A weft-faced plain weave has a repeat of two picks, and the space between the ends will have to allow for the joint diameter of two wefts. The sett can be found by winding one thread of the warp yarn and two of the weft yarn for a unit width. The turns should be pushed firmly together without overlapping. The number of warp turns wound will be the number of ends needed for the sett of the unit width (Fig 115a).

A weft-faced twill interlaces after every two ends, but requires four picks to complete the repeat and cover all warp ends. Two threads of warp yarn are wound with four threads of weft

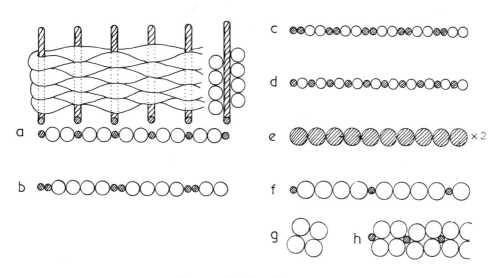

Fig 115   Unbalanced warp sett

yarn (Fig 115b), or one for warp and two for weft (Fig 115a), as the space between warp ends has to be wide enough to allow the weft of one pick to pass from front to back, and the weft of another pick to pass from back to front. The turns are pushed closely together without overlapping to give the sett. When the two-by-two twill is to be woven in opposites, two succeeding picks work like a two-ended plain weave to cover the warp. The space at the intersection has to accommodate the weft of two picks. Two warp threads and two weft threads have to be wound together (or one of each) to find the sett (Fig 115c and d).

In a warp-faced plain weave the weft does not interlace with the warp. The ends pass from the face to the reverse, enveloping the weft (Fig 90a). To find the sett for the warp, a warp thread is wound just touching for a unit width, twice the number wound is the number of ends needed for the sett (Fig 115e).

Fabrics with weft floats can be woven with both sides weft-faced by using the two opposing three-by-one shedding sequences, one for the face and one for the reverse. This does not require a change from the balanced three-by-one sett, as the number of intersections is the same for both faces.

Weaves based on the three-by-one twill can also be woven with both faces weft-faced, but only one side having weft floats. The other side has each warp end covered by one of four weft picks. The warp sett has to be spaced for two weft diameters between warp ends (one weft passing from front to back, and one passing from back to front) to allow four picks to compact into a horizontal line. One thread of warp yarn and two threads of weft yarn have to be wound together (Fig 115a and b).

In a pick of multiple weft, the total diameter is *not* the sum of the individual yarns side by side

(Fig 115f). The multiples will bunch (Fig 115g), and the sett will be nearer correct if the multiples are twisted together for winding (Fig 115h).

To increase the warp-faced effect, increase the number of ends; to increase the weft-faced effect, decrease the number of ends.

Graduations between warp-faced, balanced and weft-faced setts follow from the above guide lines. The setts depend on the yarn being used and the effect desired.

Small samples woven on a card loom are very useful for experimenting and gaining practical experience. They should be wet finished to show that wool needs a wider sett than smooth yarns, such as cotton and linen. Because of its elasticity wool is actually easier to beat into a closely set warp for a balanced weave than cotton or linen, but the cloth will be hard if the woollen yarn is not given enough space to full during the finishing process.

If you weave samples on a table or floor loom, you will have to remember that the few ends of **a narrow sample warp present little resistance to** the beat of the batten. When the loom has been dressed for its full width to weave the cloth, the greater total number of ends will make the beat much less effective. The sample should be woven with sections of different beats. If the final choice is a section where the weft has been beaten in very closely, it may be necessary to adjust the sett for the full width fabric by using a slightly wider sett (fewer ends).

WARP

Warp calculations
When the yarn has been chosen and the sett found, the warp is made by one of the methods described in previous chapters.

The amount of yarn needed for the warp can be calculated by multiplying the length by the total number of ends to be used. The count of the yarn will show the length of the yarn per **1lb, and the total length of warp yarn calculated** will show the weight required. When the count of the yarn is known, calculations for weight or length are a matter of simple arithmetic. While the count systems of yards per lb are still in use, it will be necessary to calculate the length of the warp in yards rather than metres. (See Fig 115a below.)

A warp made with 2/12s cotton, 4yd long, 30in (75cm) wide and 25 epi (10 e/cm) will have a total number of 750 ends and will need a weight of:

$$\frac{4 \times 750 \times 2}{12 \times 840} = \frac{25}{42} = \text{approx 9 to 10 oz}$$

(always round the total upwards to compensate for variations in length per lb, caused by varying moisture content).

The calculations in the fixed length system are even easier. Find the length of the warp yarn needed by multiplying the total number of ends by the length of the warp in metres, divide by the standard length (9000 for denier, 1000 for Tex), and multiply by the count to find the weight in grammes. (See Fig 115b below.)

Warp length and width
The warp always needs to be longer than the cloth to be woven. There is considerable wastage for tie-on and the part of the warp that cannot be woven (the distance from the back apron-stick through the heddles and reed), as well as the extra length needed for take-up and shrinkage. All warps require extra length for loom wastage, but the amount needed for take-up and shrinkage increases with the length of the warp, and varies for different yarns and weaves. Wool has the highest shrinkage rate, but cotton and linen have a higher take-up. Adding 10 per cent to the length of the finished cloth is necessary for wool warps, a little less is needed for the other fibres. A small amount of warp will be needed at the beginning of the cloth for adjustments in the weft texture, colour and/or beat. We also recommend extra warp length for trying some of the developments that will have occurred to you while weaving the planned cloth. This will enable you to try some of these at the end of the warp without having to weave a separate sampler.

The calculations for the length of the warp required are: length of cloth, plus loom wastage, plus 10 per cent, plus length for testing and sampling.

The calculations for the width of the warp are: width of cloth, plus 10 per cent for take-up and shrinkage.

Different structures have differing take-up. A warp-faced fabric has a large take-up in the warp and hardly any in the weft. A weft-faced

$$\frac{\text{length of warp in yards} \times \text{number of ends} \times \text{ply of yarn}}{\text{count of yarn} \times \text{standard length of 1lb of 1s yarn}} = \text{weight of warp in lb}$$

Fig 115a

$$\frac{\text{Number of ends} \times \text{length of warp in metres} \times \text{count}}{\text{standard length}} = \text{weight in grammes}$$

Fig 115b

fabric has nearly all the take-up in the weft and hardly any in the warp. Weft distortions increase the weft take-up, and warp distortions increase the warp take-up.

Raddle groups

When the sett of the warp is determined by the yarn and weave to be used, it is of advantage to use the same unit widths throughout the planning and making of the warp. As the warp is spread in a raddle, the most convenient unit width to use is the width of a raddle dent. The number of ends to pass through one dent of the raddle are counted while warping with a single end, and encircled in each group of the figure-of-eight raddle tie. When using the multiple warping method, the total number of ends needed for each raddle dent is warped together. When the total number is too large, half or a third can be warped together, and two or three groups placed in each dent for spreading. Counting the total number of ends needed for the width of the cloth is done in *groups* for the total number of groups in the width.

WEAVING

Tension

When the loom has been dressed and the warp tied to the front apron-stick, the cloth can be woven if the tension is even and there are no mistakes in entering. Faulty tension will show up if a few picks are woven in a thick contrasting weft. Single loose ends will loop and can be adjusted by pulling the loop up on the surface of the cloth and pinning it into place at the right tension. A single tight end will appear slightly lighter in colour than the other ends. The tight end can either be cut between the tie-on and the woven picks, pulled out of the web and pinned at the correct tension, or the group which contains it can be undone and retied. A whole group or area of incorrect tension will cause the weft to beat into the cloth irregularly and the fell of the cloth will be wavy. At the bottom of a wave the tension is too high (Fig 116b), at the crest it is too low (Fig 116a). It is best to undo the entire warp and re-tension. This will be found easier than trying to adjust several different sections.

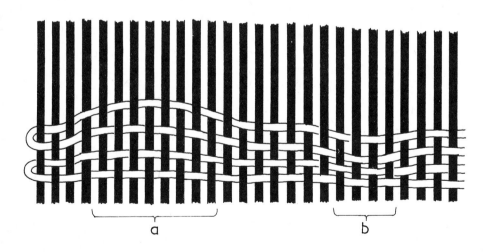

Fig 116   Warp tension

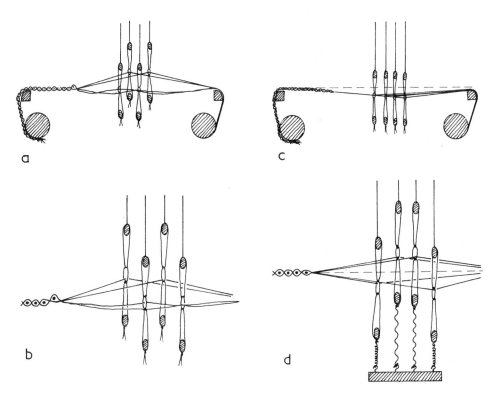

Fig 117   Adjusting a rising shed loom

Almost all table looms and some floor looms have rising sheds. The warp ends raised for a shed will take up the tension from those left at the bottom of the shed (Fig 117a). The ends in the bottom layer of the shed will become soft and rise over the last pick (Fig 117b). This should not cause any inconvenience when the web is narrow and the shed deep and clear. The softness of the bottom ends may however prevent a shuttle being 'thrown' correctly for a wide cloth, as the loose ends can be caught by the tip of the shuttle. All ends can be tensioned evenly by situating the shafts so that the heddle eyes lie below the horizontal line between the front and back bars of the loom (Fig 117c). To prevent the shafts being lifted to the horizontal by the tension of the

warp ends, springs or weights are attached to the bottom of the shafts (Fig 117d). When a table loom has insufficient depth for this, because the shafts are already touching the base of the loom when at rest, a *tension bar* can be used. The tension bar is placed under the warp, behind the heddles, and attached with strong elastic bands or springs to the top of the castle (Fig 118a and b). When a cloth structure requires different take-up for different sections of the warp (eg warp brocade) the tension bar can be used to correct the ends needing less take-up or higher tension as weaving proceeds. The bar is placed under the ends needing tensioning, over all the other ends behind the shafts, and is attached with elastic bands as before. When there is no castle, or no room on

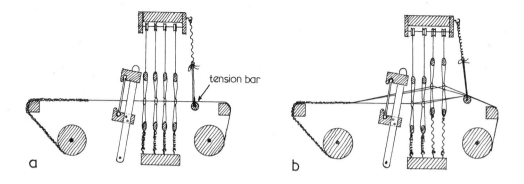

Fig 118 Tension bar

the castle, the tension bar can pass over the ends to be tensioned and under the rest of the warp. Elastic bands or weights are then attached to the bottom of the loom at a convenient spot, this will not correct a soft shed, but is effective for differential tensioning (App 9.2).

It sometimes becomes necessary to tension narrow selvage bands, eg when a firm border is required for an open weave. The tension bar is used for this.

Threading mistakes

Threading mistakes will show in the heading of contrast picks and will have to be traced and corrected before proceeding. A few pattern picks should be woven to make sure that the draft has been threaded correctly. Some common faults and their corrections are also described in Chapter 6.

Every shed to be used should be tried and examined. When two warp ends are crossed between shafts (Fig 119a), the mistake may not be easy to detect in one shed, but becomes obvious in another. When two ends are crossed between the shafts and the reed (Fig 119b) the twist will lie close to the reed and is difficult to detect in that position, but quite clear in one or more sheds.

Both ends will be left in the centre of the shed in front of the reed (Fig 119c).

An end passing through the shafts without being entered in a heddle will not take part in the shedding action. When it has by-passed the heddle, but the empty heddle is in the right place and on the correct shaft, the end is withdrawn and re-entered through the heddle and reed. When the heddle has been left out altogether, a string heddle can be tied into place on the correct shaft, with the end passing through the eye of the heddle as it is being tied (Fig 119d). When the sequence is correct with ends entered in their correct order, making the un-entered end superfluous, the end can be cut at the tie-on, pulled to the back of the loom and left hanging there. The reed will have to be re-sleyed to eliminate the gap left.

An entered, but unsleyed end will hang down between the shafts and the reed (Fig 119e). It will soon be caught into the adjoining ends, preventing these from shedding correctly. The reed has to be re-sleyed to make room for the missed end.

Even when all ends seem to be shedding correctly, the order of the entry may be incorrect. As the threading draft is a pictorial representation of the entered heddles on the shafts, the correctness of the entry can be checked by the number and position of the heddles at the top of the shafts (Fig 120a). Each repeat of the draft can be checked as a group. When the order in the group is incorrect, but the right number of ends and heddles are present, the ends can be re-drawn in the correct order. When the right number of ends are present, but because of the faulty entry, the heddles are on the wrong shafts, one or more heddles can be left empty, string heddles tied to

the right shafts (Fig 119d), and the ends entered correctly (Fig 120b and c). When the number of ends in the group is incorrect, the warp will have to be re-drawn to the nearest selvage.

Incorrect sleying, with fewer or more ends in the dents than the sett, can only be corrected by re-sleying from the fault to the nearest selvage.

DESIGN
Design starts with the fibres used for the yarn, the order or disorder of the fibres in the spun

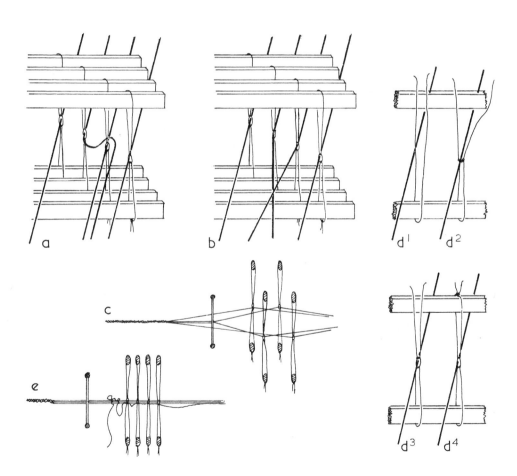

Fig 119   Threading mistakes

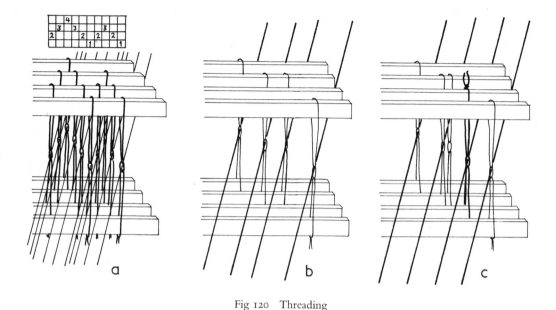

Fig 120   Threading

yarn, the tightness or softness of the spin, the count or ply and the colour, and the sett and structure of the cloth. Even the finishing process employed will have its effect on design. All woven fabrics are by their nature three-dimensional.

Every textile fulfils a function from the purely practical to the wholly decorative. The fitness of its component parts, as well as the suitability of the structure for its purpose, are therefore the main ingredients of good design. The simplest of techniques can have a result of superb design. Complex techniques and structures have their place when their special properties are needed. They will have little to do with good design when they are used for the sake of their complexity.

In Chapter 4 we have already discussed the various effects of colours and shades, as well as contrasts of textures. The variations are endless, and the more complex structures of the four-shaft weaves add the three-dimensional effect of light and shade.

When a textile has been designed with yarns, weave and texture suitable for its purpose, colour and pattern will be a matter of the individual weaver's choice. These are very much a matter of taste and fashion. The designer finds inspiration in nature and art, in fashion and daily life. Open eyes and an open mind will be of more use than any advice we could give in this book.

Keeping the technique as simple as is compatible with the effect desired, is a good starting rule however.

CLOTH FINISHING

Every fabric will need 'finishing' after it is taken from the loom. This may be only a matter of mending broken ends, fringing or hemming an edge, or tying a loop so that a hanging can be put on a wall. It may mean careful scouring and fulling, which changes the nature of the yarns used, and the fabric woven. In either case, finishing is an integral part of the design.

Mending (burling)

Burling (mending) is best done on a flat, and if possible, transparent surface with a light underneath. Alternatively the cloth can be held in front of a light or window. The effect of careful burling (mending) can be quite startling, a rather messy looking object can turn into a piece of craftmanship.

When the fabric has been removed from the loom, all pinned ends should be undone and darned into the fabric (Fig 121a and b). Weft joins are trimmed flush with the face of the cloth. Knots that have escaped attention during weaving are unpicked and the two threads are darned into the cloth just overlapping. The cloth is examined on the face and reverse for weaving mistakes. A floating end is cut, a warp thread darned in, following the weave correctly, and the faulty end is removed and trimmed from the corrected length (Fig 121c and d). A weft skip is dealt with

in a similar manner. Obvious variations of beat can sometimes be disguised at this stage by moving the weft thread with a bodkin (Fig 121e), or gently easing with the fingers.

Edge finishes

Dress and furnishing fabrics need no special edge finishing to their cut ends. At most, a row of hand or machine stitching to keep the weft in place during wet finishing is all that is required. When the edges form part of the design, as in wall hangings, table mats, rugs, blankets and bags, they can be simple or elaborate, but should be in keeping with the whole.

The warp ends can be left as a simple fringe by overstitching the last few picks with matching yarn, or knotting groups of ends in a simple thumb-knot (overhand knot) (Fig 122g) against the fell of the cloth. The fringes are trimmed to the length required by placing the fabric flat on a table with the excess hanging over the edge, and cutting along the edge. Long ends can be knotted into decorative fringes with any of the knotting techniques.

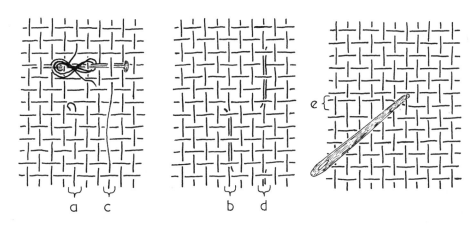

Fig 121   Burling

Hems are best done by hand with a matching or compatible yarn. When hems are impractical, and fringes are not wanted, the warp ends can be darned back into the fabric to give the appearance of another self-edge (Fig 122a and b).

A flat woven edge is produced when each warp end in turn is used as weft, and woven into the other ends (Fig 122c). The edge will be of increasing width as long as ends are added in turn. A bundle of ends will be left when the edge is completed, and these can be plaited (Fig 122d) or twisted (Fig 112e and f). Several decorative arrangements of this are possible by weaving to right or left, right and left, or in several small groups (Fig 122h).

For a twisted fringe, two or more warp ends are plied together, holding the last pick in place.

Two ends, or groups of ends, are twisted separately in the direction of the yarn twist (Fig 122e) and allowed to ply around each other in the opposite direction (Fig 122f). A thumb-knot (overhand knot) will prevent the ply from unravelling (Fig 122g). Wool yarns will felt together during wet finishing and the knots can be trimmed off.

When a thicker fringe is required than can be made with the number of warp ends available, extra yarn is knotted around a group of knotted ends, or into the fell of the cloth. The selvages can be trimmed in a similar manner.

A plain or decorative braid can be woven with a narrow warp entered in a rigid heddle and the warp ends of the fabric used as weft (Fig 123a and b). The fabric is placed at right angles along the braid warp and each end weaves at least two

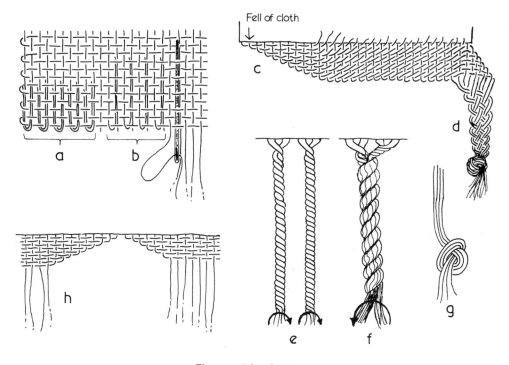

Fig 122   Edge finishes

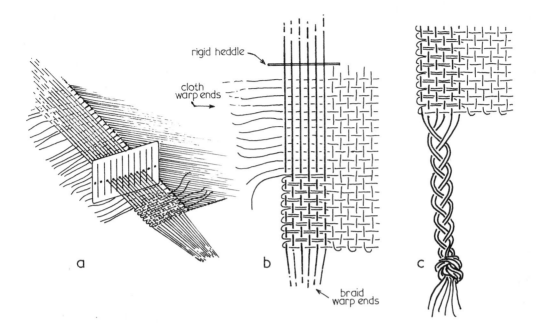

Fig 123   Woven edge finish

picks of the braid. A new selvage is formed and the ends can be trimmed close to the braid. The braid ends are finished as a tassel, plaited or plied at both ends (Fig 123c).

Warp ends can also supply the elements for coiled and rolled edges. They may be turned back into the cloth, leaving looped fringes. Techniques are endless, and you will soon find your own favourites.

The top of a wall hanging or tapestry will require an edge finish to support the weight of the hanging and ensure its proper balance. An open ended hem or binding to receive a stick or rod, will give support across the width.

A free hanging construction will have a point, or points, from which it has to be suspended for correct balance. Hanging cords of sufficient strength to support the weight of the hanging can be attached to these points.

Wet finishing
Wall hangings and rugs will not need a wet finish, unless the yarns were in oil, or the fabric got soiled. If they need cleaning, they should be washed or dry-cleaned in the way that was planned for them when they were designed. A free hanging construction can be hung out-of-doors, sprayed with soapy water, followed by clean water, till the water dripping from the bottom edge runs clear, and left to dry (provided of course, that the yarns are suitable).

Tapestries and other flat hangings may need *blocking* to correct any departure from the rectangular or other shape required. Only relatively small variations can be corrected in this way, but blocking will set the final shape and make later cleaning easier. The article is tacked to its exact shape to a block-board or frame (Fig 124), pulling out slightly tight areas and/or

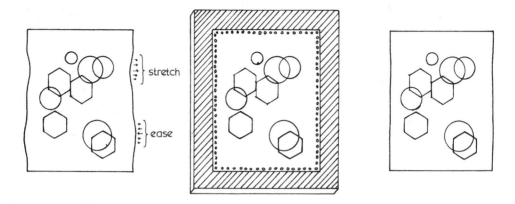

Fig 124   Blocking a tapestry on a board

easing in wide sections. The fabric is thoroughly wetted and left to dry on the board. Slow natural drying will set the yarns to the blocked shape, correcting slight differences of cloth width. Extreme buckling will not be cured, but can be improved if the cloth is steamed on the blocking board. Tapestries and flat hangings that have been blocked can be cleaned by careful washing or dry-cleaning when this becomes necessary.

Cotton or linen fabrics do not require a wet finish as an integral part of their construction. They do however shrink, and washing them before making up, will avoid later disappointment when they will have to be cleaned by washing. Cotton can be given a crisp finish by starching if desired. Ironing (pressing) should be done on the wrong side or under a cloth to avoid shiny marks caused by flattened fibres. Linen improves with every washing and pressing. As the flax fibres are flattened, the linen acquires a high lustre. This effect can be left to time or speeded up by leaving the cloth flat under heavy weights for as much time as possible.

Fabrics woven with worsted spun or plied effect yarns need to have the cloth set (the fibres

of warp and weft locked together) without fulling or felting. They are crabbed, set by heat, by steaming or boiling. The average workshop will only rarely have the room or facilities for the latter. The cloth can be sent to a commercial finisher. Most craftsmen prefer to finish the cloth themselves, and so keep control over the final result.

Crabbing (blowing) can be done with a cloth and steam iron, or a wet cloth and dry iron. Place the fabric on a lightly padded surface, with the selvages and picks straight and at right angles to each other. Cover with a very wet cloth and use a very hot iron. Place the iron on the cloth till the steam rises and lift it clear before moving on. Do not slide the iron to and fro. Crab across the width of the fabric till it is dry and move on in a similar manner along the length. When crabbing has been completed, the fabric can be washed in warm soapy water. Do not rub or wring it, but wash by squeezing and remove surplus water by rolling the cloth in a towel.

A slatted drying roller (Fig 125a) can be made, or a roller can be improvised by making a thick roll of newspaper or by using a heavy cardboard tube (Fig 125b). A piece of sheeting or clean paper is wound around the roller to prevent staining of the fabric. The fabric is wound around the roller, keeping it absolutely flat, the selvages straight, and the weft lying at right angles and straight across the width. The cloth is left on the roller till dry. The slatted roller allows air to circulate on the inside, drying the cloth evenly. When a solid roller is used, the cloth should be rewound at two-day intervals with the outside taken to the inside, making sure to keep the cloth smooth, flat and straight as before. When the cloth is dry, there will be no need to iron it, but the cloth can be softened by steam pressing.

Woollen cloth has to be *scoured* (have the oil removed by washing), and *fulled* (letting the wool fibres expand and set into cloth). Pure soap and soft water are the ingredients for both processes. A 'length' of cloth is most easily dealt with in the bath. The fabric is scoured in hot soapy water. It must on no account be scrubbed or rubbed. If the soap lather subsides before the cloth is clean, scour again in clean soapy water. When all the oil and dirt have been removed, the cloth is ready for *milling*, to full it. The cloth is worked in a thick soap solution and milled by hand, or with the feet by walking up and down, squeezing the soap through the cloth. Fulling will continue as long as milling is carried on. The amount of milling needed for the 'handle'

(texture and feel of the cloth) to reach the desired effect, depends on the yarns and weave of the cloth. It is wise to examine the result at short and regular intervals, as the fulling process is not reversible (Plate 16a). When the weave has closed up by the expansion of the yarn, and the cloth has the thickness and handle required, the cloth is rinsed to remove all the soap. Surplus water is squeezed, not wrung, from the cloth, and the cloth is set by slow drying on a drying roller. Care must be taken to keep the selvages straight and the weft picks lying at right angles to the selvages, straight across the width of the roller, while rolling the cloth on. Gentle pulling along the warp, and stroking with the palms across the width of the roller will keep the cloth flat and even. When a 'solid' roller is being used, the cloth should be rewound from time to time (taking the outside to the inside) to allow for even drying and setting. When the cloth is dry, it will be set and will not need pressing.

A woollen cloth with a special weave structure that is to be kept clear and crisp with a minimum of fulling, can first be crabbed and then very lightly milled. The crabbing is done before scouring, with the yarns still in oil.

A cloth containing both worsted and woollen yarns is crabbed first, then scoured and milled to the handle required. Woollen yarn and silk in combination needs a woollen finish, worsted

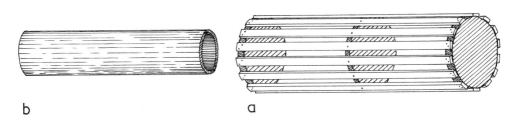

b   a

Fig 125   Drying rollers

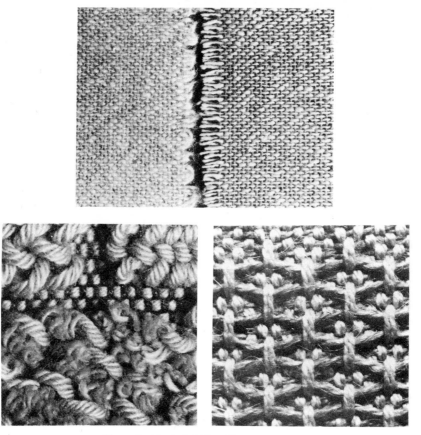

Plate 16   Cloth finishing, Texture weaves
a (above) 'Grey cloth' (loom state) and the same cloth after scouring and fulling.
b (below left) Wrapped loops. c (below right) Distorted weft-float.

yarn and silk need a worsted finish. Cotton or linen and wool require a woollen finish, and cotton and linen in combination are best finished as linen. Effect yarns not in oil will retain their special textures when they are lightly crabbed before washing. Whether they are milled at all, depends on the purpose the cloth is intended for.

Commercial finishing is available both in Britain and the United States. You will have little control over the amount of fulling in the commercial finish, unless the firm agrees to follow your instructions. You may well find your textured yarns and weaves flattened when the cloth is returned. We recommend that you do your own finishing, if at all possible.

CONCLUSION

The use of textiles is as ancient as the existence of man. Textiles have reached various peaks of development in different parts of the world, in different civilisations and at different times. Industrialisation has caused some decline of craftwork in the more prosperous nations. Automation and mass production is reaching the emerging countries and threatening their indigenous crafts. Preservation of 'primitive' conditions (in which crafts flourished naturally) is rightly out of the question. World-wide industrial civilisation requires new aims to ensure the growth and development of 'living' crafts.

The pressures and pace of life today, combined with shorter working hours, make many people feel the need to use their hands and their creative abilities. Only a few will be able to earn their living as professional craftsmen. For professional and amateur alike, the aim must surely be the attempt to create craftwork of beauty and quality. There is no point to an attempted competition with mass production, but there is every reason to produce craft objects making a personal statement.

The reproduction of a craft object, by following the step-by-step directions of an experienced craftsman, leads to hidden mass production. It can also lead to bitter disappointment when the lack of experience of the imitator produces a different (and probably inferior) result from the one illustrated.

We hope that this book will supply the reader with the relevant technical details required to create textiles of his own design.

APPENDICES

1

1.1 VEGETABLE FIBRES

Cotton and kapok are the fluffy fibres surrounding the seeds of these plants. Kapok does not spin easily because of the shortness and silkiness of the fibres. Cotton can be spun into a multitude of textures, it can be as fine as silk or thick as rope, it can be smooth or rough and can be dyed in clear, bright colours. The fibres taken from stems and leaves are spun into some of the most beautiful yarns known to man. Flax provides linen. Jute, hemp and ramie provide coarser yarns. Sisal and piña are leaf fibres. Raffia is a shredded palm leaf. Reeds and grasses can be used as textile elements. Coir is the husk fibre of the coconut.

1.2 ANIMAL FIBRES

Wool and hair are used for spinning yarns, strips of fur and leather can supply elements for fabric construction. Sheep provide most of the wool for woollen and worsted yarns. Goat, camel, rabbit, llama, alpaca, vicuña, buffalo, cow, horse and human hair are all used for spun yarns and provide a large and exciting selection of textures with differing properties.

Animal filaments

Silk is the filament secreted by the silkworm for its cocoon. Thrown silk is made from multiple strands unravelled from cocoons of the cultivated silkworm. Spun silk is made from a short staple of filaments from the broken cocoons of the cultivated or wild silkworm.

1.3 DOUBLING

Yarns wound onto cones are usually wound in an anti-clockwise direction (the cone base is turned clockwise and the yarn winds on anti-clockwise). The yarn will therefore unwind from the spool in a clockwise direction. When yarns are doubled from cones, the direction in which the yarns twist together (S twist or Z twist) will depend on the direction in which they were originally wound. The direction of ply can be used to create interesting effects in weaving (App 9.1). Empty cone bases can be used to re-wind yarns to be doubled in either direction.

Spools of yarn can be doubled in the same way as cones, using a doubling stand. As a spool is straight sided, it can be stood on end and unwound from either end, therefore the direction of twist can be determined by the way in which the spool is placed on the stand. Doubling stands can be improvised by supporting the top cone (spool) on a horizontally supported reed and placing the second yarn underneath the reed, feeding the end of the second yarn up through the reed and through the centre of the top cone or spool.

More than two yarns can be doubled, and in a variety of ways. The yarn passing up through the top cone need not be wound on a cone. A ball of yarn placed in a box or bowl under the top cone, or a staple or screw-eye fixed below the top cone with the second yarn passing through it from a spool rack, will work just as effectively.

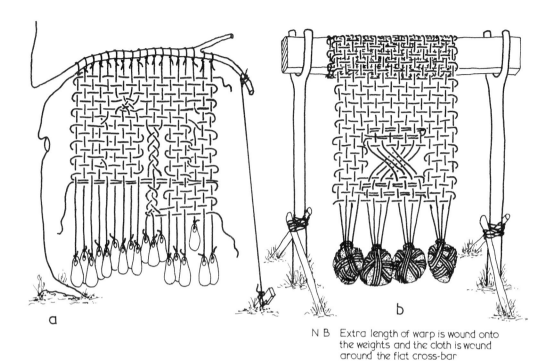

N B Extra length of warp is wound onto
the weights and the cloth is wound
around the flat cross-bar

Fig 126   Warp-weighted looms

1.4   PRIMITIVE LOOMS

Looms without a permanent framework use various devices to hold the warp under tension. The warp ends can be slung from the branch of a tree (Fig 126a) or an end-stick attached to a wall, roof beam or two uprights (Fig 126b). The ends can be weighted singly or in bundles with stones or pottery weights (Fig 126a and b). Weaving starts at the top and the cloth can be wound on with the use of a flat sided cross-bar (Fig 126b). Weaving on a *warp-weighted loom* is slow, but allows great freedom for the manipulation of warp ends. The ends can change position (Fig 126a and b), or turn into weft and back into warp again (App 2.3).

A *ground loom* uses two end sticks held by four stakes in the ground. The weaver works along the warp, sitting on the woven cloth. *Waist looms* (back-strap looms) are still being used in many parts of the world. They offer distinct advantages to the handweaver for weaving narrow cloths without space consuming equipment. One end-stick is attached to wall hooks, the tie-on stick is attached to a strap passing behind the weaver's back. The sheds can be obtained with a rigid heddle, or shed-sticks and leashes. As the weaver works up the warp, the woven cloth is wound on to the tie-stick and secured from unrolling by a second stick passing over the cloth and lashed to the tie-stick (Fig 127).

1.5 SIMPLE-LOOM TUBULAR CLOTH

Card looms can be used to weave purses, bags and cushion covers. When the first picks are

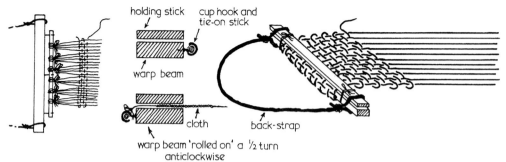

holding stick   cup hook and
                 tie-on stick

warp beam

cloth   back-strap

warp beam 'rolled on' a ½ turn
anticlockwise

N B The holding stick is tied to the warp beam (Fig 80a) each
time the cloth is rolled on.

Fig 127   Waist loom

beaten well down, and the warp ends cut at the top only, after tubular weaving, the card can be slipped out. A pocket cloth with three closed edges has been produced. The raw edges at the top can be turned back or bound, a fastener added for a purse, handles for a bag, or a cushion slipped in and the edges closed. The card loom need not be rectangular.

2

2.1   FRAME-LOOM DOUBLE CLOTH

A circular warp on a frame-loom can be used for double-width, tubular or double-cloth fabrics. The frame need not be turned as both layers of warp are visible from either side. The weft passes from front to back, and back to front on the inside of the frame uprights. Two shed-sticks are used, one for each layer of warp, for the sheds. The counter-sheds are picked up. For the surface cloth the weft passes over and under alternate warp ends of the front layer only, leaving the ends of the reverse cloth behind the pick. The reverse is woven by turning the back shed-stick on edge for the shed, and picking up all the surface ends plus alternate ends of the reverse for the counter-shed. A double cloth (Chapter 8) is bound together by lifting some of the back ends when weaving the surface cloth.

2.2   LEASH-ROD AND SHED-STICK

The leashes can be tied to a leash-rod (Fig 128a), resting on brackets or clamps attached to the uprights of the frame (Fig 128b). One hand is passed behind a group of leashes and the leashes are pulled down and forward for the counter-shed (Fig 128c). The leash-rod can be attached to strong brackets to hold the leashes under tension and the counter-shed open (Fig 128d). In this case, the shed is obtained by a shed-stick behind the leashes as before. When the stick lies flat and is pushed back, the counter-shed is open. When the stick is turned on end and brought as near to the leashes as possible, the shed is open (Fig 128d).

For double-width, tubular and double-cloth

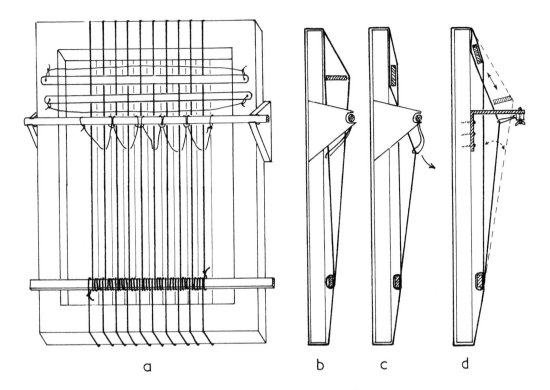

Fig 128   Leash-rod and shed-stick

weaving, two leash-rods as well as two shed-sticks are used, one of each for each side of the cloth. When a double-cloth is to be bound together, occasional stitching ends or picks will have to be picked up.

2.3   MULTI-DIRECTIONAL WARPS

The frame loom makes it possible to weave a fabric in which the warp ends leave their parallel alignment. The warp can be made on a warping-board or mill, with extra length. A strong end-stick is placed in one end loop of the warp. The warp is spread on the stick, and the stick is lashed firmly to the top of the frame. The bottom loop of the warp is cut open, and the ends are tied in

pairs to the bottom cross-bar of the frame with a bow-knot. The frame is turned so that the end-stick is at the bottom, and the bows are at the top (Fig 129). The shed and counter-shed are picked up, as shed-stick and leashes would interfere with the divergence of the ends. When two or more ends are to diverge, the bow holding these ends is undone, the ends are taken to their new position and retied (Fig 129a). The untied ends can weave as weft for one or more picks before becoming warp ends again by being retied (Fig 129b). Some picks of the ordinary weft will have to be woven to hold the warp-weft in position before these ends can be re-tensioned.

A direct figure-of-eight warp can be spread

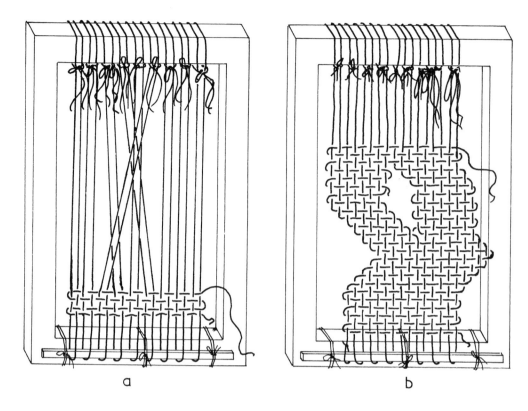

Fig 129   Multidirectional warps

evenly or unevenly. The spacing at the top can differ from the spacing at the bottom. A multi-directional warp, with ends overlapping or interweaving, can be made by looping each pair of warp ends over the top or side bar of the frame, and tying them to the opposite bar where required. Diverging and multi-directional warps are most suitable for free-woven wall hangings and room-dividers.

3

3.1 HEDDLE FRAME (FRAME SHAFT)

When a rigid heddle is not available, or is unsuitable for the sett, a *heddle frame* can be made. A strong wooden or metal frame is needed, and the heddles must be tied from strong string or cord (Fig 130). The heddles are movable on the frame and can therefore be spaced according to the sett of the warp. The frame is used exactly like the rigid heddle for shedding, but beating has to be done with a sword-stick or fork. If a

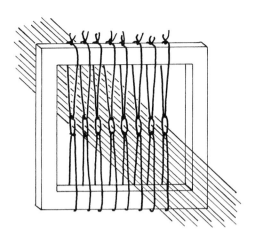

Fig 130 Heddle frame

reed is available, the ends can pass through the reed in front of the heddle frame. The reed will

keep the warp spaced, and the ends parallel, and can be used for beating.

3.2   WARPING BOARD

When making your own warping board, it is important to observe the following: use a good quality wood that will not split or warp; make sure that the pegs fit the holes firmly, but are not too tight to remove; the board needs to be thick and the holes for the pegs deep enough for the pegs to be seated well into the board; and the pegs must be strong enough not to bend under the tension of the warp.

3.3   BROKEN ENDS

When an end has broken near the fell of the cloth, but still passes correctly through its heddle and dent, the mending end can be knotted to the

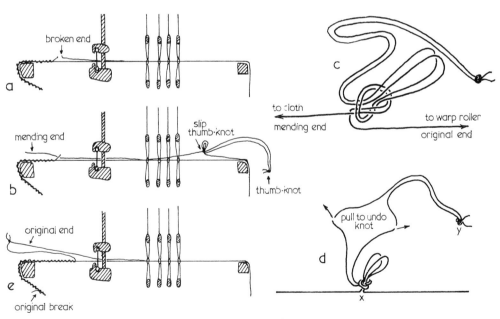

N B   Make the slip thumb-knot using the excess thread (between x and y) or the knot will undo as soon as tension is applied

Fig 131 Mending broken ends

broken end and pulled to the back (Fig 131a and b). This is quick and ensures accurate entry. When the knot has been pulled back as far as possible, a slip thumb-knot (overhand slip knot) is tied (Fig 131c) before the mending end is pinned to the cloth at the correct tension. When enough has been woven and wound on for the original end to reach the cloth, the slip thumb-knot is undone (Fig 131d), and the original warp end is pulled to the cloth by pulling the mending end forward (Fig 131e). The knot may have to be eased through the heddle eye and reed dent to make sure that it is not pulled apart. The mended end is pinned as before.

4

4.1   NOVELTY YARNS

Some of the more heavily textured novelty yarns, rely on a fine 'binder' thread to hold the component yarns in place. Care should be taken when using yarns like this in a warp as the binder may not stand up to the strain of weaving. If very fluffy yarns are used in a warp the sett should not be too close, or the yarns will chafe each other during shedding and may disintegrate during weaving. It is usually more effective to use really fluffy or hairy yarns set widely apart and, if necessary, a finer warp yarn to produce a ground cloth.

5

5.1   ANGLED WEFT

Over-slung battens rest in pivot holes or notches on the top of the loom frames and can be shifted. For an angled weft from selvage to selvage, the batten can be used. The batten is hung as far forward as possible, one side only is moved back progressively; then the other side is moved back in similar stages till the batten is level. The batten is moved forward progressively, one side first, followed by the other side, until the batten is level at the front position again. This system offers several variations. A table or floor loom with an under-slung batten on a fixed pivot excludes the use of the batten to position the angled weft. A sword-stick is used to place the weft in the desired position.

6

6.1   THREE-SHAFT WEAVES

The plain-weave draft for three shafts is a point entry with a four-end repeat (Fig 132a). Shafts 2 and 3 carry the even ends, and shaft 1 carries the odd ends. The ends on shaft 2 or shaft 3 can be used as stitching ends for a brocade weft (Fig 132b). A two-by-one twill draft is a straight entry with a three-end repeat (Fig 132c). Any one shaft can provide the stitching ends for a brocade weft. Three-shaft chevron (point twill) (Fig

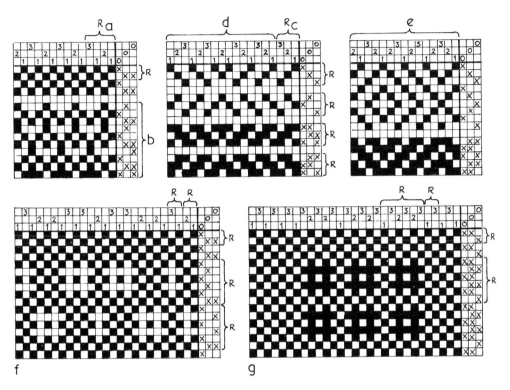

Fig 132   Three-shaft weaves

132d and e), spot (Fig 132f) and mock lace (Fig 132g) can be woven.

6.2   MULTIPLE WARP-GROUPS

Colour stripes and changes are most easily warped when the number of ends in each warp-group is related to the colour order. An end-by-end warp of alternating colours or shades, changing positions at intervals, as for the log-cabin designs, can be made without re-threading the heddle-frame by changing the turn of the group. The width of the first block is warped in the usual manner, placing the cross without turning it between pegs *b* and *c* on the way down the mill, and turning the warp-group on the way up,

before placing the cross between pegs *c* and *b*. The width of the second block is warped with a turn of the group on the way down, and no turn on the way up. In this case the turn is most easily made if the hand is taken over the warp-group and the thumb and forefinger passed through the two sheds from the opposite side. As the hand is turned to place the cross between the pegs, the group will turn. On the return journey the fingers are again introduced from the opposite side and taken to the pegs without turning the group.

Random stripes can combine all four ways of turning or not turning the warp groups at regular or irregular intervals.

6.3 RADDLE DENTING

Warp groups must not be split when being placed in the raddle dents because the order of the ends in each group can only be traced in the singles-cross. The number of threads used for multiple warping must therefore be related to the number of ends to be placed in one raddle dent for spreading the warp. When the sett requires more ends for one raddle dent than can be warped in one group, more than one group can be placed in one dent. The dentage of the raddle will depend on whether it is home-made or bought, and whether it has inch or centimetre units. Warping and spreading will involve the least amount of calculations when the unit width of the raddle dent is used throughout: for finding the sett, determining the number of ends to be used in warping and for spreading the warp. For instance: a warp 60cm (approximately 24in) wide is to be made. The raddle available has $\frac{1}{2}$in dents. When the sett required for an inch (epi) is sixteen, warp with half that number of threads, eight ($\frac{1}{2}$ epi). This will produce one group of ends for each raddle dent. Warp 48 groups (60cm = approx 24in = 48 × $\frac{1}{2}$in) for the width required. For most purposes, you will find it easiest and accurate enough to equate 5cm with 2in (actually 2in is a fraction wider than 5cm). A unit width may be any convenient measurement, matching your equipment, as long as the same unit is used throughout all calculations.

Re-setting a warp

If the raddle-cross is lost or you decide to change the sett after the warp has been made, the warp can be spread in the raddle by using the singles-cross. The warp chain is undone to expose the singles-cross, as each group of threads for each dent of the raddle will have to be counted. In order to separate the threads in the singles-cross without losing their order, the cross-sticks are

inserted and tied in place. The warp and raddle are laid on the table as before, but with the singles-cross on the same side of the raddle as the end loop. Count off the number of threads to be placed into one dent of the raddle to accord with the sett of the cloth. Check each group to make sure there are no crossed threads between the groups.

When the full width of the warp has been spread and the cap tied in place, the raddle is pulled along the length of the warp to the raddle-cross end. Do not untie the end-loop ties until a stick has been put into the loop and tied, or you will have to pick up all the loops and make sure that they are not crossed. The warp is now ready to be wound on to the loom. Leave the cross-sticks in the singles-cross (which should now be at the far end of the warp) ready for dressing the loom.

6.4 ADDING AND REMOVING HEDDLES

A narrow warp, entered from the centre may leave enough room for unused heddles to remain at the sides of the shafts. The shaft will still be balanced, as the numbers of heddles left over will be the same on either side. When the warp is too wide to clear the empty heddles, distorting and abrading the selvage ends, the extra heddles will have to be removed. To prevent the heddles from tangling, and to ease their return when they are needed again, slip a wire or string loop through the ends of metal heddles (Fig 133a or b), and tie string heddles (Fig 133c) *before* taking them off the shafts. Some looms have shaft frames that can only be opened from one side. In this case the heddles will have to be removed, and the remaining heddles centred again, before the warp ends are entered. Surplus heddles can be left empty but distributed between entered heddles when the warp is widely spaced (Fig 133d). Adding heddles to shafts is done by reversing the

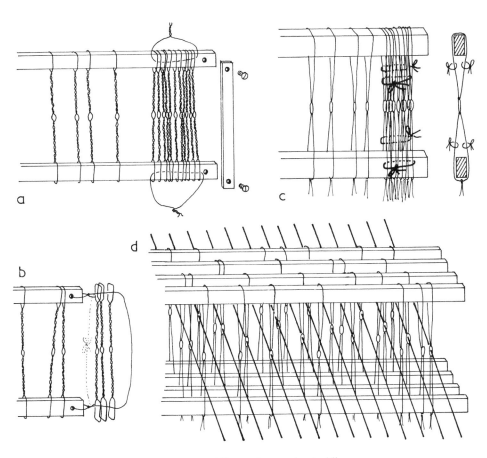

Fig 133   Adding and removing heddles

process, slipping the metal heddles on to the shafts before removing the loop, and sliding the string heddles on before removing the ties.

6.5   REED DENTAGE

It does not matter whether the reed dentage is expressed in inches or centimetres. Use which ever unit measurement you prefer. Use this unit for all your warp and cloth calculations. To relate the unit you have chosen to the reed you are going to use, hold a tape-measure from one wire dent along the reed and count the number of slits in the width of your unit. From this you can calculate how the ends should be entered for the required sett.

Make sure that the reed is suitable for the yarns and sett of the warp, by passing short lengths through the dents at the required sett. Move the threads up and down to make sure they will do so easily. When more than one end is to be entered into one dent, move the ends in one dent past each other to make sure that there is room for them to do so. A widely dented reed will present less restistance than a closely dented one. When a

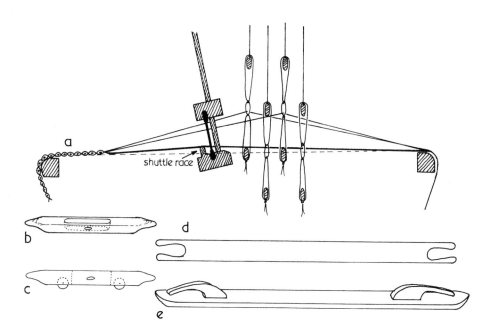

Fig 134   Shuttles and shuttle race

large choice of reeds is available, aim at two ends per dent when the warp is made of one yarn only. With yarns of widely differing counts, dent the thickest singly, adjusting the grouping of the others accordingly.

6.6   THROWING A SHUTTLE

A little practice with an empty shuttle will soon establish confidence. With confidence it is easy to achieve the steady rhythm required for easy and pleasurable weaving. A roller shuttle (Fig 134c) requires a firm base and will work best when the batten has a shuttle race (Fig 134a). Boat shuttles (Fig 134b) take slightly smaller bobbins, and therefore a little less weft, but they glide easily and quietly through the shed. Very thick weft requires the use of a stick-shuttle (Fig 134d) or ski-shuttle (Fig 134e).

7

7.1   SATIN AND SATEEN

Satin and sateen are woven on more than four shafts. Their characteristic sheen is caused by yarn floats bound into a weave at well distributed points, to cause as little disturbance of the warp or weft cover as possible. In *five-end satin* each warp end floats over four picks, being bound down by weft in a broken twill order. The warp has a close sett with few weft picks. A *five-end sateen* has weft floats over four ends and is stitched into the cloth in a broken twill order. The warp sett is wide and the weft sett is close.

7.2   OVERSHOTS

Many of the traditional extended twills have descriptive names. A small point twill, woven as a reverse twill, forming small diamonds is called birds-eye, slightly larger it becomes goose-eye. Extended to an eight-end return it is a rosepath draft. To list a few: Diamond and Cross; Honeysuckle or Pine Bloom; Orange Peel; Maple Leaf; Lover's Knot; Whig Rose; Snail's Trail; Monks Belt (a two-block brocading draft) etc.

7.3   YARN SETT AND STRUCTURE

The design of a textile includes the selection of suitable yarns and sett for the intended use of the fabric. The structure of a weave may have to be adapted for different setts and yarn. An extended twill weave, with comparatively long weft floats, can be perfectly suitable for a dress fabric when woven with woollen yarns, which will full and set with a wet finish. As the yarns are likely to be fairly fine, and the sett close, the floats will be of manageable length. The same structure employed for a furnishing fabric or floor rug in coarser yarns and a wider sett may prove impracticable. The floats extend over the same number of ends, but over a much wider area, and may catch and snag in use. The draft may have to be adapted to bind down floats at closer intervals. Wide blocks, entered on two shafts, are broken up with a stitching end at intervals, by entering an occasional end through a heddle on one of the other shafts.

Smooth or slippery yarns need a higher number of intersections than textured or rough yarns. A floor rug needs bulk and stability. A wall hanging will eventually need cleaning. A dress fabric will have to be cut, made up and worn without fraying or sagging. The yarn, sett and structure must all be planned with the purpose of the textile in mind. This need not preclude experimenting with yarns and structures for their own sake; you can always decide what to do with the resulting textile after finishing it. The experience gained will help you to design future projects, and the experimental textile may well suggest new possibilities and uses.

8

8.1   SEPARATE WARPS FOR ONE CLOTH

It is easier to dress the loom for a very wide cloth if the warp is made in two halves. Each warp is made in an identical manner, with half the warp groups required for the full width, and tied separately. The end-stick is passed through both end loops, and each half is spread from the centre of the raddle. The complete warp is wound on as before and, when the singles-cross is reached, the cross-sticks are passed through both halves. Each half-warp is entered from the centre to its edge.

The double repp weave can be used for a four-block design, one block on each shaft. Four warps are made, one for each shaft, and married on the loom. Each warp is made full length, but with only a *quarter* of the ends needed for the total warp sett. The colour order for each shaft follows the colour order for one of the four blocks. An end-stick is placed in the end loop of *each* of the four warps. They are spread in the

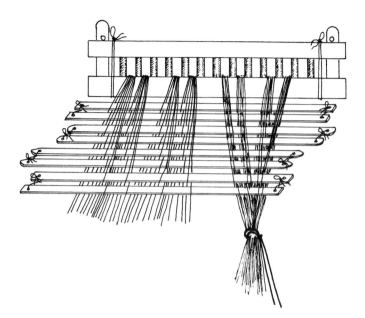

Fig 135   Entering four warps as one

raddle, one warp at a time. Each warp supplies a quarter of the ends finally lying in each raddle dent. When the warps have been spread, the four end-sticks are firmly tied together and to the apron-stick. All four warps are wound on together as one, till the singles-crosses are reached. Four sets of cross-sticks, one set for each warp, are placed in the crosses, and the warp ends are entered into the heddles as before, but taking a thread from each warp in turn (Fig 135). Each shaft will have all the ends from one quarter-warp, and therefore all the ends of one block, entered in its heddles.

9

9.1 S AND Z TWIST, EFFECT YARNS

The standard spin for a singles yarn is in a clockwise direction, producing an S twist (Fig 113a). When yarns are plied they are usually twisted in the opposite direction to the singles spin; therefore the standard spin for a plied yarn is in an anti-clockwise direction, producing a Z twist (Fig 113b). It is possible to buy some singles and plied yarns in the opposite spin (Z spun singles and S spun plied) as well as the standard spin. It is important that the two types are kept separate or 'shadow' stripes in a self-coloured fabric can spoil the appearance of the cloth. These shadow stripes are caused by the difference in light deflection of the S and Z spins. This effect can of course be used deliberately to produce subtle light reflecting stripes or checks for drapes and sheer fabrics. The effect is not only caused by light deflection, but also by the fact that S-twist yarns crossing Z-twist yarns at right angles will

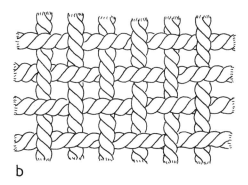
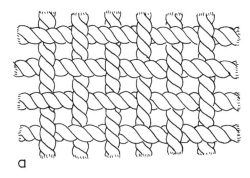

b   a

Fig 136   'S' and 'Z' twist

bed into each other, because the direction of ply produces compatible angles of spin (Fig 136b). This effect does not occur when the warp and weft are of the same spin (Fig 136a). Therefore, warp stripes of S and Z yarns used with an S *or* Z weft will bed together when the angle of spin is compatible (when the S crosses the Z, or vice versa).

Grey cloth in oil tends to curl at the corners when it has been cut from the loom. This is caused by the tension of spin in the warp and weft, when both yarns are of the same spin direction, producing a torque in the woven cloth. The torque is eliminated, or substantially reduced, by the setting process when finishing the cloth. A fabric with warp and weft of opposing twists will not be distorted by torque, as the two twists will counteract each other. Stripes of opposing twists in the warp *or* weft will produce a 'pleated' fabric if the cloth is not stretched after wet finishing.

Crêpe fabrics are produced by using alternate ends and picks of S and Z spun yarns in a balanced plain weave. Interesting effects can be achieved by varying the warp and weft with different proportions of S and Z twist, to produce areas of different crêpe effects with areas of bedded and unbedded cloth. A *crêpe yarn* has four (or more)

yarns plied in the following way: 4 × S-twist singles = 2 × Z-twist 2-ply = 1 × S-twist 4-ply, or for a final Z-twist, starting with Z-twist singles. Crêpe yarns are more elastic than ordinary plied yarns, and care must be taken to calculate the sett for warp or weft with the yarn in a relaxed condition. When the cloth is removed from the loom and the tension is released, the yarn will revert to its natural length and, if the sett was calculated on the tensioned yarn, the sett will be too close.

Other effect yarns use S and Z spins to produce different textures. It is not in the scope of this book to analyse the structures of effect yarns. The reader can un-ply various novelty and effect yarns and see how the individual yarns have been combined to produce the final effect.

The count of an effect yarn will give the approximate length to weight, but the count will give little indication of the *diameter*. An approximate average diameter can be calculated from the finest and thickest parts of the yarn.

9.2   DOUBLE WARP BEAMS

Some looms have two warp beams. When one of these beams is dressed with a ground warp, and the other with a pattern warp, no tension-bar will be required on looms with counter-

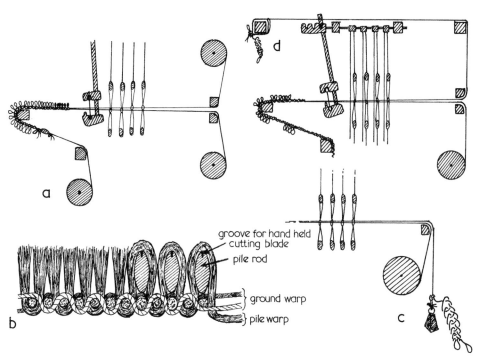

Fig 137　Double warps and pile weaving

balanced sheds. A rising-shed loom will need the tension-bar for the ground warp only. The length of the two warps can differ greatly. As each can be released independently, even extreme differences of take-up should present no difficulty. One warp can form warp-loops (eg for terry-towelling), while the other weaves a ground cloth. The looping ends will have a much larger take-up than the ground warp, and the loop-warp will have to be much longer. Warp-pile fabrics are woven with at least two warps on at least two beams (Fig 137a). The loops are formed by weaving a rod under the raised pattern warp. The rod is withdrawn after a number of picks.

When the rod (or rods) has a cutting blade, the loops are cut when the rod is withdrawn, forming a pile (Fig 137b).

When no second beam is available, a second warp can be entered without being wound on to the warp-roller. The pattern warp is left hanging over the back of the loom and tensioned with weights (Fig 137c). It can also be taken under a second back-bar, or tension-bar, brought over the top of the loom to the front, and tied to a top cross-bar (Fig 137d). It will be easy to release more length when needed. A long cord, tied through the end loop, will make it possible to reduce loom wastage.

GLOSSARY

Animal Fibres
units of wool or hair that can be combined into yarn by spinning   *see App 1.2*

Apron
cloth or cords attached to the back and front rollers of a loom

Apron-stick   *see Sticks*

Back-stick   *see Sticks*

Backstrap Loom   *see Waist Loom App 1.4*

Batten
swinging frame, holding the reed; *under-slung* when pivoted from the bottom of the loom; *over-slung* when pivoted from the top of the loom

Beam
loom rollers — back roller: warp beam; front roller: cloth beam

Binder
weft of ground cloth

Block
one pattern unit, also one colour area, forming one unit of design

Bobbin
spool of wood, paper or card for winding the weft for use in a shuttle

Bobbin Winder
geared spindle for winding bobbins

Burling
mending of cloth after removal from the loom, before wet finishing

Castle
structure across the top of a loom from which shafts (harnesses) are suspended, also serrated wooden bars to hold shafts steady while threading

Catch Thread
warp end at each selvage

Clean on Cheese
wool yarns (packaged without oil)

Cone
package of yarn wound on a conical wood or cardboard shape

Cop
package of yarn, partially supported on a short tube, mainly cylindrical, tapering to a point at one end, from which the yarn is unwound

Count   size of yarn   *see Chapter 9*

Counter-balanced   *see Loom, also Shed*

Counter-march   *see Loom, also March*

Counter-shed   *see Plain Weave*

Counting Tie
figure-of-eight tie enclosing raddle groups

Crabbing
finishing of cloth by setting with steam   *see Chapter 9*

Cross
interlacing of warp ends to keep them in order; alternating ends = singles-cross (entering cross); alternating groups of ends = multiple-cross (raddle-cross)

Cross-sticks (lease-sticks)   *see Sticks*

Cross-ties
ties in the warp at the cross to preserve the proper alternating order of the warp ends when the warp is removed from the warping board or mill

Cut
a woollen count   *see Chapter 9*

Denier
a yarn count   *see Chapter 9*

Dent
the space between two teeth of a raddle, also the space between two wires of a reed

Denting
the order and number of warp ends in a reed

Double
to ply two or more yarns together

Draft
diagram of threading order, shedding sequence and cloth structure (draw-down)

Draw-down
diagram of cloth structure

Drying Roller
slatted or solid roller for setting and/or drying cloth

END
a warp thread

END-STICK *see Sticks*

ENTERING (drawing in)
threading the warp ends through the heddle eyes; also threading the warp ends through the reed dents (sleying)

FABRIC
cloth, textile

FELL
the line of the last woven pick

FIBRE
the smallest basic threadlike unit to be spun into yarn

FILAMENT
(continuous) thread extruded by an animal (silk), or machine (man-made)

FILLING *see Weft*

FINISHING
work done on a cloth after it has been removed from the loom *see Chapter 9*

FLOAT (flush)
a length of a weft pick passing over more than two ends; also a length of a warp end passing over more than two picks

FRAME LOOM *see Loom*

FRONT-STICK *see Sticks*

FULLING
milling the cloth to expand the yarn *see Chapter 9*

GREY CLOTH
cloth in its loomstate, prior to finishing

GROUND CLOTH (backing cloth)
interlacing of warp and weft for the basic structure of a patterned cloth

GROUPING
more than one thread working as one end and/or one pick

HAND SPUN
yarn spun on spinning wheel or spindle

HANK
yarn package, also yarn count *see Chapter 9*

HARNESS
a complete set of shafts and heddles *see also Shaft*

HEADING
picks woven at the beginning of a cloth to spread the warp and to test the entry and tension

HEADING-STICK *see Sticks*

HEDDLE (heald)
a string or wire loop with an eye in the centre, suspended between shafts (harnesses), so that ends entered through the heddle eyes can be raised and/or lowered by the action of the shafts

HEDDLE FRAME *see Shaft, Harness*

HEDDLE HORSES
bars of wood, pivoted at the centre, from which shafts (harnesses) are hung in a counter-balanced loom

HEDDLE-STICK *see Sticks*

INTERLACE
to interweave warp and weft to make a cloth

JACKS
pivoted bars of wood in the top castle of a loom from which shafts (harnesses) are suspended, and through which the shafts are activated

LAMMS (lams)
pivoted levers, suspended between shafts and pedals (treadles) to centralise the shedding action

LEA
linen count *see Chapter 9*

LEASE *see Cross*

LEASE-STICKS *see Sticks*

LEASH
a loop of string or cord to raise an end of the counter-shed

LEASH-ROD
metal or wooden bar to hold leashes

LOOM
a device to keep warp threads under tension to make it possible to weave cloth by interlacing weft threads, including various devices to obtain sheds *see Leash, Rigid Heddle, Shaft, Shed-stick*
counter-balanced loom: shafts are balanced by each other
counter-march loom: shafts are balanced independently, each by its own march and counter-march *see also Chapter 6*

MAN-MADE
synthetic fibres, yarns and cloth

MARCH (lamm)
in a counter-march loom, the marches are the long lamms connected to the jacks for the rising action; the counter-marches are the short lamms connected to the bottom of the shafts for the sinking action

MENDING
darning in broken ends, correcting wrong picks

MILLING
working a hot soap solution through the cloth to expand and slightly felt the fibres

NATURAL FIBRES
animal, vegetable and mineral fibres *see App 1.1 and 1.2*

NOVELTY YARN
yarn with special effect spin, ply and/or texture

PAWL
metal tongue to engage with toothed wheel (ratchet)

PEDALS (treadles)
pivoted foot-levers to activate the lamms and shafts

PICK (shot)
  a row of weft

PICK-UP STICK   *see Sticks*

PILE
  loops or cut threads at right angles to the surface of a
  cloth

PIRN
  small cylindrical yarn package, unwinding from one
  end, for use in a shuttle

PLAIN WEAVE (tabby)
  basic weave of alternating warp ends over weft
  picks in a two-shed repeat of opposites (shed and
  counter-shed)

PLY
  to twist two or more singles yarns together, also the
  number of singles in a plied yarn count

QUILL
  a small tube (sometimes made from reeds or feathers)
  usually of paper, for the core of a bobbin

RADDLE
  a wooden bar or frame with wood or metal teeth at
  regular intervals, used to spread the warp

RADDLE-CROSS   *see Cross*

RATCHET WHEEL
  toothed wheel, preventing a roller from turning when
  engaged with a pawl

REED
  a frame with evenly spaced metal divisions, set in the
  batten in front of the shafts, to keep the warp ends
  evenly spaced and to bed or beat down the weft

REED HOOK (fish hook)
  a thin, flat hook for threading warp ends through the
  reed

RICE
  a skein holder

RIGID HEDDLE
  a shedding device; a frame with alternating slits and
  eyelets

ROLLER   *see Beam, also Drying Roller*
  to keep cloth flat after wet-finishing

SCOURING
  removing the oil and dirt from woollen cloth in hot
  soapy water

SELVAGE (self-edge)
  the two firm and closed edges of a cloth formed by the
  weft turning around an edge warp end after leaving a
  shed and entering the next

SETT (verb set)
  the number of warp ends and weft picks in a unit
  square of cloth. *Warp sett:* the number of warp ends
  in a unit width of cloth. *Weft sett:* the number of
  picks in a unit length of cloth

SETTING UP (dressing)
  spreading and rolling on the warp, entering the
  heddles, sleying the reed, tying on and preparing a
  loom for weaving

SHAFT (harness)
  frame holding heddles, also two sticks (one through the
  top loops of the heddles, the other through the
  bottom loops), suspended in a loom, used to lift
  and/or lower the warp ends entered into the heddles
  to obtain a shed

SHED
  the space between layers of warp ends for the passage
  of the weft
  rising shed: ends being lifted
  sinking shed: ends being lowered
  counter-balanced shed: some ends being raised and the
    remainder lowered for the same shed

SHED-STICK   *see Sticks*

SHEDDING
  creating the opening between layers of warp for the
  passage of the weft

SHOT   *see Pick*

SHUTTLE
  implement for carrying the weft through the shed

SHUTTLE RACE
  a wooden bar at the front of the batten, below the reed,
  to support the lower layer of warp for the passage of
  a shuttle

SINGLES
  one spun thread (unplied yarn)

SKEIN
  a yarn package, also a measure of length in woollen
  count   *see Chapter 9*

SLEYING (entering)
  drawing the warp ends through the dents of a reed

SPIN
  to twist fibres into yarn, also the amount and/or
  direction of twist

SPOOL
  small cylindrical yarn package supported on a tube

SPOOL RACK
  a free standing frame with thin cross bars for holding
  spools of yarn in such a way that they can revolve for
  unwinding

STICKS
  apron-stick: tied to canvas or cord aprons at back and
    front of loom
  back-stick: *see End-stick*
  cross-stick: one of a pair to be inserted into the two
    sheds on either side of a cross, taking the place of the
    cross-ties, to keep the ends in their proper alternating
    order

STICKS Contd

end-stick: tied to back apron-stick after passing through the end loop of a warp

front-stick: tied to the front apron-stick, warp end groups are tied to this after entering

heading-stick: used at start of weaving to provide false fell to beat first picks against

heddle-stick: one of a pair *see Shafts*

lease stick: one of a pair *see Cross-stick*

pick-up stick: used to pick up shed not available by shaft action

shaft-stick: *see Shaft*

shed-stick: broad stick darned into a warp on a simple loom to provide a shed when the stick is turned on edge

sword-stick: used in place of a batten to beat the weft into position

warp-stick: to be wound into the warp on the warp beam, to keep layers of warp firm and even

SWIFT

skein holder

SWORD

fine smooth stick used to beat (press) the weft into place

SWORDS

the side supports of the batten

TABBY *see Plain Weave*

TAKE-UP

the amount the warp and weft shorten due to bending over and under each other

TENSION BAR

rod or stick, tensioned by springs or elastic bands, used to increase or correct the tension of some or all warp ends

THREADING *see Entering*

THREADING HOOK

fine metal hook for drawing warp ends through heddles

TIE-UP

the arrangements of the cords from lamms to pedals; also the warp group ties at the front stick

TREADLE *see Pedal*

TWIST

the spin of the yarn; also the direction of the spin of a yarn (S twist and Z twist: *see App 1.1*)

VEGETABLE FIBRES *see App 1.1*

WARP

the threads running the length of a loom and held under tension and therefore the threads running the length of a cloth

WARP BEAM *see Beam*

WARP ROLLER *see Beam*

WARP STICK *see Sticks*

WARPING

the process of preparing the required number of warp ends to the required length, before dressing the loom

WARPING BOARD

a board or frame with pegs to wind the warp to the required length

WARPING MILL

a cylindrical frame for winding the warp in a spiral

WASTAGE

the length of a warp that cannot be woven and the length needed to tie the warp to the front stick

WEAVE

the order of interlacing the warp and weft

WEB

synonym for cloth

WEFT

the threads running the width of a cloth

WINDING ON

winding the warp onto a warp beam, also winding the woven cloth onto the front beam, releasing more warp

YARN

spun fibres

YARN COUNT

size of yarn *see Chapter 9*

LIST OF SUPPLIERS OF EQUIPMENT, YARNS AND INFORMATION

The authors of this book have personal experience of United Kingdom suppliers only. Readers in other countries are advised to seek information from their national craft organisations and publications.

In the United States of America, the American Crafts Council, 44 West 53rd Street, New York, NY 10019, publishes the bimonthly *Craft Horizons*. The *Handweaver & Craftsman*, 220 Fifth Avenue, New York, NY 10001, also appears every second month.

In Sweden, the Swedish Home Crafts Association, Foreningen Svensk Hemslojd, Sveavagen 44, Stockholm, will supply information, yarn and equipment.

In Germany, a magazine for handweaving 'webe mit' is published by 'webe mit' Verlag, 705 Waiblingen bei Stuttgart, Postfach 65.

In Great Britain, the Crafts Advisory Committee, 28 Haymarket, London SW1, publishes the bimonthly *Crafts*.

The Association of Guilds of Weavers, Spinners and Dyers publishes the *Quarterly Journal* of the Association and is distributed in Great Britain and Ireland by Miss Ruth Hurle, 47 East Street, Saffron Walden, Essex; overseas distribution: Mrs J. Evans, China Court, Church Lane, Petham, near Canterbury, Kent.

Hon Secretary of the Association of Guilds in Great Britain: A. E. Haynes, Moat Cottage, Siddington, Cirencester, Gloucestershire.

Hon Guild Secretaries for:

Australia: Mrs L. M. Willings, 2 Sunset Avenue, Cronulla, NSW

New Zealand: Mrs Zena Abbott, PO Box 5873, Auckland

South Africa: Mrs G. Finck, 33 Woodlands, Highstead Road, Rondebosch, Cape Province

List of suppliers in Great Britain

R. Barnett (yarns and information), 7 Ralston Street, London SW3 4DT, by appointment only

Boddy's Bookshop (equipment and books), 165 Linthorpe Road, Middlesbrough, Yorkshire

Craftsman Mark (mule-spun yarns), Trefnant, Denbigh, North Wales

K. R. Drummond (Art and Craft books), 30 Hart Grove, Ealing Common, London W5, by appointment only

Dryad Handicrafts (looms, other equipment, some yarns and books), Northgate, Leicester

A. K. Graupner (yarns), Corner House, Valley Road, Bradford 1

Handweavers Studio & Gallery Ltd (textiles, yarns, fleeces, equipment, dyes, information and tuition), 29 Haroldstone Road, London E17

Harris Looms (looms and other equipment), Dept F, Northgrove Road, Hawkhurst, Kent

F. Herring & Sons (looms and other equipment), 27 High West Street, Dorchester, Dorset

T. M. Hunter Ltd (yarns and cloth finishing), Sutherland Wool Mills, Brora, Scotland

J. Hyslop Bathgate & Co (yarns), Island Street, Galashiels, Scotland

Jackson's Rug Centre (rug yarns), Croft Mill, Hebden Bridge, Yorkshire

Lillstina (looms), 6 Granville St, Winsford, Cheshire

Linen Thread Co Ltd (linen twine), Hilden, Lisburn, Co Antrim, Northern Ireland

Mersey Yarns (yarns), M. Seagroat, 2 Staplands Road, Liverpool, L14 3LL

W. Morgan & Son (rug yarn), Wallis Factory, Ambleston, Haverfordwest, Wales

Multiple Fabric Co (horsehair, camelhair and belting yarns), Dudley Hill, Bradford 7, Yorkshire

Texere Yarns (yarns), 9 Peckover Street, Bradford 1

Uni-dye (dyes), PO Box 10, Ilkley, Yorkshire

Weavers Shop Ltd (rug yarn), Wilton Royal Carpet Factory, Wilton, Nr Salisbury, Wiltshire

The Weavers Workshop Ltd (looms, equipment, yarns, information and tuition), Monteith House, The Royal Mile, Edinburgh EH1 1SR

Yarns (yarns), Richard Edwards, 28 Upper East Hayes, Bath, Somerset

BIBLIOGRAPHY

ALBERS, ANNI. *On Designing* (Middleton, Conn: Wesleyan University Press, 2nd ed. 1962)

——. *On Weaving* (London: Studio Vista, 1966)

ALLARD, M. *Rug Making — Technique and Design* (London: Pitman, 1963; Philadelphia: Chilton, 1963)

ATWATER, M. M. *Byways in Handweaving* (New York: Macmillan, 1954)

——. *The Shuttle-craft Book of American Handweaving* (New York: Macmillan, 1933)

BAITY, E. C. *Man Is a Weaver* (London: Harrap, 1947)

BERLANT AND KAHLENBERG. *The Navajo Blanket* (Los Angeles: Praeger, 1972)

BEUTLICH, TADEK. *The Technique of Woven Tapestry* (London: Batsford, 1971)

BLACK, MARY E. *New Key to Weaving* (Milwaukee: Bruce, 1957)

BLUMENAU, LILI. *The Art and Craft of Handweaving* (New York: Crown, 1955)

CHETWYND, HILARY. *Simple Weaving* (London: Studio Vista, 1969; New York: Watson-Guptill, 1969)

CIBA REVIEW. *Textile Trade Journal* (Basle: Ciba Ltd). Reference libraries only

COLLINGWOOD, PETER. *The Techniques of Rug Weaving* (London: Faber & Faber, 1968)

DAVENPORT, ELSIE. *Your Handweaving* (London: Sylvan Press; reprinted USA, 1970)

DAVISON, M. P. *A Handweaver's Pattern Book* (Allantown, Pa: Schlecters, 1949)

——. *A Handweaver's Source Book* (J. Spencer, 1953)

EMERY, IRENE. *The Primary Structure of Fabrics* (Washington: Textile Museum, 1966)

GALE, E. *From Fibres to Fabric* (London: Allman, 1968)

GRIERSON, RONALD. *Woven Rugs* (Leicester: Dryad Press, 1952)

D'HARCOURT, RAOUL. *Textiles of Ancient Peru and Their Techniques* (Washington: University of Washington Press, 1962)

HOOPER, LUTHER. *Hand-loom Weaving* (London: Pitman, 1910)

——. *Weaving for Beginners* (London: Pitman, 1920)

HOOPER, LUTHER. *Weaving with Small Appliances* (London: Pitman, 1923)

KIRBY, MARY. *Designing on the Loom* (London & New York: The Studio Publications, 1955)

MARIET, ETHEL. *Handweaving Today* (London: Faber & Faber, 1939)

——. *Weaving Notes for Teachers* (London: Faber & Faber, 1949)

——. *Handweaving and Education* (London: Faber & Faber, 1942)

MEILACH, D. Z. AND SNOW, L. E. *Weaving Off-Loom* (Chicago: Henry Regnery, 1973)

RAINEY, SAVITA. *Weaving Without a Loom* (Davis Publications, 1968)

RHODES, MARY. *Small Woven Tapestries* (London: Batsford, 1973)

SHUTTLE CRAFT GUILD PUBLICATIONS. General editor: Harriet Tidball (Michigan, 1960 on)
The Double Weave Plain & Patterned
Surface Interest: Textiles of Today
Mexican Motifs
Peter Collingwood: His Weaves and Weaving
Undulating Weft Effects
Contemporary Tapestry
Two-harness Textiles: Loom-controlled
Two-harness Textiles: Open-work Weaves
Brocade
Twining

ROBINSON, A. T. C. AND MARKS, R. *Woven Cloth Construction* (Manchester & London: The Textile Institute, Butterworth)

TEXTILE INSTITUTE, THE. *Identification of Textile Materials* (Manchester: The Textile Institute, 3rd ed. 1961)

THOMSON, H. *Fibres and Fabrics of Today* (London: Heinemann, 1967 & 1972)

THORPE, A. S. AND LARSEN, J. L. *Elements of Weaving* (New York: Doubleday, 1967)

THURSTON, V. *A Short History of Ancient Decorative Textiles* (London: The Favil Press, 1st ed 1934, 3rd ed 1972)

TIDBALL, HARRIET. *The Weavers Book* (New York: Macmillan, 1961)

TOVEY, JOHN. *The Technique of Weaving* (London: Batsford, 1965)

VOLBACH, W. F. *Early Decorative Textiles* (Feltham, Middlesex: Hamlyn, 1969)

WATSON, W. *Textile Design and Colour* (London: Longmans, 6th ed 1954; New York: Longmans, Green & Co, 6th ed 1954)

——. *Advanced Textile Design* (New York: International Textbook Co, 3rd ed 1947)

WOOL TEXTILE DELEGATION, THE. *The Tex System* (Bradford, Yorks: The Wool Textile Delegation, 1966)

WORST, E. F. *Foot Power Loom Weaving* (London and Milwaukee: Bruce, 1924)

INDEX

Numbers in italics refer to illustrations